STUDENT'S BOOK AND WORKBOOK

with Digital Pack

COMBO A

3

CEFR B1+



# TH!NK

SECOND EDITION

Herbert Puchta,
Jeff Stranks &
Peter Lewis-Jones

CAMBRIDGE UNIVERSITY PRESS

# CONTENTS

| PRONUNCIATION | THINK! | SKILLS |
|---|---|---|
| Linking words with *up* | **Train to THINK** Reading between the lines | **Reading** Online forum: What next?<br>Blog: Before I settle down – a list<br>**Writing** An email about resolutions<br>**Listening** Conversation about success and failure |
| Initial consonant clusters with /s/ | **Train to THINK** Following an idea through a paragraph<br>**Values:** Animal rights | **Reading** Magazine article: They made a difference: The slave trade<br>Online magazine article: A short history of bathing in the UK<br>**Writing** A magazine article about someone who made an important discovery<br>**Listening** The passenger pigeon |

TOWARDS B2 First for Schools practice

| PRONUNCIATION | THINK! | SKILLS |
|---|---|---|
| Strong and weak forms: /ɒv/ and /əv/ | **Train to THINK** Identifying the main topic of a paragraph | **Reading** Article: Brand names<br>Article: Funny place names<br>**Writing** A reply to a letter asking for advice<br>**Listening** Nicknames |
| Consonant–vowel word linking | **Train to THINK** Thinking of consequences<br>**Values:** Doing the right thing | **Reading** Quiz: How honest are you? Article: How honest is that?<br>**Writing** A diary entry about a dilemma<br>**Listening** A guessing game: I wish |

TOWARDS B2 First for Schools practice

| PRONUNCIATION | THINK! | SKILLS |
|---|---|---|
| The schwa /ə/ in word endings | **Train to THINK** Thinking about different writing styles | **Reading** Blog: So you want to write a novel, do you?<br>Article series: There are always two sides to an argument: Books are always better than their films.<br>**Writing** A short paragraph expressing an opinion **Listening** Roald Dahl |
| The /ʒ/ phoneme | **Train to THINK** Understanding what's relevant | **Reading** Magazine article: How on earth does he do it?<br>Blog: Big questions – bigger answers!<br>**Writing** Explaining how things are done<br>**Listening** Conversation about a haircut |

TOWARDS B2 First for Schools practice

# WELCOME

## A THAT'S ENTERTAINMENT!

### *let* and *allow*

1 W.01 **Complete the conversation with the words. Then listen and check.**

allowed | cross | feel | get
guitar | let | look | ~~looking~~
makes | songs | sound | talent show

**Sara** Hey, Karl, what are you [0]*looking* at?
**Karl** My History book. Can't you see I'm busy?
**Sara** I'm just asking. Sorry.
**Karl** No, I'm sorry. I don't [1]______ great today.
**Sara** You don't [2]______ very happy. What's the matter?
**Karl** My dad [3]______ me so [4]______ .
**Sara** That doesn't [5]______ so good. Why?
**Karl** He says I'm not [6]______ to be in the band.
**Sara** What?! So he won't allow you to play in the [7]______ at the weekend?
**Karl** No. He says no music until after my exams.
**Sara** But that's four weeks from now!
**Karl** I know. He wants me to study and forget about writing [8]______ . He won't even [9]______ me practise the [10]______ .
**Sara** But you need some time to relax.
**Karl** I know. I [11]______ so angry when I think about it. It just isn't fair.

2 W.01 **Listen again. Answer the questions.**

1 Why is Karl angry?
2 How long is it until the exams finish?
3 What does Sara think about the situation?
4 Who do you agree with: Karl or his dad? Why?

3 SPEAKING **What do your parents allow you to do during exam time? What don't they let you do? Make lists. Then compare with a partner.**

### Music

4 **Sort the words into two groups. Label the groups. Then think of four more items for each one.**

classical | drums | guitar | jazz
piano | pop | rap | violin

### Verbs of perception

5 **Complete the sentences from the conversation with the correct forms of (*not*) *look*. Then match them with the rules.**

1 You __________________ very happy.
2 Hey, Karl, what __________________ at?

**RULE:** We use verbs of perception (*look, smell, feel, taste*) …
- in the present continuous to talk about actions. ☐
- in the present simple to talk about states. ☐

6 **Complete the mini-dialogues with the correct forms of the verbs.**

1 taste
**A** What are you doing?
**B** I ______ the soup … It ______ great.

2 smell
**A** My socks ______ really bad!
**B** Then why ______ you ______ them?

3 feel
**A** Why ______ you ______ that jumper?
**B** Because it's so soft. I like the way it ______ .

7 SPEAKING **Work in pairs. Karl tries to persuade his dad to let him play in the talent show. Write a conversation of eight lines. Then read it out.**

## The big screen

**8** SPEAKING **Work in pairs. For each type of film, think of an example that you have both seen.**

action | animated | comedy
drama | horror | romantic comedy
science fiction | thriller

**9** **Read the article. What types of films does it mention?**

**10** **Read the article again and answer the questions.**

1 When did Columbus start making films?
2 Who are his films especially popular with?
3 Where did he learn about filmmaking?
4 What does he do apart from direct films?
5 Who started a company with him?

**11** SPEAKING **Work in pairs. Think of your favourite film director and discuss these questions.**

1 What films has this director made?
2 What do you like about his/her films?

## Present perfect tenses

**12** **Complete the sentences. Use the present perfect simple or continuous form of the verbs and choose the correct words.**

1 They ______________________ (play) *for / since* 87 minutes and neither side has scored yet.
2 I *yet / still* ______________________ (not see) the final, so please don't tell me which singer won.
3 ______________________ you ______________________ (see) last night's show *still / yet*? Bradley Cooper and Lady Gaga were guests.
4 The children ______________________ (sit) in front of the TV watching *SpongeBob for / since* seven o'clock this morning.
5 It's the funniest programme on TV. I ______________________ (not miss) an episode *still / yet*.
6 The Prime Minister ______________________ (say) the same thing *for / since* weeks now. No one believes her.

# BEHIND THE CAMERA

## CHRIS COLUMBUS

**A 12-year-old who gets left behind when his family go on holiday, a teenage magician fighting to save his world and the troubled son of a Greek god living in modern-day America: these are just three of the characters brought to life on the big screen by director Chris Columbus. With films such as *Home Alone*, *Harry Potter and the Chamber of Secrets* and *Percy Jackson: Sea of Monsters*, Columbus has certainly shown that he knows how to get teenagers into the cinema.**

Columbus, who studied film at New York University, has been making films for more than 30 years and has become one of the most successful film directors of all time. Since he directed his first film, *Adventures in Babysitting*, in 1987, Columbus has been involved in some of the biggest films as both a director and a producer.

But Columbus doesn't only make action films for the teenage market. He's also made a number of successful films for adults. Comedies such as *Mrs. Doubtfire*, dramas such as *The Help* and science fiction films such as *Bicentennial Man* have all helped make Columbus one of Hollywood's most popular filmmakers. And in 2014, he formed a production company with his daughter Eleanor.

## TV programmes

**13** SPEAKING **Work in pairs. Look at the sentences in the previous exercise. Match them with the types of TV programme.**

cartoon | chat show | sitcom
sports programme | talent show | the news

**14** **Choose a type of TV programme from the list below. Write a sentence about it using the present perfect simple and/or continuous. Don't include the type of programme in your sentence!**

drama series | game show
reality show | soap (opera)

*I've been watching it for weeks, but no one has won the million-dollar prize yet.*

**15** SPEAKING **Read out your sentence. Can the rest of the class guess the type of TV programme?**

## B TIME TO ACT

### Our endangered planet

1 SPEAKING **Work in pairs. Describe the photos. What problems do they show?**

A

B

C

2 W.02 **Listen to three conversations. Match them with the photos.**

3 W.02 **Listen again. In which conversation do you hear these words? Write the number.**

a rubbish ☐
b climate change ☐
c litter ☐
d pollution ☐
e fumes ☐
f smog ☐
g flooding ☐

### Question tags

4 **Complete these sentences from the recording with the question tags.**

are they? | aren't they? | does it? | did they? | is it? | isn't it? | weren't they? | doesn't it?

1 I guess they're just lazy, ____________
2 But it only takes a few people to spoil everything, ____________
3 Yes, it's all those fumes from the factory, ____________
4 They didn't ask us if we wanted it here, ____________
5 Even if they do, it doesn't make our lives any better, ____________
6 Hundreds of homes were damaged, ____________
7 And the politicians aren't really doing anything to help, ____________
8 It isn't the sort of thing you'd expect to see here, ____________

5 **Complete the sentences with question tags.**

1 You haven't told Ron, ________ ?
2 You're going to do something about it, ________ ?
3 It sounds quite dangerous, ________ ?
4 It didn't work, ________ ?
5 It won't be easy, ________ ?
6 She wrote to her local politician, ________ ?

### *So do I / Neither do I*

6 **Look at the questions and complete the answers with *so* or *neither*.**

1 **A** I don't really believe in all that.
**B** ____________ do I.
2 **A** I think we should do something.
**B** ____________ do I.

7 SPEAKING **Complete the sentences so that they are true for you and read them out. Agree (or disagree!) with your partner's sentences.**

1 I really like ____________ .
2 I don't like ____________ .
3 I believe ____________ .
4 I don't believe ____________ .

### Accepting and refusing invitations

8 W.03 **Put the sentences in order to make a conversation. Then listen and check.**

[1] **Mandy** Marco and I want to do something to help the flood victims.
☐ **Mandy** Yes – 20 km! Want to join us?
☐ **Mandy** That's a shame. But you will sponsor us, won't you?
☐ **Mandy** We're going to do a sponsored walk next Sunday.
☐ **Jamal** Of course I will.
☐ **Jamal** Are you going to walk a long way?
☐ **Jamal** What are you going to do?
☐ **Jamal** I'd love to, but I can't. I'm busy.

9 SPEAKING **Work in pairs. Write a conversation using the underlined phrases from Exercise 8.**

You and your friend are tired of all the rubbish in the street and have decided to do something about it. What are you going to do? Invite another friend to join you.

## Party time

**10** **Work in pairs. Imagine you're organising a party. Make a list of important things to do.**

**11** **Read the article. Does it mention the things on your list?**

# HOW TO PLAN A PARTY

**The first question to ask is, 'Why am I having a party?' (It's someone's birthday; it's the end of term; your team won a big championship; just to have fun with friends.)**

A really good party has a theme. What's going to be the theme for yours? Beach party? 1970s disco? Something else? Then you have to find [1]______ to have your party. Wherever you decide to have it, it's always a good idea to [2]______ permission from your parents first.

Now, it's time to [3]______ the guest list. Are you going to invite [4]______ you know, or just some of your friends? It's important to think hard about how many people you can afford to invite. Once your list is ready, you can [5]______ the invitations. A good time is about a fortnight before the party. Any sooner, and people might forget about it; any later, and some of the people on your list might already have other plans.

OK, so now you've got two weeks to get everything ready. Don't panic – it's plenty of time: just don't leave [6]______ until the last minute. If you want to [7]______ a DJ, start looking now. Remember that they might ask you to [8]______ a deposit, so make sure you've got money for that. Then you need to [9]______ the food and [10]______ the room, although these things can be left until the day before.

Last but not least, keep cool, get some sleep, and in the afternoon before the party, just check it's all ready. Then – have fun!

**12** **Read the article again and complete it with the missing words.**

decorate | draw up | everyone | everything | get | hire | organise | pay | send out | somewhere

## Indefinite pronouns

**13** W.04 **Complete the conversation with suitable indefinite pronouns (*everyone, somewhere, nothing*, etc.). Then listen and check.**

**David** Have you got [1]______ ready for the party?

**Joanna** No, [2]______ is ready. We haven't found [3]______ to have it, for a start. We've looked [4]______.

**David** Have you invited [5]______ yet?

**Joanna** Yes, we've invited 50 people and [6]______ is coming!

**David** So you've got 50 people coming, but [7]______ for them to come to?

**Joanna** That's right.

**David** Well, we've got to do [8]______. How about using my house?

**Joanna** What about your parents?

**David** They won't mind. They're going [9]______ for the weekend. I'll make sure [10]______ is clean and tidy when they get home.

**14** **Read the next part of the story and continue the conversation. Write four more lines. Use at least one indefinite pronoun.**

*It's the day after the party. David's mum and dad arrive home and open the door ...*

**Mum** What's happened? Look at our house!

**Dad** David! DAVID!

**David** Oh, hi, Mum. Hi, Dad. You're home early. Did you have a good time?

## Arranging a party

**15** SPEAKING **Work in pairs to organise a party. Be creative! Think about:**

- what it's for
- the theme
- who to invite
- where it will be
- food and drink
- music

# C IN MY OPINION, ...

## Feeling under the weather

1 W.05 **Listen to the conversation. What's the matter with Angie?**

2 **Complete the conversation with the words.**

appointment | better
energy | get | operation
physically | should | took

**Mum** You don't look well, Angie. What's up?

**Angie** I'm just tired all the time, Mum. You know, I haven't got any [1]______ .

**Mum** Are you sleeping OK?

**Angie** Not great, no. I often wake up in the night.

**Mum** Well, you know, Angie, you [2]______ take more exercise. That would help.

**Angie** Really?

**Mum** Yes. I mean, if you [3]______ more exercise, you'd be more tired [4]______ and then you'd sleep better.

**Angie** You're joking, right? I run, I go swimming, I go for long walks. My problem isn't exercise.

**Mum** Yes, you're right, of course. Well, perhaps you'd [5]______ see a doctor. I can ring and make an [6]______ for you if you like.

**Angie** A doctor? I don't think so. I don't feel sick – just tired. I'm sure I'll [7]______ better soon.

**Mum** OK, well, we can talk about it later. I'm going out to see a friend of mine who had an [8]______ last week.

**Angie** OK, Mum. Hope your friend's all right. And don't worry about me. I'll be fine.

3 **Match the verbs (1–6) with the nouns and adjectives (a–f) to make phrases. Sometimes there's more than one possible combination.**

| | |
|---|---|
| 1 feel | a an appointment |
| 2 get | b an operation |
| 3 have | c exercise |
| 4 make | d a doctor |
| 5 see | e better |
| 6 take | f sick |

4 **Write down as many words related to health as you can think of. Then compare with a partner.**

*sick*
*nurse*
*hospital*
...

## Giving advice

5 **Complete the sentences with *better*, *should* or *ought*.**

1 It's late – you'd ______ go.
2 If you aren't well, you ______ to see a doctor.
3 Jane's in hospital. We ______ go and visit her.
4 The doctor is very busy, so you ______ make an appointment. Don't just turn up.
5 Your knee hurts? Well, you'd ______ not play football today, then.
6 If you want to get better, you ______ to rest as much as possible.

6 **Match the problems (1–3) with the advice (a–c). Then write one more piece of advice for each problem. Use *had better*, *should* and *ought to*.**

1 My hand really hurts. ☐
2 I think I'm going to be late for school. ☐
3 I can't do this homework. ☐

a You'd better hurry.
b Perhaps you should phone a friend.
c You ought to see a doctor.

7 SPEAKING **Work in pairs. Write mini-dialogues including the problems and advice in Exercise 6. Add two or three lines to each. Then act them out.**

## Better or worse?

**8 Read the blog entry. Mark the sentences T (true) or F (false).**

1 The writer likes awards ceremonies. ☐
2 *A Star is Born* won Best Film at the 2019 Oscars. ☐
3 The writer thinks the song in *A Star is Born* is the coolest he's ever heard. ☐
4 Dave thinks the writer is very intelligent. ☐

**9 SPEAKING Work in pairs. Discuss these questions.**

1 What other awards ceremonies do you know of?
2 Do you like awards ceremonies? Why or why not?
3 Do you think it's fair to compare different movies, actors, music, etc. and choose one as the best?

## Comparisons

**10 Complete the sentences with the correct form of the adjectives and adverbs. Add any other necessary words.**

1 The weather tomorrow won't be ________ (cold) as today.
2 This is the ________ (good) pizza I've ever eaten.
3 Do you think this is ________ (difficult) than the other test?
4 This book's OK, but it isn't the ________ (interesting) one I've ever read.
5 She learns things ________ (easy) than I do.
6 I'm not very good at tennis, but I'm ________ (bad) as Janice!
7 Hurry up! Can't you walk ________ (quick) than that?
8 Do you speak ________ (loud) as your sister?

**11 SPEAKING Work in pairs or small groups. Discuss these statements. Do you agree or disagree with them? Why?**

1 The best things in life are free.
2 If something is more expensive, it's always better.
3 It's more important to work hard than to play hard.
4 Exercise isn't as important as good sleep.

**12 Choose two things or people from one of these categories. Write a paragraph comparing them.**

sports that you like | actors that you like
towns or cities that you know
school subjects | books that you have read

# WHY ALL THESE awards?

**I'm really tired of awards ceremonies and prizes. Why do we have to compare things? Everywhere you look, there's something going on about who or what is 'the best' or 'the most comfortable' or 'the biggest', and so on. And sometimes the prize winners aren't the best anyway!**

Here's an example: the Oscars in 2019. I saw the film *A Star is Born* and it was the most wonderful film I'd ever seen. But did it win the Oscar for Best Film? No! They gave the award to *Green Book*! Can you believe it? It wasn't as good as *A Star is Born*.

OK, *A Star is Born* got lots of nominations – seven, I think – but I don't think that's enough. Lady Gaga was fantastic as Ally Maine. In my opinion, I think she's much better than Olivia Colman, who won Best Actress. But the good thing is that *A Star is Born* won Best Original Song for *Shallow* – I've never heard anything as cool. And was the acting good? It was great! No other film had acting as brilliant as that.

I said all these things to my friend Dave the day after the Oscars. I told him I thought the judges were the craziest people in the world. Dave asked me how many films I'd seen in 2018. I said, 'One – *A Star is Born*.' Dave says he doesn't know anyone as silly as me.

# D HELP!

## Reported speech

**1** **Read the story and answer the questions.**

1 What had happened to the caller's computer screen?
2 What three things did Vicky ask the caller to do?
3 Why couldn't the caller switch on the lights?
4 What did Vicky finally say to the caller?
5 What happened to Vicky in the end?

### We asked readers to tell us about a time when they tried to help someone. Here's one from Vicky Hastings.

I used to work in IT for a big company, but I was fired because I got angry with a manager. Here's what happened.

I answered the phone one day and said, 'Hi. Can I help you?' A voice said, 'Hi. I'm a manager in the Sales Department and I've got an IT problem. I need your help.' 'What's the problem?' I asked, and he told me his computer screen had suddenly gone black.

[1]______ , I couldn't think why it had happened. I asked him to check that the screen was still connected. He said it was. [2]______ I asked him if he'd pressed any buttons by mistake. He said, 'No, I was downloading a program when, suddenly, it went "pooff".'

[3]______ a few seconds, I said, 'OK, please check that your computer is still plugged in at the wall. Sometimes it gets disconnected accidentally.' The manager asked me to wait a bit. Then he came back and said, 'I can't see behind my desk where the plug is. It's very dark.' So I told him to switch the light on. Do you know what he said? 'Oh, I can't do that, the electricity went off five minutes ago.'

I tried to keep quiet. But [4]______ , I had to say something. I warned him never to waste my time again, ever. He complained to my boss and I was fired. How fair is that, do you think?

**2** **Rewrite the sentences in reported speech.**

0 'I need your help.'
He said that *he needed my help.*

1 'What's the problem?'
I asked him ______

2 'I can't see here because it's very dark.'
He said that ______

3 'Please check that your computer is still plugged in.'
I asked him to ______

4 'I can't put the light on because the electricity went off five minutes ago.'
He said that ______

## Sequencing words

**3** **Match these words with spaces 1–4 in the story.**

a After ☐ c finally ☐
b Then ☐ d At first ☐

## Asking for and offering help

**4** **Put the words in order to make questions.**

1 I / you / Can / help / ?
2 help / something / you / me / Could / with / ?
3 me / you / Can / a / lend / hand / ?
4 you / Do / help / any / need / ?
5 you / minutes / got / a / Have / few / ?

**5** **Look at the sentences in Exercise 4 again. Mark them A (asking for help) or O (offering help).**

**6** SPEAKING **Work in pairs. Choose a situation and write a conversation in which A asks B for help. Use expressions from Exercise 4. Then act it out.**

- A has a problem with some homework.
- A isn't feeling well.
- A's computer isn't working.
- A wants to have a party, but doesn't know where to hold it.

## IT problems

7 SPEAKING Work in pairs. What do the pictures show?

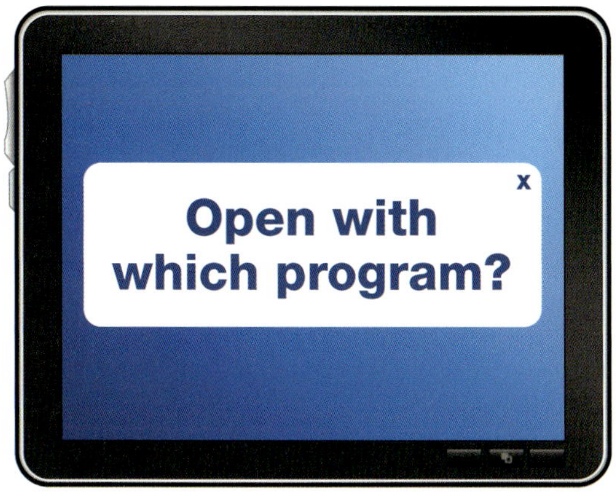


A ☐

B ☐

C ☐

8 W.06 **Listen to three conversations. Match them with the pictures in Exercise 7.**

9 W.06 **Listen again. In which conversation do you hear these words? Write the number.**

| | | | |
|---|---|---|---|
| a attachment | ☐ | e install | ☐ |
| b coverage | ☐ | f online | ☐ |
| c downloaded | ☐ | g program | ☐ |
| d file | ☐ | h upload | ☐ |

## IT vocabulary

10 **Choose the correct words.**

1 *go / have* online
2 *post / file* a message
3 *install / key in* your password
4 *install / go* a program
5 *attach / activate* a file
6 *go / download* a file
7 *upload / key* a photo
8 *key / delete* a message
9 *open / install* an attachment
10 *post / buy* an app
11 *upload / activate* flight mode
12 *have / go* network coverage

11 **Match the verbs with the nouns. Make as many combinations as you can.**

a message | a photo | flight mode | a password
an attachment | a program | a file | an app

0 install *install a program / an app*
1 attach ______
2 download ______
3 upload ______
4 open ______
5 post ______
6 delete ______
7 activate ______
8 key in ______

## Passive tenses

12 **Complete the sentences from the conversations with the verb forms.**

is being repaired | was taken | is installed

1 The photo ______ on a safari trip.
2 Just click on it and the program ______ automatically.
3 The network ______ out here.

13 **Rewrite the sentences in the passive.**

0 Someone posted a message.
*A message was posted.*
1 Someone is downloading a program.
______
2 Someone has installed a new program.
______
3 Someone has keyed in the password.
______
4 Someone is repairing the anti-virus software.
______
5 Someone deleted the message.
______

14 **Describe one of these processes using the passive.**

- downloading an app to your mobile phone
- uploading a photo to a social networking site
- installing a program on your computer

# 1 BIG DECISIONS

**Get THINKING**

**Watch the video and think: are you good at making decisions?**

**OBJECTIVES**

**FUNCTIONS:** talking about the future; complaining

**GRAMMAR:** present tenses (review); future tenses (review)

**VOCABULARY:** making changes; life plans; phrases with *up*

A

B

C

D

E

## READING

1 **What are the people doing in the photos? Are these things you do or would like to do? Why?**

2 **Tick (✓) the things you would like to do when you finish school. Then add two more ideas of your own.**

- ☐ travel to other countries
- ☐ go to university or college
- ☐ go into business
- ☐ get any job you can find
- ☐ do any job you can and spend time on your hobbies
- ☐ find work that provides training on the job
- ☐ do volunteer work

3 SPEAKING **Work in pairs. Compare your ideas from Exercise 2. Give reasons for your choices.**

4 **Read John's blog post on the next page and the replies to it quickly. Which three photos show activities that these people do now?**

Amy ☐ Mark ☐ Pauline ☐

5 1.01 **Read the article again and listen. Mark the sentences T (true) or F (false).**

1. John is unsure what to do when he leaves school. ☐
2. John is worried about his exam results. ☐
3. Amy went to Thailand to learn the language. ☐
4. Amy has got plans for when she leaves Thailand. ☐
5. Mark's advice is to do a course. ☐
6. Pauline got a job before she finished her university course. ☐

# What next?

## John *posted 2 hours ago*

**My time at school is almost up, and of course I'm thinking about the big question: what next? Perhaps I've left it a bit late to start thinking about it, but that's how I am. I think I'll do well in my exams, so maybe I'll go to university or college and get more qualifications – but I've been asking myself if it's better to just find a job and start a career that way. On the other hand, if I do go on to study further, should I do it right away or perhaps take a year off – a 'gap year'? Helpful comments and ideas, please! Thanks.**

Like Share Reply

## Amy *posted 5 minutes ago*

Hi, John. I'm doing a gap year right now. I saved up some money and went to Thailand, but after two months of 'holiday' I got bored and the money was running out. Then I learned about a volunteer medical organisation working in poor parts of the country and they let me join as a driver. Now I'm working, struggling with the Thai language (I spend up to an hour a day practising with friends) and learning lots about myself. I've made a resolution, too – when I go home, I'm going to study medicine, to be a doctor or a nurse. So my advice? Do a gap year, but don't just travel around – do some volunteer work somewhere. For me, it's been life-changing.

Like Share Reply

## Mark *posted 28 minutes ago*

Hey! I left school three months ago and I didn't want to go to university or travel. So I'm doing a course. I'm studying to become a yoga teacher. I took up yoga a couple of years ago and I've loved it ever since. I was quite lazy at school, but I've changed my ways and now I study really hard. The course starts every day at 7.00, so I've had to get into the habit of waking up early. But that's fine – I love what I'm doing. That's the important thing – do what you love, if you can.

Like Share Reply

## Pauline *posted 1 hour ago*

Hi there! Here's my advice. Do what feels right for you now, but keep an open mind and be prepared to change. Some of my friends went travelling after school, but I didn't have the courage; I just went to university. It was OK and I was having a good time. Then one day an old friend from school phoned me and said he was going to start an online company and asked me to join him. So, I gave up the university course and went to work with him. It was the best thing I've ever done. I wasn't intending to leave university, but I took the chance to try something different, and I don't regret it.

Like Share Reply

## Train to TH!NK

### Reading between the lines

*Sometimes a writer doesn't tell us everything directly: we need to draw conclusions from the information the writer gives. We call this 'reading between the lines'.*

**6 Answer the questions and give reasons for your answers.**

0 Is John worried about his abilities as a student?
*No, he says he'll do well in his exams and he's thinking about university.*

1 Has Amy been enjoying her work with a medical organisation?

2 Is Mark different now to when he was at school?

3 Did Pauline want to travel after leaving school?

## SPEAKING

**7 Work in pairs. Discuss these questions.**

1 What resolutions are you going to make for this school year?

2 What do you think is the secret of changing your life for the better?

*Plan carefully.*

*Do work first, play later.*

*Listen to your parents.*

## GRAMMAR
### Present tenses (review)

**1 Match sentences (1–4) with the tenses (a–d) and then complete the rule with the names of the tenses.**

1 I'm thinking about the big question: what next?
2 I've been asking myself if it's perhaps better to just find a job.
3 I spend up to an hour a day practising with friends.
4 I've made a resolution.

a present perfect continuous
b present simple
c present continuous
d present perfect

**RULE:**
We use the [5]______ to talk about something that happens regularly.
We use the [6]______ to talk about what's happening at or around the time of speaking.
We use the [7]______ to talk about past actions without saying when they happened.
We use the [8]______ to talk about actions that started in the past and are still happening.

**Look**

We can use the present continuous with *always* to complain about behaviour that we don't like and find annoying.

*My dad's always telling me what to do.*

**2 Complete the text with the correct present tense forms of the verbs. Sometimes more than one tense is possible.**

It's 2 am and I [1]________ (lie) in bed. I [2]________ (try) to get to sleep, but I can't. I [3]________ (have) trouble sleeping for about a month now. I [4]________ (try) different things to help me sleep, but nothing [5]________ (work). My mind [6]________ (not want) to stop. A lot [7]________ (happen) in my life right now. It's exam time, so I [8]________ (study) a lot. There's also the question of next year. I [9]________ (think) about it for ages. Mum and Dad [10]________ (want) me to go to university, but I'm just not sure what to do.

**3 SPEAKING Work in pairs. Think about a problem you've been having and tell your partner.**

*I've been fighting a lot with my little brother recently. I've tried to ignore him, but it's impossible.*

→ workbook page 10

## VOCABULARY
### Making changes

**4 Match the phrases with the definitions.**

0 make a resolution [f]
1 give something up [ ]
2 do well [ ]
3 struggle with something [ ]
4 take something up [ ]
5 take the chance (*to do something*) [ ]
6 get into the habit (*of doing something*) [ ]
7 change your ways [ ]

a stop doing something
b start doing something regularly
c use an opportunity
d find something difficult
e start a new hobby or interest
f decide to make a positive change
g do things differently (usually for the better)
h be successful

**5 Complete the email with the missing verbs.**

**Sam**
Sam@thinkmail.com

New Year's resolutions?

Last year I [1]______ loads of resolutions and decided to [2]______ my ways. I tried to [3]______ the habit of getting up early. For two months I got up at 8 am, and I even [4]______ running before going to school. But I started falling asleep in the afternoon, so I soon [5]______ that idea! Then I stopped eating meat. I was [6]______ well until Mum made roast beef. I just had to eat it. I also [7]______ the chance to start learning the piano when my school offered extra classes. But I [8]______ with finding time to practise, so I stopped. This year I've only made one resolution: not to make any resolutions!

**6 SPEAKING Work in pairs. Discuss these questions.**

1 What subjects are you doing well in at school?
2 What subjects do you struggle with?
3 What was the last thing you gave up doing? Why?

→ workbook page 12

## LISTENING

**7** SPEAKING **Work in pairs. Discuss these questions.**

1 What do you know about these people?
2 Can you match the information with each person?

A ______________________ was a famous painter.
B ______________________ is a film actress.
C ______________________ started a film studio.

**8** 1.02 **Listen and check.**

**9** 1.02 **Read the questions carefully. Listen again and make notes.**

1 What is Alan worried about?
2 Why does Becky tell Alan about Carey Mulligan?
3 Why was Walt Disney unsuccessful at first?
4 What does Alan not like about the example of Van Gogh?
5 How does Alan compare himself to Van Gogh?

**10** SPEAKING **Work in pairs. Compare your answers to Exercise 9.**

Grammar rap! 02

## GRAMMAR
### Future tenses (review)

**11 Look at the sentences from the listening. Complete them with the correct future forms of the verbs. Then complete the rule with the present continuous, *going to* or *will*.**

1 We ______________________ (have) a party at our place.
2 Are you ______________________ (apply) to other drama schools?
3 I'm sure one of them ______________________ (say) yes.

> **RULE:**
> - To talk about future arrangements, we often use the [4] ______ .
> - To make predictions, we often use [5] ______ .
> - To talk about intentions, we often use [6] ______ .

**12 Choose the best tense.**

1 *We'll go / We're going* to the beach this Friday. Do you want to come?
2 I don't think *I'll finish / I'm finishing* this homework.
3 *I won't go / I'm not going* to university this year. I want to take a year off.
4 I've got an appointment with the dentist tomorrow. *I'm seeing / I'll see* her at 10 am.
5 Daisy's learning to fly. *She'll be / She's going to be* a pilot.
6 I'm not *eating / going to eat* chocolate. That's my resolution for next year.
7 Argentina *will win / are winning* the next World Cup. That's what I think.
8 *We're flying / We'll fly* on Friday. I'm so excited.

**13 Write down:**

1 two arrangements you've got for this week.
2 two intentions you've got for this year.
3 two predictions for your life.

→ workbook page 11

# READING

**1** SPEAKING **Tick (✓) the statements you agree with. Add one more thing you think is important. Then discuss in pairs.**

A good life means …

- ☐ getting rich.
- ☐ having friends who care about you.
- ☐ settling down and having a family.
- ☐ liking what you've got and not thinking about what you haven't got.
- ☐ doing work that's important for you.

**2** 1.03 **Listen and read the text. Put the phrases (a–f) into the correct spaces. Listen and check.**

| | |
|---|---|
| a that's the point | d a good experience |
| b play live | e is allowed |
| c ~~really scares me~~ | f raise money |

**3** SPEAKING **Work in pairs. Discuss these questions.**

1 Which of the things on this list would be on yours, too?
2 What other things would be on your 'before I settle down' list?

## BEFORE I SETTLE DOWN – A LIST

***A British billionaire once said: 'You only live once, but if you do it right, once is enough.' I love that quote, but what does 'doing it right' mean?***

**I suppose my grandparents did it right. They both left school, went to university (where they met) and got degrees. They started careers (he was an accountant, she was a doctor), then they got married and started a family. They got promoted at different times and then they both retired at 60. And off they went to travel the world. They've been happy, I think. However, it's just not really what I want – not yet, anyway. Before I settle down, when I'm 30 or so, I want to do all kinds of things. Here are some of them.**

1 *Do something that [0] __c__. I'm terrified of heights, so sky-diving would be perfect!*

2 *Sleep on a beach under the stars. Where? Somewhere warm, of course, where sleeping on the beach [1] ______.*

3 *Take a really long train ride. The destination doesn't matter, it's the journey that's important. Train travel is brilliant – you can see the places you're passing through, you can meet and chat with other travellers, you can leave your seat and walk around. I love it!*

4 *Go somewhere where they don't speak English and I don't speak the language (Nepal?). It'll be hard, of course, but [2] ______!*

5 *Run a marathon. I'm not a good runner and perhaps I'm not up to a marathon, but I'd really like to try. And perhaps I can [3] ______ for my favourite charity (cancer research).*

6 *Learn how to cook at least ten things that I love to eat. Right now I can only cook two!*

7 *Have dinner with a friend in one of the world's best restaurants.*

8 *See lots – lots! – of my favourite bands [4] ______.*

9 *Do some kind of volunteer work for a while. In other words, work in order to help other people, not myself (though it'll be [5] ______ for me, too).*

10 *Make a list of other interesting things to do before I'm 40!*

**OK, that's my list. It's up to me to try to do these things. What would be on your list?**

# VOCABULARY
## Life plans

**4 Match the phrases with the pictures. Write 1–8 in the boxes.**

1 retire
2 travel the world
3 start a career
4 get a degree
5 start a family
6 settle down
7 get promoted
8 leave school

**5 Complete the text with phrases from Exercise 4. Use the correct forms of the verbs.**

My uncle has always done things differently. He [1]__________ when he was 18 because he wanted to see other places. He spent the next twenty years [2]__________ , working in restaurants and hotels in many different countries. When he was in his early forties, he decided to return to the UK. He went to university and [3]__________ . He did really well, and when he finished, he [4]__________ as a translator. Because he was good at his job, he [5]__________ quite quickly and he soon became Head Translator. When he was 48, he met the love of his life and they decided to [6]__________ and [7]__________ . Now he's 55, with three young children. He says he wants [8]__________ soon. He wants to stop working and take the whole family around the world with him. I wouldn't be surprised if he does.

→ workbook page 12

## WordWise: Phrases with *up*

**6 Match the phrases in bold with the definitions.**

1 **What's up**, Alan?
2 I spend **up to** an hour a day practising with friends.
3 What are you **up to** tomorrow night?
4 My time at school is almost **up**.
5 It's **up to me** now to try to do some of the things.
6 Perhaps I'm not **up to** a marathon.

a finished
b doing
c what's the matter?
d capable of
e as long as / to a maximum of
f my responsibility

**7 Use words and phrases from Exercise 6 to complete the sentences.**

1 What have you been ______ recently?
2 The time is almost ______ . Two more minutes!
3 Oh, no! You look really unhappy. ______ ?
4 It isn't my decision. It's ______ you to decide.
5 He's 75 now, so he isn't ______ long walks.
6 This car can carry ______ six people.

→ workbook page 12

**PRONUNCIATION**
Linking words with *up* Go to page 120.

# WRITING
## An email about resolutions

**8 Write an email to an English-speaking friend in another country. Describe your resolutions for the coming school year. Write about:**

- bad habits you're changing
- new classes you're taking
- activities you plan to take up
- why you're doing all of this

# DEVELOPING SPEAKING

**1** 🔊 1.06 **Look at the photo. How is the girl feeling? Listen and read to check.**

**Martin:** Hi, Sandra. I haven't seen you for ages. Where have you been hiding?

**Sandra:** Hi, Martin. Hiding? Nowhere. I've just changed some of my routines. I was feeling so stressed a few months ago that I thought, 'Sandra, you've got to make some changes.' So I did!

**Martin:** What kind of changes? Exercise? Sleep?

**Sandra:** Well, where shall I start? I'm eating better. And now you mention it, I'm trying to get seven hours sleep a night, minimum. But the big thing is my attitude.

**Martin:** And how has that changed?

**Sandra:** Well, I read an article about stress and it said something like 'Look at the big picture. How important is this problem? Is it going to matter in three months' time?' And I thought, that's right – the problem is, I worry about little things too much. So I'm trying to worry less.

**Martin:** But can you do that? If I'm honest, I'm a terrible worrier, too. But I can't stop.

**Sandra:** Don't be silly. Anyone can stop worrying – not overnight, but you can do it little by little.

**Martin:** Now I'm getting stressed about being someone who can't stop worrying.

**Sandra:** Let's go and have ice cream and talk more.

**Martin:** Thanks, Sandra. You're a star.

**Sandra:** Here we go, then! Ice cream coming up! And don't worry, I'll pay!

**2** 🔊 1.06 **Read and listen again to the dialogue. Answer the questions.**

1 What areas of her life does Sandra say she's changed?
2 How much sleep is she trying to get?
3 What advice did she get from the article?
4 What is Martin getting stressed about?

**3** SPEAKING **Discuss the questions in pairs. What do you think?**

1 Do things like diet and sleep help with stress?
2 Does the article give good advice? Why or why not?
3 Is it possible to slowly reduce how much you worry?

## Phrases for fluency

**4** **Find the underlined expressions in the dialogue. How do you say them in your language? Use the expressions to complete the conversations.**

1 **A** You look tired. Has it been a busy day?
**B** Busy? ______________________ ? First, I had a Maths test. Then I had Drama club at lunchtime. Then it was a five-kilometre run in PE …
**A** Well, you just sit down and I'll get you something to eat.
**B** Thanks, Mum. ______________________ .

2 **A** ______________________ , Annie? I haven't seen you for days.
**B** I haven't been anywhere. You're the one who disappeared.
**A** ______________________ , I have been quite busy.

3 **A** It's ten o'clock. Time for the test.
**B** ______________________ ! I'm really not ready for this.
**A** Me neither. I've got a feeling I'm not going to pass.
**B** ______________________ . You always pass.

## FUNCTIONS

### Expressing dissatisfaction

**KEY LANGUAGE**

I'm not happy with (my attitude).
The thing / problem is, (I worry too much).
If I'm honest, (I'm a terrible worrier, too).
My parents are always (telling me to work harder).

**5** **Match the parts of the sentences.**

1 I'm not happy with ☐
2 He's always ☐
3 If I'm honest, ☐
4 The problem is, ☐

a he just laughs when I complain about it.
b I don't like his attitude.
c borrowing my things without asking me.
d the things my brother does.

ROLE PLAY **Work in pairs. Student A: go to page 127. Student B: go to page 128.**

# LIFE COMPETENCIES

Stress can cause health problems, emotional problems and relationship problems. Finding ways to reduce or manage stress helps you feel healthier and happier, and be a better friend.

1 ▶ 03 **Watch the vlog. Why is Leo feeling stressed?**

2 ▶ 03 **Watch the vlog again and make notes about:**

a three symptoms of stress.
b three things you can do to deal with stress.

3 **Compare your notes with a partner.**

4 **Read this online article about stress. When can stress be useful?**

## ALL ABOUT STRESS

We tend to think of stress as negative, but in fact it's something normal. Stress is our body's natural way of reacting to a difficult situation. Stress improves our ability to perform under pressure and to avoid danger. Cavemen hunting dangerous animals for food felt stress, and famous singers perform better on stage because of stress. However, stress becomes a problem when it reaches high levels and continues for a long period of time.

People seem to feel more stress these days. Money is one source of stress. Not having any money at all is very stressful, but for most of us, the problem is that we always want something better or newer. And we worry unnecessarily about things we can't afford.

Things like mobile phones can be a problem, too. We spend our lives moving from screen to screen, responding to a huge number of messages and images instead of really relaxing. Exercise is great for reducing stress, but technology in the form of smartphones and computers also means that we do much less exercise now than people did in the past.

The level of stress in our daily lives means that when we have to face really challenging situations, like doing exams or performing in public, our bodies are often less able to cope with them in a positive way.

5 SPEAKING **Work in pairs. Answer the questions.**

1 When does stress have a negative effect on us?
2 Why does the writer think people are more stressed these days?
3 Do you agree that the things mentioned in the article cause stress?
4 Can you think of any other reasons why people feel stressed?

### Me and my world

6 **Make notes under the headings to show how your *family*, your *friends* and *school* might cause stress.**

FAMILY
__________
__________
__________
__________

FRIENDS
__________
__________
__________
__________

SCHOOL
__________
__________
__________
__________

7 SPEAKING **Think of a time when you were stressed. Talk to your partner about:**

- how you felt.
- what you did.
- what you would do differently in the future.

## TIPS FOR MANAGING STRESS

- **Tell people how you are feeling. Being strong means sharing, not hiding feelings.**
- **Be patient – try not to worry about things you can't control.**
- **Get enough sleep and exercise, and eat healthily.**

# 2 A HARD LIFE

**OBJECTIVES**

**FUNCTIONS:** talking about the past

**GRAMMAR:** narrative tenses (review); *would* and *used to*

**VOCABULARY:** descriptive verbs; time periods

**Get THINKING**

▶ 04

**Watch the video and think: would you like a demanding job when you leave school?**

## READING

1 **Look at the pictures and answer the questions.**

1 What do the pictures illustrate?
2 Where were the people from?
3 What happened to them?

2 **Read the article quickly. What is the big difference between James Ramsay and Mary Prince?**

3 🔊 2.01 **Read and listen to the article. Write R (Ramsay) or P (Prince) after each statement.**

1 Showed no discrimination __
2 Tried to escape their life __
3 Was separated from their parents when only a child __
4 Came from a family of slaves __
5 Was not popular with the local slave owners __
6 An event on a ship changed their life __
7 Their life became the subject of a book __
8 Helped slaves with their medical problems __

# THEY MADE A DIFFERENCE

## THE SLAVE TRADE

From the 16th to the 19th century, millions of people in Africa were taken from their homes and forced into lives of slavery. By the late 18th century many people had realised this was wrong and wanted to stop it. These people became known as 'abolitionists' and together they helped demolish one of the cruellest systems in the history of our world. Here are two of the men and women who made a huge difference.

One day in November 1759, the British ship *Arundel* was sailing the West Indies when a slave ship approached it, begging for help. Many of the slaves on the ship had died of disease and the others were living in horrible conditions. One person from the *Arundel* went to help – a young doctor called James Ramsay. He was horrified by what he saw and he never forgot this experience. Soon after this, he went to work on the island of St Kitts in the Caribbean. There he enraged local businessmen as he helped the slaves who worked for them and treated them for injuries and disease. He also worked as a church minister and he insisted on opening his church up to slaves as well as the white people. When Ramsay returned to England, he wrote books about his experiences. The vivid details he included shocked many people. He was also a huge influence on William Wilberforce, the leader of the anti-slavery movement in the UK and a politician who worked tirelessly to smash the laws and eventually succeeded in doing just that.

Mary Prince was born in Bermuda in 1788. As her mother and father were slaves she was a slave, too. She was sold a total of four times in her life. The first time with the rest of her family, but when she was 12, she was separated from them and went to work as a maid. She had been working at this job for a few months when she ran away to be with her mother, but she was soon captured and sent back. The third time she was sold to work in the salt ponds. The work was long and hard and the sun caused blisters on her body. She was also treated cruelly by her owners, who often struck her for the smallest of things. When she was 40, new owners took her to England. Slavery was illegal in the UK, so she was able to go and work with the abolitionists. In 1831, the Anti-Slavery Society published a book about her life story called *The History of Mary Prince*. Lots of people read the book and it helped many change their minds about slavery.

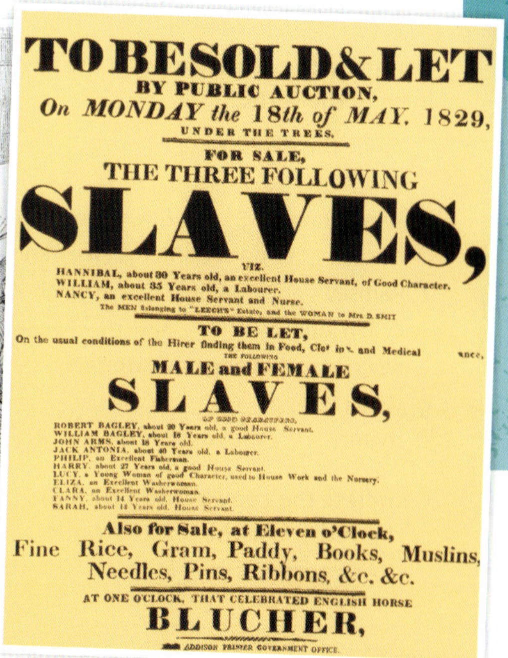


### Train to THINK

#### Following an idea through a paragraph

*It can be difficult to follow what a writer is trying to say in a longer paragraph. We need to read carefully to understand fully what the writer is saying.*

**4 Answer the questions.**

In paragraph 2 it says: 'he wrote books about his experiences.'

1 Look back at the paragraph. What were his experiences? Make a list of them.

Near the end of paragraph 3 it says: 'the Anti-Slavery Society published a book about her life story.'

2 Look back at the paragraph. What things might the book include?

### SPEAKING

**5 Work in pairs. Discuss these questions.**

1 Who would you suggest for the 'They Made a Difference' series?

2 Why would you include this person?

Grammar rap!

# GRAMMAR
## Narrative tenses (review)

**1 Match the sentences from the article on page 21 with the tenses. Then complete the rule.**

1 The British ship *Arundel* **was sailing** the West Indies when a slave ship approached.
2 Many of the slaves on the ship **had died of disease**.
3 She **had been working** at this job for a few months when she **ran away**.
4 In 1831, the Anti-Slavery Society **published** a book about her life.

a past perfect simple
b past simple
c past continuous
d past perfect continuous

**RULE:**
We use ...
[5] ______ to talk about finished actions in the past.
[6] ______ to set the scene or to talk about longer actions in the past interrupted by shorter actions.
[7] ______ to talk about actions before a certain time in the past.
[8] ______ to talk about actions that continued for some time before a certain time in the past.

**2 Complete the sentences with the past simple or past continuous form of the verbs.**

0 While the slaves *were working* in the fields, a fire *started* . (work / start)
1 When Ramsay ______ how serious the situation was, he ______ he ______ to do something. (see / know / have)
2 Ramsay ______ to help a slave when the man ______ . (try / die)
3 While Ramsay ______ how the owners treated the slaves, he ______ thinking how wrong it was. (watch / start)
4 While Ramsay ______ to the slave owners, many of them ______ the room. (talk / leave)

**3 Complete the conversation with the correct form of the verbs. Use the tenses from Exercise 1.**

burn | do | go | open | run | see | sit | walk

**Ian** I had a real scare yesterday. As I [1] ______ up to our house, I [2] ______ smoke coming from the window.
**Oli** [3] ______ something ______ ?
**Ian** Fortunately not. I [4] ______ into the house, [5] ______ the kitchen door and there was my brother. He [6] ______ on the floor in shock. He [7] ______ science experiments! One of them [8] ______ wrong and exploded.

→ workbook page 18

# VOCABULARY
## Descriptive verbs

**4 Certain verbs make narratives sound more dramatic. Find these words in a dictionary and write down:**

1 what they mean.
2 their past simple and past participle forms.

beg | demolish | enrage | ~~force~~ | shock | smash | strike

**5 Replace the underlined words with words from Exercise 4. Change the form if necessary.**

0 He was made to eat his vegetables by his mum. *forced*
1 The sad news surprised the people. ______
2 He asked urgently for help, but people just carried on walking. ______
3 It made me very angry when I heard what they had done. ______
4 They knocked down the houses to make space for new shops. ______
5 The car lost control and hit another vehicle. ______
6 He dropped the mirror and it broke into lots of pieces. ______

→ workbook page 20

**PRONUNCIATION**
Initial consonant clusters with /s/
Go to page 120.

## LISTENING

**6 Look at the picture. Why is this bird special?**

A It is the rarest bird in the world.
B It was once the most common bird in the world.
C It has a very unusual song.

**7 2.04 Listen to the interview with Chris Oddie. Check your answer to Exercise 6 and answer these questions.**

1 Who or what was Martha?
2 When was the last passenger pigeon seen in the wild?

**8 2.04 Listen again. Choose A, B or C for each question.**

1 What do we learn about passenger pigeons in Sarah's introduction?
   A They flew in enormous groups at night.
   B They lived up to the age of 50.
   C Their numbers dropped dramatically in the 19th century.
2 Which of these did not help lead to the extinction of the passenger pigeon?
   A a shortage of food
   B a big increase in hunting
   C better communication systems
3 Why did the US government law fail to help the passenger pigeon?
   A because people didn't respect the law
   B because no one cared about passenger pigeons
   C because they introduced the law too late
4 What does Chris hope we have learned from the extinction of the passenger pigeon?
   A All animals are equal.
   B Humans need to make sure animals are protected.
   C We need better programmes in zoos to help species in danger.

## THINK values

### Animal rights

**9 Read the scenarios. Match them with statements 1–6. There are two statements for each scenario.**

**Scenario A:** ☐ / ☐
Work on a huge multi-million-pound shopping centre has been stopped because nests of an extremely rare frog have been found in the area. It is one of only five places where this frog breeds. The property developers are putting pressure on the local government, saying it will be a disaster for the economy if they aren't allowed to finish the job.

**Scenario B:** ☐ / ☐
An elderly lady lives on her own. She has family, but they all live far away. A relative has suggested buying her a parrot for her 80th birthday. Other family members are against the idea of keeping an animal in a cage.

**Scenario C:** ☐ / ☐
There is a hotel that's very popular with tourists because it's close to a beautiful forest. The forest is home to a species of large spider. Although it's harmless, people working in the hotel have been given strict orders to kill any spiders that get into the guest rooms.

1 A bird in a cage can be a great companion for a person who lives alone, so it's the right present.
2 Creating places where people can relax is more important than worrying about a few animals.
3 We can't afford to lose any species of animal.
4 Places where endangered animals have their natural habitat belong to the animals, and not to people.
5 Spiders are ugly and disgusting, and many people are scared of them. Of course they should be killed.
6 Birds need to fly, and they need space to be able to do that. Cages should be forbidden.

**10 SPEAKING Which of the statements 1–6 do you agree and disagree with? Why? Make notes of your answers. Then compare your ideas in pairs or small groups.**

## READING

1 SPEAKING Work in pairs. Look at the pictures. What are the problems with baths like these?

2 2.05 Read and listen to the article. Then check your answers.

# A short history of bathing in the UK

**These days most people in the UK have access to hot water by simply turning on a tap. People know how important it is to keep clean and take baths and showers daily. But of course, it wasn't always so easy.**

In medieval times most people knew that washing your body with water was a good thing to do and there were instruction books that explained the importance of keeping your body clean. Some, though, offered rather strange advice, such as to avoid taking a bath in the summer or not to take long baths because they would make you fat.

In the palaces and houses of the rich, people enjoyed bathing in a wooden bathtub that servants filled with hot water. They would often add perfumes and flower petals to make the water smell nice. Having your own private bath was a sign of importance and King John, for example, used to take his bathtub with him whenever he travelled.

Most people had no bath of their own, but they might visit one of the many public baths that started to appear in most cities by then. These were often beside bakeries, and the heat from baking the bread was used to warm up the water.

People with no access to public baths would wash using only cold water and a cloth. When the weather was warm enough, they would jump in the nearest river for a wash.

By the early 1800s there were serious concerns about the dreadful conditions in crowded cities and people started to recognise the importance of hygiene. Some now bought metal bathtubs for their homes, although for most people there was no bathroom and the water still had to be carried in from outside and heated up. Many people still didn't use to have baths in their homes, but some could afford to make a weekly visit to the new public baths that opened in the 19th century. At the same time, bathing in the sea became popular as people looked to saltwater to help cure skin problems.

Bathing habits changed for good in the late 19th century when pipes could carry water directly into homes. Bathing became a lot easier and people started taking many more baths. However, many homes in the UK, especially those in rural areas, had to wait until as late as the 1960s before they had running water directly connected to them.

3 2.05 Read and listen to the article again. Mark the sentences T (true) or F (false).

1 In medieval England many people believed water was important for your health. ☐
2 Flower petals helped to keep people clean. ☐
3 King John had a bathtub made for him everywhere he went. ☐
4 Bathing in rivers was common in medieval times. ☐
5 By the early 1800s some people had hot water in their homes. ☐
6 In the early 1800s bathing in the sea was thought to help skin problems. ☐
7 Most homes in the UK had running water by the 1940s. ☐

4 SPEAKING Work in pairs. Discuss these questions.

1 How do medieval bathing habits compare with those of today?
2 How might bathing habits change in the future? Why do you think this?

## GRAMMAR
### *would* and *used to*

**5 Complete these sentences from the article on page 24. Then complete the rule with *used to / didn't use to* and *would(n't)*.**

1 King John ______ take his bathtub with him whenever he travelled.
2 People … ______ wash using only cold water and a cloth.
3 Many people still ______ have baths in their homes.

**RULE:**
To talk about habits and repeated actions in the past, we can use ***used to / didn't use to*** or ***would(n't)***.
- We use $^{4}$______ with both action and stative verbs.
- We use $^{5}$______ only with action verbs.

**6 Choose the correct words. Sometimes both options are possible.**

1 When I was a child, I *would / used to* play a lot with my sister.
2 We *would / used to* have a cat, Tubby.
3 We *would / used to* like her a lot and play with her all the time.
4 It's funny, but I *would / used to* think I'd never learn to read.
5 I *would / used to* sit and talk to my grandmother for hours.
6 My sister and I *would / used to* be such good friends!

**7 Complete the sentences and conversations with the correct form of *used to*.**

1 A ____________ you ____________ have a pet when you were a child?
B Yes, I ____________ have a cat.
2 We ____________ have a car. We used to walk everywhere.
3 A ____________ you ____________ watch a lot of TV when you were younger?
B Yes, I ____________ watch it every day when I got home from school.
4 I ____________ like vegetables, but I love them now.
5 A ____________ your dad ____________ read you stories before you went to bed?
B No, he didn't, but my mum ____________ .
6 I ____________ like having birthday parties. I was a really shy child.

→ workbook page 19

## VOCABULARY
### Time periods

**8 Look at phrases (1–9) and match them with categories (a–c).**

a the present
b the recent past
c a long, long time ago in history

1 from 1995 until 2004 ☐
2 in medieval times ☐
3 in this day and age ☐
4 these days ☐
5 in the olden days ☐
6 in the last century ☐
7 nowadays ☐
8 a decade ago ☐
9 not so long ago ☐

→ workbook page 20

## FUNCTIONS
### Talking about the past

**9 SPEAKING Work in pairs. Choose a topic for your partner and a period in the past. Your partner makes a comparison between the present and that time period. Take turns.**

food | games | home | school | technology | travel

*games in the 1930s*

*Well, children would play with teddy bears or dolls. These days, many children have electronic games.*

# Culture

**THINK**
Living in different climates

1 SPEAKING **Work in pairs. Look at the photos and try to match each one with a part of the world.**

Australia | the Himalayas | the Philippines | the Andes

2 2.06 **Read and listen to the article. Check your ideas.**

## CREATIVE CLIMATE SOLUTIONS

A

**Climate change is the biggest threat to our planet. As temperatures increase, the ice caps and glaciers around the world are starting to melt, meaning sea levels will get higher. We are already seeing the results of climate change with an increase in extreme weather events such as hurricanes and wildfires and serious shortages of water.**

**All over the world there are people living in difficult conditions. But difficult conditions often inspire creative solutions.**

Every year the Philippines are hit by huge tropical typhoons. These violent storms often kill hundreds of people and cause billions of dollars in damage to the islands. In an attempt to fight back, one company has come up with a house that is designed to stand up to the strongest of winds. The houses are built in a dome shape and the curved surfaces are much better at surviving in storms than traditional flat roofs and walls. They are also better at surviving earthquakes.

Wildfires often cause massive destruction in many places around the world, destroying land, homes and lives. In 2015 bush fires burned down vegetation in a large area of South Australia leaving nothing but bare earth. This made the land difficult to farm as strong winds blew the soil away. A farmer called Brian Fischer had a brilliant idea to stop the problem. With the help of his sons he ploughed the fields in spirals. This means that it doesn't matter which way the wind blows because it can never blow away the soil.

One man who wanted to tackle global warming directly was inventor Eduardo Gold. He used the idea that light colours reflect the sunlight to try to stop mountains in the South American Andes from heating up and losing their glaciers. His plan was simple; with the help of a few friends he started painting the mountains white in the hope it would keep their surfaces cooler. Although his idea was included in the World Bank's '100 ideas to save the planet' in 2009, Gold died in 2014 and his work had limited success.

A lack of water is one of the most serious problems we can face. In the Himalayan Desert water is very difficult to find during the spring months. To help solve this problem, the Ice Stupa project has come up with a very clever solution. In winter, a pipe takes water from higher up in the mountains down to the desert, where it rushes out as a fountain. Because it is so cold in the desert, the water freezes and makes frozen towers of ice. In the spring the ice melts giving the farmers the water they need for their land.

B

C

D

3 **Read the article again. Answer the questions.**

1 What shape are the houses in the Philippines and why?
2 What caused the problem in Australia and how did one farmer try to solve it?
3 What problem does an ice stupa solve?
4 What did Eduardo Gold do and why?

4 SPEAKING **Work in pairs. What other areas of the world are difficult to live in and why?**

5 VOCABULARY **There are eight highlighted words or phrases in the article. Match the words with these meanings. Write the words.**

1 to survive by resisting ______
2 large parts of frozen land ______
3 a structure that forces water up in the air ______
4 material on the surface of the ground ______
5 to motivate ______
6 to find an answer to ______
7 something there is not enough of ______
8 to send light back ______

## WRITING
### A magazine article about someone who made an important discovery

1 INPUT **Read the article. What discovery did John James Audubon make?**

2 ANALYSE **Find examples in the article of:**

1 a sentence containing the past simple and the past continuous.
2 the past perfect simple.
3 the past perfect continuous.
4 expressions referring back to the past.

3 **Read the essay again and make notes to complete the table.**

| | John James Audubon |
|---|---|
| His background | |
| What he discovered and how he discovered it | |
| Other information | |

4 PLAN **Think of someone who made a discovery.**

- Do some internet research to find out more about them.
- Choose the most important and interesting details.
- Organise the information into paragraphs. Write notes in the table above.
- Think about the language you'll need to describe the person and what they did.

5 PRODUCE **Write an article for your school magazine about a person who made a discovery (200 words).**

# John James Audubon

**John James Audubon was an American bird expert and wildlife painter. He was born in 1785 in Saint-Domingue in the Caribbean. He was brought up in France, but at the age of 18 his father sent him to live in the US.**

Audubon had always had a fascination for wildlife and, in particular, birdlife. He spent much of his time outdoors, studying and drawing nature. One of the things he had been wondering about was whether the same birds returned each year to his farm after disappearing for the winter months. One day, while he was drawing, he had an idea to test his theory. He caught a few birds and tied some cotton around their legs. The next year when he saw a bird with the cotton around its leg return, he knew his ideas were correct. He was one of the first people to start to understand bird migration and popularise birdwatching.

As well as his important studies into bird life, Audubon was an amazing artist. His *The Birds of America* is considered to be one of the best bird books ever written. These days it's also one of the most expensive: an original copy was recently sold for $7 million. He also identified 25 new species of birds and is regarded as a true hero of early American conservation.

# TOWARDS B2 First for Schools

## READING AND USE OF ENGLISH
### Multiple-choice cloze

→ workbook page 17

**1 For questions 1–8, read the text below and decide which answer (A, B, C or D) best fits each gap. There is an example at the beginning (0).**

0 A stopped B finished C ended D not

Do you ever stop and think about how easy the internet has made our lives? I know there are times when it's slow or has [0] ___A___ working altogether, times when maybe you feel like [1]______ your computer into pieces. But just think of all those things you use it for. You want to buy a new book – you can [2]______ online and buy it. You need to [3]______ some research for your homework – you can find it all there on the web. You feel like a [4]______ with your best friend, so you Skype them. You just want a [5]______ from your homework, so you start up Minecraft or whatever game it is you prefer and start playing. These [6]______ , everything we need is just a click of a button away.

Of course, it wasn't always like this. Only a few decades [7]______ , people had to do things like go to the shops if they wanted to buy something and often those shops were closed! They had to look in very large, heavy books called encyclopedias to find information. They had to [8]______ up the telephone if they wanted to talk, and if their best friend wasn't at home, they simply couldn't talk to them. That's how tough life was! And these poor people who had to suffer such hardships were … our parents! Makes you feel sorry for them, doesn't it?

| | A | B | C | D |
|---|---|---|---|---|
| 1 | begging | striking | forcing | smashing |
| 2 | come | enter | click | go |
| 3 | do | make | find | ask |
| 4 | talking | chat | question | speak |
| 5 | break | stop | end | fix |
| 6 | times | ages | years | days |
| 7 | after | since | ago | past |
| 8 | take | pick | grab | hold |

## SPEAKING
### Interview

→ workbook page 25

**2 In pairs, ask and answer the questions.**

1 Who do you spend the most time with at the weekends, and what do you do with them?
2 What kind of films do you like best? What do you like about them?
3 Where did you go for your last holiday? What was it like?
4 What's your favourite sport to play? What do you like about it?
5 What things do you enjoy doing the most with your parents?
6 What is your favourite room in your home and why do you like it?
7 If you could be anywhere now, where would it be and why?
8 What things do you like to do at home on a rainy day?
9 Who is your best friend and what do you like the most about him/her?

# TEST YOURSELF UNITS 1 & 2

## VOCABULARY

**1 Complete the sentences with the words in the list. There are four extra words.**

change | demolished | do | forced | form | give up | got into | got promoted | make | retire | settle | strike | struggle | travel

1 It would be wonderful to ____________ the world one day.
2 I'm happy I ____________ the habit of exercising every day.
3 He would always arrive late, and no one could make him ____________ his ways.
4 Good luck with the test – I'm sure you'll ____________ really well.
5 Every 31 December, I ____________ a resolution to do something, but I usually break it!
6 Mum makes more money now because she ____________ .
7 On her 65th birthday, she decided to ____________ and never work again.
8 I need more time to study for my exams, so I'm going to ____________ my judo classes for a while.
9 The hurricane ____________ more than 50 homes in the town.
10 As the flames got closer many people were ____________ to leave their homes.

/10

## GRAMMAR

**2 Complete the sentences with the phrases in the list. There are two extra phrases.**

was looking | would look | 'm seeing | are going to | go to | used to love | see | 'll love

1 I ____________ my aunt and uncle once a month.
2 Four or five of us ____________ eat curry tonight.
3 Have fun at the concert – I'm sure you ____________ it!
4 When I was a kid, I ____________ going to the river to swim.
5 I'm not very well, so I ____________ the doctor tomorrow.
6 When I saw her, she ____________ in a shop window.

**3 Find and correct the mistake in each sentence.**

1 When he was young, my dad used to reading books about nature.
2 When I got to the house, there was no one there. The party finished!
3 I am running in the park every morning before school.
4 We're really excited because we will go on holiday next week.
5 He was tired because he had been running two kilometres.
6 While I was cycling in the park, I was falling off my bicycle.

/12

## FUNCTIONAL LANGUAGE

**4 Choose the correct words.**

1 A I'm angry with Mike. He's *always* / *often* making jokes about me.
B I know. He's horrible. *I don't like* / *I'm not liking* him at all.
2 A You know, in the *past* / *olden* days, people didn't have the internet.
B I know! But *these days* / *not so long ago* we can get information so quickly!
3 A Gina and I *have* / *are having* lunch tomorrow. Why don't you come, too?
B Great – thank you! *I see* / *I'll see* you at the restaurant!
4 A No one *uses* / *is using* typewriters any more.
B Not in *nowadays* / *this day and age*, no!

/8

MY SCORE /30

22–30 | 10–21 | 0–9

# 3 WHAT'S IN A NAME?

**Get THINKING**

**Watch the video and think:**
**do you have a favourite logo? Why do you like it?**

**OBJECTIVES**

**FUNCTIONS:**
giving advice; expressing obligation; giving recommendations, warnings and prohibitions

**GRAMMAR:**
*(don't) have to / ought to / should(n't) / must; had better (not); can('t) / must(n't)*

**VOCABULARY:**
making and selling; expressions with *name*

## READING

1 **Look at the names and logos and answer the questions.**

1 These are the names and logos of various companies. What kind of products do they offer?

*Jaguar sells cars.*

2 Add two more names of companies or products that are famous around the world.

2 SPEAKING **Work in pairs. Some people think the name of a brand is very important. What do you think is the reason for this?**

3 **Read the blog entry on the next page quickly. Which of the brands shown above does it mention?**

4 3.01 **Read the blog entry again and listen. Answer the questions.**

1 Why do companies think a lot about a brand name?
2 What makes a good brand name?
3 Why were each of these names chosen?
   - Jaguar • Pret A Manger • WhatsApp
4 Why was Nova a bad name for a car in Spain?
5 Why do some teenagers choose to buy more expensive products (like clothes)?

**Train to THINK**

### Identifying the main topic of a paragraph

*Writers use a new paragraph when they want to change the topic. The opening line of a paragraph usually gives you a clue about its topic.*

5 **Look at paragraphs 3 and 4. What is the topic of each paragraph? Tick (✓) two options.**

A what teenagers wear to school ☐
B brand names are important in the teenage market ☐
C some really bad brand names ☐
D ways to pick a brand name ☐

# Brand names

**1** OK, so imagine you've thought of a great idea for a product to make and sell – a game, or an app, or clothes, for example. You know you can sell millions of them, but first of all, you must give the product a name – a brand name. And that may not be as easy as you think.

**2** The brand name is the thing that distinguishes your product from all others, and it's really important that it makes an impact. Businesses spend a lot of time thinking about brand names; when the name has been picked, it's very difficult to change, so companies have to get it right first time.

**3** So how do you choose a name? A brand name ought to be unique, memorable and easy to understand. It should create some kind of emotional connection with people who buy the product – the target market. Some companies use the family name. When Henry Ford started making cars, he just called the company Ford. But you don't have to use a family name – you can go for an image. Staying with cars, think about the brand name Jaguar, a beautiful but dangerous wild cat. What does that say about the manufacturer's product? Some companies use wordplay. It's a common technique for naming apps, for example WhatsApp (from the English expression 'What's up'?). Others like to use foreign words because they sound special or different. For example, in Britain, in Europe and in the US there's a chain of sandwich shops with the French name Pret A Manger, which means 'ready to eat'. And what do you have to be careful about when choosing a name? Well, you shouldn't choose one that might not work in certain countries or cultures. Many years ago, a car company launched a new car that they called Nova. They thought it suggested something nice and new, but in Spanish it can be read as *no va* ('it doesn't go'). Not a good name for a car in Spain, then!

**4** These days, the choice of brand name is particularly important if your product is targeted at the teenage market. Teenage consumers are perhaps more concerned with brand names and company logos than any other group. When a brand, especially a clothing brand, becomes popular with teenagers, then there's a lot of pressure to wear those clothes and have the name and/or logo visible. A teacher in an American high school said: 'I certainly see that kids are obsessed with brand names. They won't buy something that's almost identical – and cheaper – simply because they feel they must wear something with the right logo.' So if you want to get into the teenage market, you have to find a product and a brand name that works with that age group, and create some great advertisements, too.

**5** Companies know that the name isn't everything – the product itself has to be good, of course – but it's an essential part of the package.

## SPEAKING

**6 Work in pairs. Discuss these questions.**

1 Can you think of any more brand names which:
   - a use a family name?
   - b try to create an image?
   - c are in another language?

2 Have you ever bought or wanted something just because of the brand? Give examples.

*'I'm so glad that we don't have to wear school uniforms any more!'*

## GRAMMAR
### *(don't) have to / ought to / should(n't) / must*

**1 Complete the sentences from the article on page 31. Then complete the rule with *have to, don't have to, ought to, should, shouldn't* and *must*.**

1 First of all, you ______ give the product a name.
2 Companies ______ get it right first time.
3 A brand name ______ be unique, memorable and easy to understand.
4 But you ______ use a family name.
5 And what ______ you ______ be careful about?
6 Well, you ______ choose a name that might not work in certain countries or cultures.

> **RULE:** We use [7]______ or ______ to say 'this is important or necessary'. We use [8]______ to say 'this isn't important or necessary'. We use [9]______ or [10]______ to tell someone that something is a good idea. We use [11]______ to tell someone that something isn't a good idea. (***Ought to*** isn't as frequent as ***should***. It is used mostly in writing, and the negative form is rare.)

**2 Complete the conversation with the correct form of *have to*.**

**Mandy** Mum, there's a new mobile phone out. It's brilliant. I [1]______ get one!
**Mum** No way! Your mobile phone is fine. You [2]______ buy another one.
**Mandy** But you know what it's like at school. Everyone [3]______ have the latest product!
**Mum** Yes, and it's terrible. Why [4]______ you all ______ wear the same clothes, for example?
**Mandy** Because it's what teenagers do. You were young once. Don't you remember?
**Mum** I see. And I [5]______ go to work to pay for all these things, right?
**Mandy** Oh, Mum! You [6]______ be difficult!

**3 Complete the conversation with suitable modal verbs. There is often more than one possible answer.**

**Gill** The new café is great – you [1]______ go there.
**Jack** I've heard it's a bit expensive.
**Gill** Yes, that's true. You [2]______ go there every day. But you [3]______ try the cakes – they're delicious!
**Jack** OK. What's the place called, anyway?
**Gill** Can you believe it's called The Coffee Shop?!
**Jack** What a boring name! You [4]______ be a genius to think of that! They [5]______ have a foreign name, like Le Café.
**Gill** Well, OK. But it [6]______ be easy to pronounce. There's a shop in town called Arighi Bianchi and no one knows how to say it.
**Jack** But the owner is Italian. It's his name!
**Gill** I guess I [7]______ know that. Anyway, I [8]______ go home and do my homework for tomorrow.
**Jack** You [9]______ worry about that. It's easy.
**Gill** Really? OK, so let's go to the cinema. There's a new film that we [10]______ see!

→ workbook page 28

## VOCABULARY
### Making and selling

**4 Complete the sentences with the words.**

advertisement | brand | chain | consumers
image | logo | manufacturer | products

1 They make cleaning ______, like washing powder.
2 The prices have gone up a lot, so now ______ have to pay more.
3 I always buy the same ______ of shoes – they're so comfortable.
4 It's a ______ that has shops in every town.
5 That shop has a really funny ______ on TV.
6 The Nike ______ is a large tick.
7 When the company's director went to prison, it damaged the company's ______.
8 If it doesn't work, send it back to the ______.

**5 SPEAKING Answer the questions. Then work in pairs and compare your answers.**

Can you name …
1 three places where you find advertisements?
2 a manufacturer of mobile phones?
3 a chain of shops and a chain of restaurants?
4 one thing you always buy the same brand of?

→ workbook page 30

## LISTENING

**6** 3.02 **Listen to Paul talking to Alexandra. What is their conversation about? Choose the correct option.**

A why it's good to have a nickname
B how people get their nicknames
C why some people don't like their nicknames

**7** 3.02 **Listen again. Mark the sentences T (true) or F (false).**

1 There are at least two shortened versions of the name Alexandra. ☐
2 Paul got the nickname Smithy because he lived in a town called Smith. ☐
3 Paul's brother liked his nickname. ☐
4 Sting got his nickname because he liked bees. ☐
5 Miley Cyrus's real name is Destiny. ☐
6 Lady Gaga got her name from a text message. ☐

## GRAMMAR
### *had better (not)*

**8 Complete these sentences from the listening. Then choose the correct words to complete the rule.**

1 We ______________________ go now.
2 You ______________________ tell anyone at school.

**RULE:** We use ***had ('d) better*** to warn someone that something bad will happen if they [3]***do / don't do*** something. We use ***had ('d) better not*** to warn someone that bad things will happen if they [4]***do / don't do*** something.

**9 Complete the sentences with *had better (not)*.**

1 The bus goes in two minutes. You ______________________ run.
2 I'll lend you my pen – but you ______________________ break it!
3 It's going to rain. We ______________________ go inside.
4 You have to get up very early tomorrow, so you ______________________ go to bed. It's 1 am.
5 You ______________________ eat any more sweets. You'll be sick.

→ workbook page 29

## FUNCTIONS
### Giving advice

**10** 3.03 **Put the sentences in the correct order to make two conversations. Then listen and check.**

1 ☐ **Liam** Why? What's her name?
☐ **Liam** What's the matter, Jo?
☐ **Liam** Well, you'd better get some help – quickly!
☐ **Jo** It's something like Sharita Wass Ikonor.
☐ **Jo** I've got to phone someone and I've no idea how to pronounce her name.

2 ☐ **Bob** Well, I wrote the wrong name in my birthday card to her son. I called him Jason, not Jacob.
☐ **Bob** I know. She's really cross.
☐ **Bob** My sister's really angry with me.
☐ **Mia** Why?
☐ **Mia** You'd better not do that again!

**11** SPEAKING **Work in pairs. Imagine you forgot your best friend's birthday. Write a conversation using *had better (not)*.**

## SPEAKING
### People and their names

**12 Complete the questionnaire with 1–5 (1 = I strongly agree; 5 = I strongly disagree).**

1 It's cool to have a nickname. ☐
2 I only remember the names of people I like. ☐
3 I hate it when people forget my name. ☐
4 Your name is an important part of who you are. ☐
5 I feel sorry for people who have unusual names. ☐

**13 Compare your answers in small groups. Which question(s) do you agree on?**

## READING

1 **Can you match these American cities with their nicknames?**

1 New York ☐  a The Windy City
2 Chicago ☐  b The Big Apple

2 **Here are seven names of real towns. What country do you think each city town is in? Choose from the list.**

Austria | Belgium | Scotland
the Netherlands | the US (x2) | Turkey

3 3.04 **Read and listen to the article and check your answers to Exercise 2.**

4 **Read the article again. Answer the questions.**

1 How did Mr Deakins choose which land to take?
2 What or who is an Accidental?
3 Why was Levi Davis's store in a good position?
4 When did the place name Hot Coffee become official?
5 What problem did the village of Lost have?
6 How did they solve this problem?
7 How did the city of Batman probably get its name?
8 Why was the mayor of Batman annoyed with Christopher Nolan?

# FUNNY place names

**Around the world, there are lots of names for towns and villages that sound funny in English – for example, Monster in the Netherlands, Egg in Austria and Silly in Belgium. Here are a few of my favourites.**

In around 1751, George Deakins was offered some land in the US by King George II of England as payment for a debt. 'You can choose a piece of land anywhere in Western Maryland,' the king said. Mr Deakins sent two teams of engineers to find the best land, without actually working together. The two teams came back with their maps and to their surprise, they discovered they had chosen exactly the same piece of land. Mr Deakins called it, 'The Accident Tract', and that's how the town got its name. And guess what a person from Accident is called: an Accidental!

In Mississippi, in the late 1800s, you had to travel a long way to take your crops to market and to buy food and provisions. When Levi Davis built a store halfway between Natchez and Mobile, it provided a welcome break. He always offered tired travellers a good pot of hot coffee which he advertised as 'the best coffee around'. Soon his store became well known as a place to stop for hot coffee and the surrounding area became known as Hot Coffee, too. In the 1920s, the name Hot Coffee began appearing on maps. Today, you can still see the road signs to Hot Coffee, but maybe it's not really 'the best coffee around' any more.

There is a little village in Aberdeenshire, Scotland called Lost. (The name comes from the word *Lòsda* in Scottish Gaelic.) Visitors loved the name and local road signs were often stolen. In fact, the longest time a sign stayed there was for three months, and the council became so fed up with this that they decided to change the name to Lost Farm. However, the local people complained. 'We're happy with the name,' they said. 'You mustn't change it.' So the name wasn't changed and instead the council made the road signs stronger. Now people can't take the signs, but they can still have their photograph taken beside them.

The Turkish city Batman takes its name from a river and not from the comic book superhero. The river's name was probably inspired by the Bati Raman Mountain. However, there is still a connection with the Batman we've seen on the screen. In 2008, the mayor of Batman said that Christopher Nolan, the director of *The Dark Knight*, should have to pay money to the city for using the name Batman without permission. 'There is only one Batman in the world', he said. 'The American film producers used the name of our city without informing us.' Of course, Nolan didn't have to pay, though. It's true that filmmakers can't steal information and ideas, but the name Batman has been around since the character was created in 1939.

## SPEAKING

**5 Work in pairs. Discuss these questions.**

1 Do you know how your town or city got its name?
2 What funny or unusual town names are there in your country?

## GRAMMAR
### *can('t) / must(n't)*

**6 Complete these sentences from the reading. Then complete the rule with *can*, *can't* and *mustn't*.**

1 'You ______ choose a piece of land anywhere in Western Maryland'.
2 'We're happy with the name. You ______ change it.'
3 It's true that filmmakers ______ steal information and ideas.

**RULE:** To talk or ask about permission, we often use the modal verb [4]______ . To say what isn't allowed, we often use [5]______ or ______ .

**7 Complete the sentences with *mustn't* and the verbs. Then match them with the pictures.**

be | miss | run | talk

1 You ______ so loudly!
2 I ______ late.
3 I ______ the goal!
4 You ______ .

A

C

B

D

**8 Rewrite the sentences using modal verbs from this unit and the pronouns in brackets. There is often more than one possible answer.**

0 Diving isn't allowed. (you) *You can't dive here.*
1 It isn't necessary for us to wear uniforms. (we)
2 It's a good idea to buy a new phone. (you)
3 It's OK for you to use my laptop. (you)
4 It's necessary for them to work harder. (they)
5 Are we allowed to play here? (we)

→ workbook page 29

## VOCABULARY
### Expressions with *name*

**9 Match the underlined expressions with the definitions.**

1 Tony Hawk is a big name in skateboarding.
2 He's upset because some of the other kids call him names.
3 Jay-Z isn't his real name – it's his stage name.
4 Fish, meat, vegetables, fruit – you name it, I eat it.
5 Look! It's what's-his-name / what's-her-name.
6 We want to get married, but we haven't named the day yet.
7 I know you don't want to do the exams, but it's the name of the game for university entry.
8 He made a name for himself as a great actor.

a decide the date of an event, often a wedding
b someone whose name I can't remember
c something necessary that you have to accept
d a person who is important or famous in their profession
e a name that an actor or musician uses in their profession
f use rude names about, or to, a person
g become known or respected by many people
h anything you say (or choose)

**10 Complete the missing word(s).**

1 She's been to Europe, Asia and Australia – you ______ ______ , she's been there!
2 Hard work is the ______ of ______ ______ if you want to do well in your exams.
3 My uncle's a doctor. He's a ______ ______ in the field of cancer research.
4 Some of her classmates ______ her ______ . It's horrible for her.
5 You're engaged? That's wonderful! When are you going to ______ ______ day?
6 Oh look! There's ______ -his- ______ – you know, that boy who lives in your street.
7 She made a ______ for ______ on a reality TV show and became a famous singer.
8 Bruno Mars is the ______ name of Pete Gene Hernandez.

→ workbook page 30

**PRONUNCIATION**
Strong and weak forms: /ɒv/ and /əv/
Go to page 120.

# Fiction

1 **Read the introduction. What kind of story is this?**

## How I Met Myself

by David A. Hill

John Taylor is an Englishman living in Budapest with his wife and daughter. One day he is knocked over in the street by a man who looks exactly like him – his 'doppelgänger'. He starts to look for more information about the man, and learns that he is a Hungarian called János Szabó. But he also learns that Szabo died in the 1956 Hungarian Revolution.

2 3.07 **Read and listen to the extract. What does the Hungarian word *szabó* mean in English? Why is this important for John?**

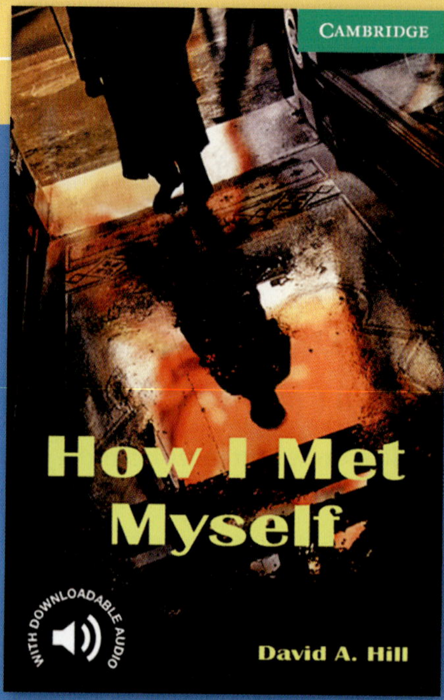


The next day, I was walking home from work. [...] As I went along a street I saw some men putting up a new sign on an old shop. There was the owner's name in red, and below it the word *szabó* in green. In the window there were suits, jackets and trousers. *Szabó*. Tailor. The tailor's was getting a new sign. '*Szabó*,' I thought. Then I said 'János Szabó' out loud. Then I thought, 'Janos the tailor. John the tailor. John Taylor.' I stopped in the street. János Szabó was John Taylor! My doppelgänger and I shared a name. John Taylor was the English for the Hungarian János Szabó. My hair stood up. Here was something new and important: we shared the same name!

I [...] thought about what I had discovered. I tried to decide what to do. Should I tell Andrea about this? Perhaps it would help her to believe me? I didn't know. [...] I decided to go and see Mrs Fischer again. I walked quickly round to [...] her flat.

'Do you remember I came to ask you about János Szabó, Mrs Fischer?' I asked when she let me in.

'Oh, the poor young man,' she said, looking at me sadly. 'And do you know something – you look so like him, too.'

This was quite a surprise. 'Really?' I asked.

'Come here under the light,' she said.

I moved under the strong light in the hall.

'Yes,' she said, looking at me carefully. 'You look very much the same. The eyes, the nose, the mouth. Very much the same. I didn't look at you carefully when you came last time. Oh, the poor young man.'

I felt myself getting very hot.

'Mrs Fischer, I came to ask you something different,' I said. Then I went on very slowly, because I was so afraid of her possible answer. 'Can you remember the names of the wife and daughter who were killed in the cellar?'

'Well, I know the wife was called Andrea,' she started, and I felt my face go white, 'but as for the little girl ... let's think ...'

I waited for a moment. She didn't seem able to remember.

'It wasn't ...' I waited, and then said, 'It wasn't Kati, was it?'

Mrs Fischer looked at me and smiled. 'Yes, that was it,' she said. 'Quite right. Andrea and Kati. The poor young things.'

I thanked her and left as quickly as I could. My head was turning round and round. I felt sick. Outside in the cold street, I stood against the wall of the building. There were too many new things inside my head to understand at once: my doppelgänger had the same name as me – Szabó, or Taylor – I looked like him, and his wife and daughter had the same names as mine!

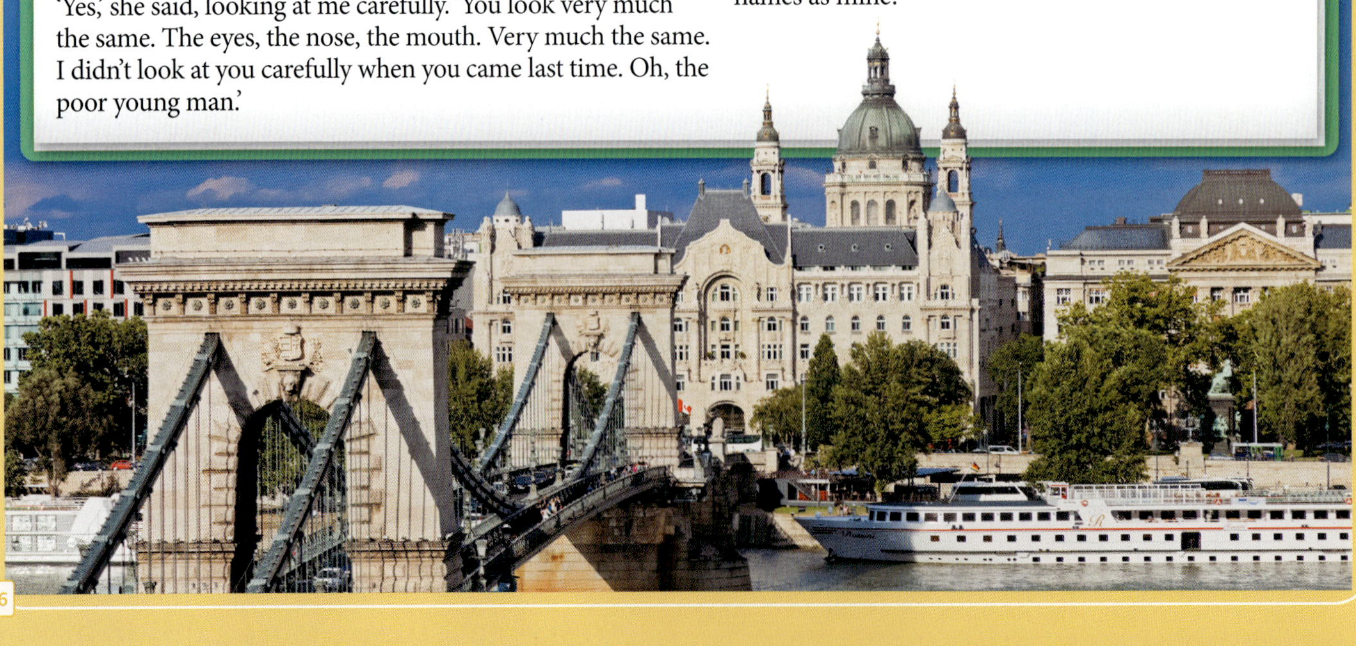

**3 Read the extract again. Mark the statements T (true) or F (false).**

1 John Taylor goes into a shop to buy a suit. ☐
2 He realises that János Szabó is a translation of John Taylor. ☐
3 John's wife Andrea doesn't believe something he told her. ☐
4 It is not the first time he has talked to Mrs Fischer. ☐
5 He is scared to ask Mrs Fischer about the wife and daughter's names. ☐
6 He is happy when he leaves Mrs Fischer's flat. ☐

**4 SPEAKING Work in pairs. Discuss these questions.**

1 Why does Mrs Fischer call Szabó 'the poor young man'?
2 What do you think happened in the cellar?
3 What might happen next to solve this mystery?
4 Would you like to meet someone who looks exactly like you and has the same name? Why or why not?

## WRITING

### A reply to a letter asking for advice

**1 INPUT Read the letter and the reply. Then answer the questions.**

1 What is Alan's problem?
2 What question does Susannah suggest that Alan asks himself?

**2 Complete the missing words from Susannah's reply.**

1 This is the first question you ______ ______ ask yourself.
2 If the answer is no, then maybe ______ ______ end the friendship now.
3 ... you ______ ______ talk to him about the name-calling ...
4 ... and explain that he ______ ______ stop saying those things.
5 Finally, ______ ______ ______ ______ to talk to your parents.

**3 ANALYSE Read Susannah's reply again. In which paragraph does she ...**

1 offer advice to make the friendship work?
2 outline Alan's problem?
3 tell him to speak to others about his problem?
4 ask Alan to think more carefully about the situation?

**4 PLAN Read another letter to Susannah. Write three pieces of advice for Lara.**

**5 PRODUCE Write a reply to Lara (150–200 words). Say what you think she should do.**

## SUSANNAH'S ADVICE PAGE

***Write with your problem and Susannah will give you advice. This week's letter is from Alan in Salisbury, UK.***

**Dear Susannah,**

Last month, we moved to a new town. My parents quickly made friends with the people who live next door. They've got a son of about my age. He's friendly and invites me to do things with him. But the thing is, when we see other kids, he calls them names and makes horrible comments. He wants me to join in, but I don't want to.

What can I do? If I tell my parents, it'll be hard because they really like his parents. And to be honest, I haven't got many other friends yet. If I stop hanging out with him, maybe he'll start calling me names, too.

What should I do?

***Alan, Salisbury***

Dear Alan,

It's often difficult to make new friends when you move to a new town, so it was almost perfect that your new neighbours had a son your age and that he wanted to be your friend. What a shame that you're finding it difficult to spend time with him.

You don't say in your letter if you think you could be friends if his behaviour was better. This is the first question you ought to ask yourself. If the answer is no, then maybe you'd better end the friendship now. Don't worry – I'm sure you'll soon make lots of friends when you start school.

However, if you think you could be friends, then you should definitely talk to him about the name-calling and explain that he had better stop saying those things. If he's going to be a good friend, he'll listen to you. If he ignores you, then this friendship probably isn't going to work.

Finally, it's a good idea to talk to your parents. They're the people who know you best and are often the best people to give you advice.

Good luck!

***Susannah***

**Dear Susannah,**

I have very bad eyesight and need to wear glasses. Because of this, some people at school call me names. I tried not to let it bother me too much, but the problem is that it happens quite often. I've always enjoyed school and had lots of friends, but I'm starting to hate going there. My grades are also getting worse and some of the teachers have said they're disappointed with me. I know I should talk to the teachers, but I'm sure this is only going to make things worse. Can you help?

***Lara, Ipswich***

# 4 WHAT WOULD YOU DO?

**OBJECTIVES**

**FUNCTIONS:** talking about hypothetical situations; expressing wishes; apologising and accepting apologies

**GRAMMAR:** first and second conditional (review); time conjunctions; *wish* and *if only*; third conditional (review)

**VOCABULARY:** being honest; making a decision; *now*

**Get THINKING**

Watch the video and think: are you always honest with your friends?

A

C

B

D

## READING

1 **Read the definition. Then look at the pictures. What dilemmas do you think they show?**

> **dilemma:** a situation in which a difficult choice has to be made between two or more alternatives

2 **Read the quiz on the next page quickly. Match each picture with a question.**

3 4.01 **Read and listen to the quiz. Then take the quiz and compare with a partner.**

4 **Match these responses with the quiz questions.**

a I'd keep quiet and run back to the middle of the pitch. ☐

b I'd ask if I could change it for another one. ☐

c I wouldn't look because I'd be scared of getting caught. ☐

d I'd tell the person who did it that they should tell the truth. ☐

e I'd put it in my pocket as quickly as I could. ☐

f I'd make the door dirty to try and cover it up. ☐

# HOW HONEST ARE YOU?

**Take our quiz! For each question choose A, B or C.**

## What would you do if ...

**1 you gave a £10 note to buy a £5 item, but the assistant gave you £15 change by mistake?**

- A I'd take the money and walk out quickly.
- B I'd tell the assistant he had made a mistake and give ten pounds back.
- C I'd take the money and give it to a homeless person.

**2 your grandparents gave you a shirt as a present, but you didn't like it?**

- A I'd say thank you but never wear the shirt.
- B I'd say thank you but tell them it really wasn't my style.
- C I'd say thank you but only wear it when I was with them.

**3 you scored a goal in a football match, but you knew it wasn't legal because the ball had hit your hand without the referee seeing it?**

- A I'd celebrate my goal in the usual way.
- B I'd tell the referee that the ball hit my hand, so it wasn't a goal.
- C I'd say sorry to the players on the other team but tell them it was the referee's mistake, not mine.

**4 you kicked a stone outside your house and it made a dent in the neighbour's car door?**

- A I wouldn't do anything.
- B I'd ring my neighbour's doorbell and tell them I'd damaged their car.
- C I'd tell the neighbours that their car was damaged but I didn't know who did it.

**5 you couldn't answer a question in a test, but you realised you could see another student's answer?**

- A I'd try to copy their answer.
- B I wouldn't look, but would just try to answer the question myself.
- C I'd look a little bit to help myself think more clearly.

**6 your school principal wanted to know who broke a classroom window, and you knew who the person was?**

- A I wouldn't say anything.
- B I'd go to the principal's office and say who did it.
- C I'd write a note to the principal, saying who did it but without putting my name on the note.

## RESULTS

**MOSTLY A:** Sometimes you take the easy way out. Be careful, because it may cause you problems. You don't want people to think of you as dishonest.

**MOSTLY B:** You're basically an honest person. You understand that if you always tell the truth, people will trust you. But don't forget that the truth can hurt a little, too, sometimes!

**MOSTLY C:** Perhaps you should ask yourself why you are taking this middle path between being dishonest and being completely honest? Perhaps you'd feel better if you always acted 100% honestly.

## Train to TH!NK

### Thinking of consequences

*In order to make a good decision, it's important to think of all the possible consequences for others and for yourself.*

**5 Choose four of the questions in the quiz. Think of possible consequences for each option.**

| Question | Action | Consequence |
|---|---|---|
| 1 | *I tell the man about his mistake.* | *I don't get an extra £10.* |
| | *I take the money.* | *Maybe the man loses that money from his wages that week.* |

## SPEAKING

**6 Work in pairs. Discuss these questions.**

1. Which of the situations in the quiz is the most / least serious?
2. Do you agree with what the results say about you?

# GRAMMAR

## First and second conditional (review)

**1 Complete these sentences from the quiz on page 39 with the correct forms of the verbs. Then match them with the parts of the rule.**

1 What ______ you ______ (do) if you ______ (kick) a stone and it ______ (make) a dent in the neighbour's car door?

2 If you always ______ (tell) the truth, people ______ (trust) you.

**RULE:**
We use the first conditional to talk about real situations and their consequences. We form it with *if* + present simple / future (*will*) clause. ☐
We use the second conditional to talk about hypothetical or very unlikely situations and their outcomes. We form it with *if* + past simple / (*would*) clause. ☐

**2 Complete the conditional sentences with the correct forms of the verbs. Think carefully about whether each one is a first or second conditional.**

### What should I do?

Why is Jan so mean to me? If Jan [1]______ (not be) so mean to me, I [2]______ (want) to invite her to my party. The problem is, she's so popular. If she [3]______ (not have) so many friends, nobody [4]______ (care) if she was at my party or not. I have to invite her. If I [5]______ (not invite) Jan to my party, nobody [6]______ (come) to it. Maybe I shouldn't have a party. But if I [7]______ (not have) a party, I [8]______ (not get) any presents and I want presents! Why are birthdays always so much trouble? If it [9]______ (not be) my birthday next week, my life [10]______ (not be) so complicated. If I [11]______ (know) what to do, I [12]______ (do) it. But I don't!

→ workbook page 36

## Time conjunctions

**3 Complete the sentences with the words.**

as soon as | if | unless | until | when

1 I don't know where he is, but I'll tell him ______ I see him.
2 I'm meeting him later, so I'll tell him ______ I see him.
3 It's really important. I'm going to tell him ______ I see him.
4 I won't tell him anything ______ he asks.
5 I'll work ______ he arrives and then I'll stop.

**4 Complete the sentences so that they are true for you. Tell your partner.**

1 As soon as I get home tonight, I …
2 If the weather is good this weekend, I …
3 When I'm 18, I …
4 Unless I get lots of homework this weekend, I …
5 I'm going to save all my money until …

→ workbook page 36

# VOCABULARY

## Being honest

**5 Write the words in the correct columns.**

~~cheat~~ | get away with something
hide the truth | do the right thing | tell a lie
be open about something | tell the truth
own up to something

| Positive behaviour | Negative behaviour |
|---|---|
| | *cheat* |

**6 Compete the conversation with the correct form of the verbs from Exercise 5.**

**Dan** I've got a dilemma. The other day I [1]______ in a test. I copied from Ben.
**Ana** Why?
**Dan** Well, I thought I could [2]______ away with it, but now the teacher wants to know who copied who. I said it was Ben.
**Ana** You should [3]______ up to it and say it was you.
**Dan** I know, but it's too difficult to [4]______ the truth.
**Ana** But you can't [5]______ the truth now! What about poor Ben? What were you thinking?
**Dan** It's Maths. I just find it so difficult.
**Ana** Well, you need to [6]______ about this. First, say sorry for cheating and explain why you [7]______ a lie. Then tell your teacher what the problem is.
**Dan** You're right, of course. It's just so difficult to [8]______ the right thing sometimes.

→ workbook page 38

## LISTENING

7 SPEAKING **Work in pairs. Look at the photo. What do you think they are doing?**

8 4.02 **Listen to the conversation. Were you right? What did they decide to do?**

9 4.02 **Listen again. Choose the correct answers.**

1 Why are the teenagers there?
   A they are going on a long journey
   B they are waiting for a friend
   C they are going home
2 What do they decide to play?
   A a card game invented by Angie
   B a guessing game invented by Stuart
   C a traditional children's game
3 Why does Maria say 'a cartoon animal, perhaps'?
   A because animals aren't usually tall
   B because the game can only have fictional characters
   C because Stuart is thinking of a non-human character
4 Why does Angie give three clues at the same time?
   A because Jenny's bus is arriving
   B because she wants to make the game easier
   C because she's bored with the game
5 Why is Angie wrong to make Gru say,'I wish I could steal the moon'?
   A because in the film, Gru steals the moon
   B because in the film, Gru doesn't steal the moon
   C because Angie is reading *The Lord of the Rings*

## GRAMMAR
### *wish* and *if only*

10 **Read the sentences. Which fictional characters might say them? Complete the rule. Use the sentences to help you.**

1 'If only I **spoke** Luke Skywalker's language.'
2 'I wish I **could** get the ring back.'
3 'I wish those three girls **would** go to sleep.'

**RULE:**
- We use *wish* / *if only* + the [4] ______ tense to express how we would like our current situation to be different.
- We use *wish* / *if only* + [5] ______ to say that we'd like the ability to do something.
- We use *wish* / *if only* + [6] ______ to say that we'd like something to happen or someone (else) to do something.

**Look**

We can use *was* or *were* after a singular subject (*I*, *he*, *she* or *it*) when we express wishes.

*I wish I was older. / I wish I were older.*

11 **Complete the sentences with the correct forms of the verbs.**

be | go | have | knock | like | not have

1 I wish I ______________ taller.
2 I wish you ______________ me more.
3 If only I ______________ a more interesting book to read.
4 I wish I ______________ this awful headache.
5 If only I ______________ to sleep.
6 I wish you ______________ before you come into my room!

12 SPEAKING **Play 'famous wishes' in groups of four.**

- Choose a famous fictional person and write three wishes.
  (Remember: they should be about the present situation, not the past.)
- Read out your sentences. The other students have to guess who you are.

→ workbook page 37

## READING

1 4.03 **Read and listen to the stories. Match the stories (1–3) with the pictures (A–C).**

2 **Read the stories again. Who do you think said these things?**

1 'I found this in your bin.'
2 'I was very surprised when I read the letter.'
3 'They let you out too soon.'
4 'It's incredible that you brought it back to us.'
5 'OK, you can go now.'
6 'It was a long time ago, but I've always been sorry for what I did.'

3 SPEAKING **Work in pairs. Decide what you would have done in each situation. Then compare with other students.**

A

B

C

## HOW HONEST IS THAT?

### 1 MAKING IT RIGHT – MANY YEARS LATER

The manager of a shop in Seattle was very surprised one day in 2011 when a man came in, gave him an envelope and left. The manager opened the envelope and found a $100 note and a short letter. The letter said: 'I stole $25 from this store in 1961. Now that I've got some money, I want to give it back. If you had put it in the bank, it would have grown to $100. So here it is.'
The newspapers wanted to know who the man was, but the manager didn't release his name.

### 2 BACK TO PRISON

In 2011, Luis Lopez was sent to prison in Florida for a year. After three months, the prison guards came and told him he could go home. Amazed, Lopez asked the guards if they were sure – they said yes, so he left. But it didn't feel right to Lopez, so when he got home, he called his lawyer. The lawyer told him that in fact the local court had made a mistake. He advised Lopez to go back and finish his prison sentence – and that's what he did. If he hadn't gone back to prison, he would have had bigger problems.

### 3 A LITTLE MONEY, A LOT OF HONESTY

Now and again, people throw things away by mistake. One day, rubbish collector Jimmy James found a $50 store gift card amongst the rubbish outside a home. He went on working, but later that day, Jimmy went back to the house, rang the doorbell and gave the family the card. They were very surprised because $50 didn't seem like a lot of money to them. But Jimmy just said he thought it was the right thing to do. The family gave him a $75 reward to say thank you.

## GRAMMAR
### Third conditional (review)

4 **Complete these sentences from the story with the correct forms of the verbs. Then complete the rule.**

1 If Lopez ____________ (not go) back to prison, he ____________ (have) bigger problems.
2 If you ____________ (put) it in the bank, it ____________ (grow) to $100.

**RULE:**
We use the third conditional to talk about imagined situations and their outcomes in the past. We form it with:
*if* + [3] ______ + *would(n't) have* + [4] ______ .

5 **Complete the third conditional sentences.**

0 If the court *hadn't made* a mistake, Lopez *wouldn't have left* prison early.
1 If the store ____________ (release) the video, everyone ____________ (know) the man's name.
2 If Jimmy James ____________ (keep) the card, he ____________ (not get) the reward.

6 **Complete the sentences so that they are true for you.**

1 If I hadn't gone to school today, …
2 I'd have been really happy if …
3 If I'd been born 100 years ago, …

→ workbook page 37

# VOCABULARY
## Making a decision

**7** **Match a–h with the underlined words and phrases in the text below.**

a for a long time ☐ e make ☐
b a good ☐ f thought again about ☐
c a bad ☐ g original idea ☐
d decide ☐ h made a new decision ☐

My [1]first thought was to go with the blue. But then I thought [2]long and hard and [3]changed my mind. Maybe the red was better. But had I made [4]the right decision? Had I? I [5]reconsidered my choice. Red or blue? Red or blue? Why was it so difficult to [6]make up my mind? Well, I didn't want to make [7]the wrong decision, did I? So I called my sister. Maybe she could help me [8]come to a decision.

'I don't know why you're asking me,' she said. 'You only ever wear blue.'

**8** SPEAKING **Work in pairs. Discuss these questions.**

1 What's the biggest decision you've ever made?
2 Have you ever made the wrong decision? What was it?
3 How good are you at making your mind up about small things?
4 What sort of things do you usually need to think long and hard about?
5 Do you ever reconsider decisions you've made?
6 Who do you ask to help you come to important decisions?

→ workbook page 38

## WordWise: Phrases with *now*

**9** **Look at the words and phrases in bold in these sentences from the unit. Match them with the definitions.**

1 OK, you can go **now**.
2 **Now that** I've got some money, I want to give it back.
3 **Now and again**, people throw things away by mistake.
4 I looked at the station sign **just now**, but it doesn't say.
5 Do you want to have a go **now**, Angie?

a in the near future
b at this moment
c a moment or two ago
d because finally
e sometimes

**10** **Use words and phrases from Exercise 9 to complete the sentences.**

1 I've finished my work, so ______ I'm going to hang out with my friends.
2 I don't listen to this music all the time, but ______ I like to play it.
3 Sally was here ______ , but she's gone out.
4 I'll eat later. I'm not hungry ______ .
5 I don't walk to school ______ I've got a bike.

→ workbook page 38

## THINK values
### Doing the right thing

**11** **Think about a time when you had to make a difficult decision. Make notes.**

1 What decision did you make?
2 What were the consequences?

**12** **Write a short paragraph. Include a third conditional sentence.**

*Last year, there was a new student in my class. Nobody wanted to sit next to him, so I did. I'm really happy I did. If I hadn't sat next to him, he wouldn't have become my best friend. What a good decision I made!*

**13** **Read your paragraph out to the class. Then vote on the best story.**

# WRITING
## A diary entry about a dilemma

**14** **Choose one of these situations or use your own idea. Write a diary entry about it (150–200 words). Try to use language from this unit.**

1 Explain the problem.
2 Think about two possible solutions and their consequences.
3 Decide what you're going to do and why.

- You've got a detention. If you tell your parents, you won't be allowed to go to a party.
- It's your mum's birthday this weekend, but you spent all your money on clothes and haven't got any left to buy her a present.
- You saw your best friend's boyfriend / girlfriend at the cinema with another boy / girl.

**1** 4.04 **Look at the photo. Who do you think the two people are and what are they talking about? Listen and read to check.**

**Dad:** What's with the worried face, Tom?
**Tom:** Well, I'm thinking about what to study if I go to university.
**Dad:** Well, I'd like to help if I can. Any chance?
**Tom:** Of course, Dad! Believe it or not, I really like it when we talk together.
**Dad:** Well, me too. OK, so if I remember rightly, you're torn between doing Spanish or Economics.
**Tom:** Exactly. And between you and me, I'm pretty good at both. They just seem to lead in different directions.
**Dad:** How do you mean?
**Tom:** Well, if I carry on with Economics, I think I'll end up in an office job. But do I want that?
**Dad:** And Spanish?
**Tom:** Well, then I could live in a Spanish-speaking country, like Peru or Ecuador, and that could be exciting. But do I want to live so far away? And what job would I do? Teaching? I don't know. It's a dilemma.
**Dad:** Listen, don't overthink it. There's no hurry. You've got six months before you have to choose. And if you still can't decide – well, just go with your instinct.
**Tom:** Thanks, Dad. I'll do that. Can we keep talking about this?
**Dad:** Of course. Now Tom, I was wondering if you could help me with a dilemma. Should I cook dinner or should I ask you to?
**Tom:** Dad! Are you out of your mind? You're a hopeless cook! I'll do it!

**2** 4.04 **Read and listen to the dialogue again. Answer the questions.**

1 What is Tom's dilemma?
2 What are his worries about doing Economics?
3 What are his worries about doing Spanish?
4 What does he think of his father's cooking?

**3** SPEAKING **Discuss the statements in pairs. What do you think?**

1 Tom's dilemma is an important one.
2 Tom should probably choose Spanish because then he can travel.
3 His father gives him good advice.

## Phrases for fluency

**4** **Find the underlined expressions in the dialogue. How do you say them in your language? Use the expressions to complete the mini-dialogues.**

1 A Andy, ____________________ you could come and help me choose my next tattoo?
B Sorry, no. ____________________, I don't think tattoos look good on you at all.

2 A Hi, Steve. Wow! ____________________ those really old football boots?
B They're ancient, aren't they? ____________________, my dad used to wear them when he was at school. I need new ones.

3 A Listen, Jane. I love that new necklace of yours. ____________________ I could borrow it tonight?
B ____________________? It's really expensive! I wouldn't lend it to anyone!

## FUNCTIONS
### Apologising and accepting apologies

**KEY LANGUAGE**

No problem.
That's / It's OK.
Don't worry about it.
I'm so ashamed.
I feel awful about this.
I don't know what to say.
No worries.
I'm so sorry.

**5** **Write the expressions from the Key Language box in the correct columns.**

| Apologising | Accepting apologies |
|---|---|
| | |

**6** SPEAKING **Work in pairs. Imagine you're in these situations and act out conversations. Use expressions from the Key Language box.**

- A has spilled a drink on B's trousers.
- A has arrived very late for a meeting with B.
- A has bumped into B and B has fallen over.
- A has completely forgotten B's name.

**PRONUNCIATION**
Consonant–vowel word linking Go to page 120.

# LIFE COMPETENCIES

We all act on instinct at some point in our lives, and acting on instinct can have positive or negative consequences.

1 ▶ 11 **Watch the vlog. What is Serena's dilemma?**

2 ▶ 11 **Watch the vlog again and answer the questions.**

1 What are the bad things about Mandy?
2 What are the good things about Nadia?
3 What did Serena do with the kitten on the street?
4 What happened with the cake in the fridge?
5 What is Serena's final decision?

3 **Read the start of Marta's story. What do you think she should do?**

In the summer holidays my friends and I met up for a picnic and a game of football. We had a great day, the weather was good and we all had fun. My friend Ellie needed to be home by 9 pm and by this time it was getting dark. The cycle ride back to her house takes her along a quiet footpath in the woods and across a main road. Ellie was happy to walk back to her house by herself, but I felt worried about her.

## TIPS FOR ACTING ON INSTINCT

- **If something doesn't feel right, take some more time to think about it.**
- **If your friends are all doing one thing but you feel it isn't right, don't feel pressured into behaving in a way you don't agree with. If your instinct says no, don't do it.**
- **Acting on instinct can be a good thing. If you think your actions will benefit or help someone else, go ahead and do what you feel!**

4 **Now read endings A and B. What was the result of Marta's actions in each ending?**

**A**

It was nearly dark; what if she met a stranger in the woods or got lost? I said I would walk with her, and then we would call my dad from her house to pick me up. At first, Ellie said she was fine, she didn't want me to have to call my dad. But when I insisted I was worried about her, finally she agreed and we both got home safely.

**B**

It was getting dark, but I thought she'd think I was being silly if I told her how I felt. I asked her to text me when she got home. At 10 pm Ellie's mum called me. She was at the hospital with Ellie. On her way home, she had twisted her ankle, and couldn't walk on it. Because she was on her own, she had been frightened and upset, but she had managed to call her mum on her mobile phone.

5 **Answer the questions about the story.**

1 How would you have acted in the situation?
2 What was Marta's instinct in ending A?
3 How do you think Marta feels in ending B?

## Me and my world

6 SPEAKING **Work in pairs. What is your instinct in each of the situations? Would you normally act on your instinct? Why or why not?**

A You are at the local skate park. Your friend is about to do a dangerous jump. He's not wearing a helmet.
B You are with a group of friends. A few of them are being unkind to another friend in your group.
C You have always wanted to buy a particular thing but it's very expensive. One day you see it in a sale, 40% off the original price – but it's still more than you can really afford. Your friend offers to lend you the money to buy it.

# TOWARDS B2 First for Schools

## LISTENING
### Multiple choice

→ workbook page 35

**1** 4.07 **You will hear people talking in eight different situations. For questions 1–8, choose the best answer (A, B or C).**

1 You hear a boy talking about how he got his name. Why was it hard for his parents to name him?
- A They each wanted different names.
- B There weren't many possibilities for a name that worked in two languages.
- C He was born two weeks early.

2 You hear a girl talking on her phone. What is her problem?
- A She doesn't want to invite Lucy to her birthday celebration.
- B Her mum said that Lucy can't come for a sleepover.
- C She really wants to have a big party.

3 You hear part of an interview with a footballer. What does he find most difficult about his job?
- A not being free at weekends
- B having to work out every day
- C the comments some of the fans make

4 You hear two friends talking about a camping trip. What advice does Alan give Steve?
- A to take a comfortable sleeping bag
- B to get a lift to the campsite
- C not to take things that weigh too much

5 You hear a local news report. What did Clive Roberts think when he found the money?
- A I'm £10,000 richer.
- B How can I return this to the owner?
- C Could I keep this? Would anybody ever know?

6 Two friends are talking about a party. Why did Chloë miss the party?
- A Her dad said she had to go cycling with him.
- B She fell asleep in the middle of the day.
- C She was watching TV and forgot the time.

7 You hear a girl talking about a difficult decision. Why did she find it hard to choose which exams to take?
- A She had no idea about what career she wanted to do.
- B She didn't want to disappoint her dad.
- C She wanted to make sure her exams would help her get a well-paid job.

8 You hear a book review on the radio. What did Carla like best about the book?
- A that she was able to understand the story
- B that it was a love story
- C the way the characters developed during the story

## WRITING
### Story

→ workbook page 43

**2 Your English teacher has asked you to write a short story for the school's new website. The story must begin or end with the following words:**

*I still don't know why I didn't tell the truth.*

**Write your story in 140–190 words.**

## VOCABULARY

**1 Complete the sentences with the words / phrases in the list. There are four extra words / phrases.**

brand | call | chain | cheat | consumers | get away with | image | logo
manufacturer | make | name | own up to | products | tell

1 He worked hard for a long time before he started to ____________________ a name for himself in cinema.
2 The company was in trouble until they started making some new ____________________.
3 If you ____________________ during the exam, we'll take you out of the exam room and destroy your paper.
4 I like so many different kinds of fruit. Basically, you ____________________ it, I like it!
5 He tried to look at another boy's test, but the teacher saw him so he didn't ____________________ it.
6 Other kids used to ____________________ me names, but it never upset me.
7 Our website has been redesigned – and if you visit it, you'll see that we have a new ____________________, too.
8 It's not always easy, but it's important always to ____________________ the truth.
9 We started with just one shop, but now we have a ____________________ of 20.
10 I know you took my things without asking. Why don't you just ____________________ it?

/10

## GRAMMAR

**2 Complete the sentences with the words in the list. There are two extra words.**

better | go | if | ought | unless | until | went | when

1 It's pretty late – I think I have to ____________________ now, OK?
2 I really wish we ____________________ out to eat more often.
3 I'll call you ____________________ the film finishes, OK?
4 I'm not going to bed ____________________ I finish this book – it's brilliant!
5 You'll never be his friend ____________________ you go and talk to him!
6 It's a secret, so you'd ____________________ not tell anyone else!

**3 Find and correct the mistake in each sentence.**

1 You shouldn't to talk to a teacher like that. It isn't respectful.
2 If they wouldn't be so expensive, I'd buy those trainers.
3 I wish you don't live so far away.
4 Your eye looks bad – I think you better go to the doctor.
5 If it hadn't rained, we had gone for a walk yesterday.
6 If only we can see you more often.

/12

## FUNCTIONAL LANGUAGE

**4 Choose the correct words.**

1 A I think we *should* / *ought* to go now.
B That's a shame. If only you *could stay* / *stayed* a little longer.
2 A Listen, we *mustn't* / *don't have to* miss the last bus tonight.
B You're right. *I'd better not* / *I don't have to* forget to set an alarm on my phone.
3 A Sorry, but you *don't* / *can't* come in. You're too young!
B I know. But I really want to see the film. I wish I *would be* / *were* 18 already!
4 A Patrick *wouldn't have* / *won't have* come to the party if he'd known Sue was going to be there.
B Yeah, it's a shame – if only *we'd told* / *we've told* him earlier.

/8

MY SCORE /30

22–30 | 10–21 | 0–9

# 5 STORYTELLING

**OBJECTIVES**

**FUNCTIONS:** telling a story

**GRAMMAR:** relative pronouns; defining and non-defining relative clauses; relative clauses with *which*

**VOCABULARY:** elements of a story; types of story

**Get THINKING**

**Watch the video and think: what makes a really good story?**

## READING

1 SPEAKING **Think of an example of each of these things. Then work in pairs and share one or two of your ideas.**

- a story or a favourite fairy tale from your childhood
- a favourite film
- a thriller (either a book or a film) that really grabbed you
- an anecdote or a joke you've heard recently

2 SPEAKING **What are the ingredients of a good story? Discuss with a partner. Then compare your ideas with the rest of the class.**

3 5.01 **Read and listen to the article on the next page. Were your ideas the same as the writer's?**

4 **Choose the correct answers to the questions.**

1 What advice does the writer give about getting started?
   A Think carefully about how all the events in the story will develop.
   B Choose your best idea and just start writing.
   C Write the first thing that comes into your head.

2 What does the writer say is important for a good plot?
   A a happy ending
   B a fight between good and bad
   C a situation where there is conflict

3 What does the writer suggest about the theme of a novel?
   A You should try to make it as clever as possible.
   B It is more important than your plot.
   C Your reader should work it out for themselves.

4 What does the writer suggest about the characters?
   A Get to know them as you write.
   B Make sure you tell your reader exactly what they look like.
   C Let them make mistakes.

5 What advice does he give about writing style?
   A Keep your reader in mind.
   B Take your time to think of the right words.
   C Try to copy the style that other writers use.

# SO YOU WANT TO WRITE A NOVEL, DO YOU?

About | Blog | Latest posts | Archives

What's stopping you? Time? Ideas? Self-belief? Well, let me help you. Time: find half an hour to write every day. You'll be surprised to see how quickly the pages start filling up. Ideas: write down loads and then choose the best. You only need one main idea. Start writing and the rest will soon come. Self-belief: what can I say? You can do it. I know you can. Remember, your novel, which will be fun to write, doesn't need to be 600 pages long. You could start with a short one.

What else do you need to know? Here are a few rules I always follow that might help you:

I always like to start with the plot. That's because I like a novel with a good story. And a good story comes from conflict. Many of the best novels start in a good place where the main character is happy with their life. Then something goes wrong and as the situation gets worse, our hero is thrown into conflict. The plot is then driven by how they can make things better. But in their struggle to right these wrongs the character should learn something about themselves.

The theme, which is basically the message that the story is trying to get across, is also important. This is something you should never tell your reader directly. No one likes to be told what's right or what's wrong. The best thing to do is to let your reader work out the message on their own. That way your novel will make them feel clever and they'll want to read your next one!

Characters. They're important! Before you start writing, get to know the people whose stories you will be telling. Ask yourself questions about them. Get inside their heads and answer your questions. Don't spend too much time describing what they look like. What's important is what they're like inside. Who are they? What motivates them? Why are they doing those things? And they shouldn't be perfect. They're humans (presumably). They need to make mistakes from time to time, and as they try to deal with the conflict in their life, they should develop and change.

Finally, you might want to think about your own writing style – the words you are going to use to write your story. You don't need to use long complex sentences or words that will leave your readers confused (but some variety in words is good!). You can keep your style simple. Think about the people who might want to read your story. Think about how to keep them interested. But be yourself. Write the words that come most naturally. These will always be your best words. So there you have it: plot, theme, characters and style. Follow these golden rules and you'll never go wrong. Of course, though, don't forget – rules are often there to be broken.

## Train to TH!NK

### Thinking about different writing styles

*Writers use different techniques to bring their texts alive.*

**5 Answer the questions.**

1 What technique does the writer use in the title of the article?
2 How many times does he use this technique in the article?
3 Why do you think he does this?

**6 Choose the correct option.**

1 When people ask a rhetorical question, they …
  A expect an answer.
  B don't really expect an answer.
2 They ask a rhetorical question to …
  A introduce a subject they want to talk about.
  B find out what you're thinking.

**7 Some of the paragraphs don't contain any rhetorical questions. Think of a rhetorical question that you could add to the final paragraph.**

## SPEAKING

**8 Work in pairs. Discuss these questions.**

1 What kind of stories do you enjoy most? Give an example.
2 What kind of story would you like to write most?

Grammar rap!

# GRAMMAR

## Relative pronouns

**1 Complete these sentences from the article on page 49. Then complete the rule.**

1. Think about the people ______ might want to read your story.
2. Get to know the people ______ stories you will be telling.
3. The theme, ______ is basically the message ______ the story is trying to get across, is also important.
4. Many of the best novels start in a good place ______ the main character is happy with their life.

> **RULE:**
> We use relative clauses to give extra information. We use …
> 5 ______ to refer to people.
> 6 ______ and ______ to refer to things.
> 7 ______ to refer to possessions.
> 8 ______ to refer to places.

**2 Combine the sentences by replacing the <u>underlined</u> words with relative pronouns from Exercise 1.**

1. One of the world's greatest storytellers was Roald Dahl. <u>He</u> wrote wonderful books for children.
2. Many people love his children's stories. <u>The children's stories</u> are fun for all ages.
3. The best storyteller I know is my uncle. <u>He</u> lived in India for several years.
4. We love listening to our English teacher. <u>Her</u> stories are fascinating.
5. At our school we have a great library. We like to relax and read <u>there</u>.

→ workbook page 46

## Defining and non-defining relative clauses

**3 Complete these sentences from the article on page 49. Then read the rule.**

1. Remember, your novel, ______ will be fun to write, doesn't need to be 600 pages long.
2. You don't need to use long complex sentences or words ______ will leave your readers confused.

> **RULE:**
> We use a defining relative clause to identify an object, a person, a place or a possession. Without this information, it's hard to know who or what we're talking about.
> *We don't often see the people.* (Which people?)
> *We don't often see the people* ***who live next door.***
> We use a non-defining relative clause to add extra information. We don't need this information to understand the sentence. We put commas around it.
> *Roald Dahl was a famous writer.*
> *Roald Dahl,* ***who was British,*** *was a famous writer.*
> (Extra information: he was British.)

**4 Complete these defining relative clauses with *who, where, whose* or *that*.**

1. The house ______ I grew up is next to a school.
2. A book ______ has lots of short chapters is perfect for the bus ride to school.
3. A person ______ knows a lot of jokes is usually a good public speaker.
4. We went to hear a lecture by a writer ______ books are always on the bestseller list.
5. The author ______ wrote the famous teen novel *The Outsiders* was only 16.

> **Look**
> We can only use *that* in defining relative clauses. In non-defining clauses we must use *which*.
> We can use *that* for people as well as things.

**5 Tick (✓) the sentences which contain non-defining relative clauses and add commas.**

1. My brother is someone who just doesn't like listening to jokes. ☐
2. Fairy tales which were written for children are now being adapted for the cinema. ☐
3. The Brothers Grimm whose stories have fascinated millions of children lived in the 19th century. ☐
4. It's difficult to read in places where people are talking on mobile phones. ☐

→ workbook page 46

## VOCABULARY
### Elements of a story

**6 Match the words with their definitions.**

character | dialogue | ending | hero
opening | plot | setting | villain

1 the story of a film, play, etc.
2 a person in a story
3 the last part of a story
4 the main (usually good) character in a story
5 a character who harms other people
6 the words that the characters say to each other
7 the beginning of a story
8 the time and place in which the action happens

**7 Think about these things for two minutes. Make notes.**

- a film or book with a great plot
- the setting of the last film you saw or story you read
- a film or book with a great opening
- a good film or book with a disappointing ending
- a film or book with a memorable villain

→ workbook page 48

**8 SPEAKING Work in pairs or small groups. Share your ideas.**

*I really enjoyed the latest Spider-Man film – the plot was brilliant!*

*I don't think the ending of the book is very good.*

*All the characters in the story are fascinating, but the villain is the best!*

## LISTENING

**9 Find out how much your class knows about Roald Dahl. Then read the fact file.**

# Roald Dahl FACT FILE

- Dahl was born in 1916 in Cardiff, Wales.
- His parents were immigrants from Norway.
- He was a fighter pilot during the Second World War.
- His first children's book was *The Gremlins*, which was published in 1942.
- His most famous book, *Charlie and the Chocolate Factory*, has sold over 13 million copies.
- Many of his books have been made into successful Hollywood movies, including *Charlie and the Chocolate Factory*, *Fantastic Mr Fox* and *The BFG*.

**10 5.02 Listen to two teenagers talking about a short story by Roald Dahl called *The Hitchhiker*. In the story, he uses an invented word: 'fingersmith'. What does a fingersmith do?**

**11 5.02 Listen again and answer the questions.**

1 Why is Annie surprised that Lucy is reading Roald Dahl?
2 What was *Tales of the Unexpected*?
3 What was Roald Dahl's connection to it?
4 Who are the two main characters in *The Hitchhiker*?
5 Why does the policeman stop them?
6 What does the policeman write down in his book?
7 What does the hitchhiker do to show how good he is with his fingers?
8 Why isn't the hitchhiker worried about the policeman?

**12 SPEAKING Compare your answers in pairs.**

## READING

1 **Look at the titles. Have you seen any of the film versions of the books? What did you think of them?**

LORD OF THE FLIES

THE MAZE RUNNER

THE HUNGER GAMES

The Lord of the Rings

The Jungle Book

2 **Read the magazine article and title quickly. Decide which paragraph is *for* and which is *against* the argument.**

3 5.03 **Read and listen to the article. Answer the questions.**

1 What does Ellie like doing when she's reading a book?
2 Why wasn't she disappointed by the film of *The Lord of the Rings*?
3 Why didn't she like the film version of *The Maze Runner*?
4 Why does Ben prefer films to books?
5 What did he think of *The Hunger Games* books?
6 Why does he try and watch films of the books he has to read for school?

4 SPEAKING **Work in pairs. Discuss.**

1 Which do you prefer to do first: read the original book or watch the film version of it?
2 Think of a film that you think was much better or worse than the book. Say why.

## WRITING

### A short paragraph expressing an opinion

5 **Write a paragraph giving your ideas on the statement: 'Books are always better than their films.'**

1 Say what your opinion is and why.
2 Give examples from books you've read and films you've seen.

# THERE ARE ALWAYS TWO SIDES TO AN ARGUMENT

## BOOKS ARE ALWAYS BETTER THAN THEIR FILMS.

When you read a book, you can imagine it all in your head: what the characters look like, where the action takes place – that sort of thing. Then when you see the film, you can compare your ideas with those of the director, which is always interesting. If you see the film first, you don't get to use your own imagination because you just see things the way they were in the film. It's a shame and I don't really see the point in doing it. For example, I read *The Lord of the Rings* and had all these wonderful images in my head. When I saw the films, which were directed by the great Peter Jackson, some of it was quite different from how I had imagined it, but it didn't matter. His visions were so brilliant and I wasn't disappointed. It doesn't always work like that, though. Sometimes the film version can be a real disappointment. I saw *The Maze Runner* a few weeks ago. I loved that book, but the film just wasn't right for me. In my opinion, the characters were all wrong and they'd changed some of my favourite bits. I didn't bother to see the other films in the series. I didn't want to spoil my own personal memories of the books.

***Ellie***

I hardly ever read books, so I nearly always see the film first. I think it's probably because I'm a bit lazy. It takes me weeks to finish a book whereas I can watch the film in 90 minutes, which leaves me time to do other things. But sometimes I enjoy a film so much that it makes me want to go and read the book. I love fantasy and science fiction stories and so I did that with *The Hunger Games* series. The films were amazing, so I went out and bought the books. It took me a bit of time to get through them, but they were worth the time and effort. I really enjoyed them, even though I knew what was going to happen. It was also quite interesting seeing where the film and book were a bit different. When our teacher asks us to read books for school, I always see if I can get a film of the book first. That helps me get into the books, which are often quite difficult. If I already know what the story is about, it helps me understand better when I'm reading. I did this with *Lord of the Flies* and *The Jungle Book*. Seeing the films first really helped me enjoy the books more.

***Ben***

## GRAMMAR
### Relative clauses with *which*

**6 Complete these sentences from the article on page 52. What does *which* refer to in each of the sentences? Complete the rule.**

1 I can watch the film in 90 minutes, ______ leaves me time to do other things.

2 You can compare your ideas with those of the director, ______ is always interesting.

> RULE: The pronoun [3]______ normally refers to a noun, but it can sometimes refer to the whole of the previous clause. We cannot use [4]______ or *that* in the same way.
> *She was late, which made her nervous.*

**7 Join the pairs of sentences using *which*.**

0 I often play the drums on Sunday mornings. This annoys the neighbours.
I often play *the drums on Sunday mornings, which annoys* the neighbours.

1 She's lost all her money. This means she'll be in trouble.
She's lost ____________________ in trouble.

2 Nobody in class learned the new words. It was frustrating for our teacher.
Nobody in class ____________________ for our teacher.

3 Fairy tales have been turned into successful teen films. This has surprised many people.
Fairy tales ____________________ many people.

4 It's quite amazing that the author manages to write several books per year.
She ____________________ quite amazing.

5 It's fascinating that most of his books have been made into films.
Most of his books ____________________ fascinating.

**8 Complete the sentences so that they are true for you.**

0 My favourite singer *is giving a concert in our town next month*, which is fantastic.

1 ____________________ last year, which made me feel really proud.

2 I heard on the news that ____________________, which I was really upset about.

3 ____________________, which really isn't easy.

**9 SPEAKING Work in pairs. Share your sentences. How long can you keep each conversation going?**

*My favourite singer Dua Lipa is giving a concert in our town soon.*

*Wow! I like her songs, too. Do you know when ...?*

→ workbook page 47

## VOCABULARY
### Types of story

**10 🔊 5.04 Match the types of story with the book covers. Write numbers 1–7 in the boxes. Then listen and check.**

1 crime novel
2 science fiction novel
3 historical novel
4 horror story
5 (auto)biography
6 romantic novel
7 fantasy novel

**11 Which type of story is non-fiction?**

**12 SPEAKING Which types of story do you like reading most?**

→ workbook page 48

## SPEAKING

**13 Work in pairs. If you had to choose one of the books in the previous exercise, which would it be and why?**

*I'd choose ... because the cover looks / the title sounds (exciting / funny / interesting / ... ).*

**14 Prepare a one-minute talk about reading. Think about the following points and take notes.**

- if you prefer articles, short stories, novels, etc.
- where and when you like reading

**15 Take turns giving your talks in small groups.**

THINK

Storytelling in the Caribbean

# Culture

**1 Look at the photos and answer the questions.**

1 What can you see in the photos?
2 What do you think the person is doing?
3 Would you like to visit this place? Why or why not?

**2** 5.05 **Read and listen to the article. Find out who Paul Keens-Douglas and Tanti Merle are.**

## Storytelling in the Caribbean

Storytelling plays a big part in the childhood of most people growing up on the Caribbean Islands. It is a tradition that was brought over from Africa by their ancestors many years ago and is a way of keeping their shared culture alive. The stories are a way of remembering the past and making sure it's not forgotten in the future.

And despite the modern distractions of television and video games, many Caribbean families still gather on the steps outside their homes, with the full moon in the sky and the wind blowing gently through the palm trees, to hear stories that they have already heard many times before.

The storyteller has an important position in Caribbean society. But it is not an art that is learned quickly. Good storytellers take years to perfect their performances. First, they must collect a catalogue of good stories, which are often short and simple and should work well for people of all ages. They must then practise these on family members to test out their material before moving on to larger crowds in local community centres. From there they may choose to become travelling storytellers and move from town to town looking for new audiences to share their tales with. And the very best storytellers make it onto the international stage and travel the world. More recently many storytellers have started using film to reach even more people.

With many Caribbean islands and people originating from many African countries, there are lots of types of stories to be told. One common feature though is the performance tradition known as 'crick crack'. Although this may differ a little in each country, the basic idea is that the audience participates in the storytelling. For example, in St Lucia, where stories are usually told in French, the storyteller (known as the 'conteur') announces that he or she wants to tell a story by shouting out 'Crick!' and the audience show they want to listen by responding 'Crack!' Throughout the performance, the storyteller continues to involve the audience by inviting them to answer questions and riddles and to make comments. In this way, the storyteller and the audience become an almost equally important part of the whole experience.

But as well as the many traditional tales and myths there are to be told, storytellers also create their own characters, and the most successful of these have become part of cultural life. One of the most famous storytellers in the West Indies is Paul Keens-Douglas, who was born in Trinidad but grew up in Grenada. Probably his most popular character, Tanti Merle, is known throughout the region and appears in many of his stories. Tanti Merle is a woman who is not afraid to say what she thinks and Keens-Douglas uses her as a lovable comic figure to make comments on everyday life in the Caribbean.

**3 Read the article again. Mark the sentences T (true) or F (false).**

1 Children in the Caribbean don't use modern technology. ☐
2 Storytellers have to learn long detailed stories. ☐
3 Audiences play an important part in the storytelling. ☐
4 You should shout 'crack' if you want to hear a story. ☐
5 Storytellers only tell traditional stories. ☐

**4** SPEAKING **Work in pairs. Discuss these questions.**

1 How does the Caribbean storytelling tradition compare with storytelling in your country?
2 What stories are there about places near where you live?

5 VOCABULARY There are eight highlighted words or phrases in the text. Match the words with these meanings. Write the words.

1 short word puzzles
2 lots of people together
3 is present
4 the art, stories and history of a place
5 takes part in something
6 a collection of something
7 normal
8 things that take your attention from what you are doing

## SPEAKING

6 Look at the pictures. Put them in order and use them to tell a story.

7 5.08 Listen and compare your story to the one you hear.

**PRONUNCIATION**
The schwa /ə/ in word endings Go to page 120.

## FUNCTIONS
### Telling a story

8 5.08 Annie uses these expressions to bring her story to life. Match them with the correct places in the conversation. Then listen again and check.

☐ you'll never believe what
☐ The strangest thing happened to me the other day.
☐ Well, let me finish …
☐ That was the annoying thing.
☐ What are the chances?

**Annie** [1] ____________
**Mac** What?
**Annie** I woke up with this song in my head and I couldn't stop singing it all day long. It was really annoying.
**Mac** What was it?
**Annie** [2] ____________ It was a song I knew, but I couldn't remember what it was. I even sang it to a few of my friends, but they didn't know what it was either.
**Mac** So what was so strange about that?
**Annie** [3] ____________ I got home from school (with the song still in my head) and I went upstairs to do my homework. I decided to put on the radio to try and forget the song, and [4] ____________ they were playing!
**Mac** Go on.
**Annie** They were playing the song that I'd been singing all day!
**Mac** So you'd just been singing a pop song that you'd forgotten the name of.
**Annie** Yes, but the strange thing is that it wasn't a pop song from now. It was some obscure song from the 1980s that you never hear any more. It was a song that my dad used to play when I was really small. I hadn't heard it for years. And they were playing it on the radio! [5] ____________
**Mac** Yes, that is pretty weird.

9 Think of a strange story that happened to you or to someone else.

- Write down the main events in note form.
- Think how you can use some of the expressions.
- In groups, tell your stories.

# 6 THAT'S IMPOSSIBLE

**OBJECTIVES**

**FUNCTIONS:**
talking about sequence; explaining how things are done

**GRAMMAR:**
present and past passive (review); *have something done*; future and present perfect passive (review)

**VOCABULARY:**
extreme adjectives and modifiers; *make* and *do*

## Get THINKING

**Watch the video and think: what is your favourite magic trick?**

## READING

**1** SPEAKING **Work in pairs. Discuss these questions.**

1 What magicians can you name?
2 What magic tricks have you seen?
3 Can you do any tricks yourself? What are they?

**2** **Read the article about David Copperfield quickly. Which three of his tricks does it mention?**

**3** 6.01 **Read and listen to the article again and match the sentences (a–g) with the spaces (1–6). There's one extra sentence which doesn't belong in the text. Check your answers.**

a It was very dark and he fell. ☐
b The audience is absolutely amazed. ☐
c Where had he gone? ☐
d Time and time again, people have wondered: ☐
e There was nothing there. ☐
f He walked in one side and out the other. ☐
g People who catch one are invited to come up onto the stage. ☐

## Train to THINK

### Understanding what's relevant

*To write a good text, a writer must make sure that each sentence is linked to what comes before it. Understanding how this is done will help you to do tasks like Exercise 3.*

**4** **Choose the sentence which *doesn't* have any relevance to the first.**

David Copperfield made the Statue of Liberty disappear.

A He was watched by millions on TV.
B He performed in front of a live audience.
C People from all over the world visit the statue every year.
D He used a large sheet to hide the statue.

**5** SPEAKING **Work in pairs. Use this sentence to make a similar task for your partner.**

Gavin Cox was injured in one of David Copperfield's magic tricks.

A ____________ C ____________
B ____________ D ____________

# HOW ON EARTH DOES HE DO IT?

**Perhaps the world's most famous magician, David Copperfield has entertained his audiences for years with his fantastic magic tricks and thrilling illusions. [1]_____ 'How did he do that?'**

## The Great Wall

In a 1986 TV special, Copperfield appeared to walk *through* the Great Wall of China. [2]_____ First, he stepped into a box and the audience could see his silhouette on the white screens around the box. Then, he appeared to enter the wall. Minutes later his silhouette could be seen pushing out through the wall into a similar box on the other side. The white screens were lifted and there stood the magician, on the other side of the wall.

## The Statue of Liberty

A live TV event was staged in April 1983. A huge audience sat on Liberty Island in New York Harbour, facing the Statue of Liberty. There was a column on each side of the stage and the statue was visible between the two columns. A white screen was raised and the statue was hidden from view. Minutes later, the screen was lowered, and to the amazement of the audience, the statue had disappeared. [3]_____ Then, as the stunned audience watched, the screen was raised again. But this time, when it was lowered, the Statue of Liberty was there again.

## Lucky 13

Imagine the scene at one of David Copperfield's shows. From the stage, 13 soft balls are thrown into the audience. [4]_____ These 13 volunteers enter a cage, which is raised above the stage. The people inside are given torches to shine at the audience, and then a cover is lowered over them. When the magician lifts the cover, the cage is empty – but then, moments later, the 13 people reappear at the back of the theatre, still holding the torches they were given. [5]_____ This is David Copperfield's famous Lucky 13 trick, which he performed for nearly 20 years. How did he do it?

## The secret revealed

Normally magicians guard their secrets, but this time we know the answer. In 2013, 55-year-old chef Gavin Cox was at one of Copperfield's shows in Las Vegas. He was called up to the stage by the magician to take part in the Lucky 13 illusion. As soon as the cage was covered, he and the other 12 volunteers were pushed quickly into a secret passage and outside the theatre. In the confusion, Mr Cox was injured. "They were shouting 'Hurry! Run, run, run'," he said. He didn't know where he was going. [6]_____ After the accident, there was a court case and Copperfield had to reveal the trick and the technique of his famous 'disappearing audience' illusion.

## SPEAKING

**6 Work in pairs. Discuss these questions.**

1. What other magic tricks can you think of?
2. How do you think the Great Wall and the Statue of Liberty tricks were done?

**PRONUNCIATION**
The /ʒ/ phoneme Go to page 120.

## GRAMMAR
### Present and past passive (review)

**1 Complete these sentences from the article on page 57. Use the correct form of *be*. Then complete the rule with *by*, *be* and *past participle*.**

1 Gavin Cox ______ called up to the stage by the magician.
2 Thirteen soft balls ______ thrown into the audience.
3 The white screens ______ lifted.
4 The cage ______ raised above the stage.

> **RULE:** We form the passive with a form of the verb [5]______ and the [6]______ .
> We use the preposition [7]______ to say who or what does the action, but only if this is important.

**2 Complete the instructions with the correct active or passive forms of the verbs.**

cut | get | hide | hold | pull | push | ~~use~~

0 A long box *is used* for this trick.
1 One woman ______________ at one end of the box.
2 A second woman ______________ into the box.
3 She puts her head out of one end and ______________ her legs to her chest with her arms. At the same time, the first woman ______________ her legs out of the other end.
4 The box ______________ in half by the magician.
5 The ends of the box ______________ apart to show that it has been cut in two.

→ workbook page 54

## VOCABULARY
### Extreme adjectives and modifiers

**3 Look at these phrases from the article on page 57. What do the adjectives in bold mean?**

1 As the **stunned** audience watched, the screen was raised again.
2 A **huge** audience sat on Liberty Island.
3 David Copperfield has entertained his audiences for years with his **fantastic** magic tricks and **thrilling** illusions.

**4 Match the gradable adjectives (1–8) with the extreme adjectives (a–h).**

| | |
|---|---|
| 1 good | a hilarious |
| 2 funny | b fascinating |
| 3 happy | c huge / enormous |
| 4 big | d freezing |
| 5 small | e great / fantastic / wonderful / brilliant / amazing |
| 6 bad | f delighted |
| 7 cold | g tiny / minute |
| 8 interesting | h terrible |

> **Look**
> We use:
> - *very* with gradable adjectives.
> - *absolutely* with extreme adjectives.
> - *really* with gradable and extreme adjectives.

**5 Look at these examples of adjectives with the modifiers *very*, *really* and *absolutely*. Which combinations are correct and which are incorrect? Mark them ✓ or ✗.**

| | | | |
|---|---|---|---|
| 1 really good | ☐ | 4 very hilarious | ☐ |
| 2 really amazing | ☐ | 5 absolutely small | ☐ |
| 3 very funny | ☐ | 6 absolutely tiny | ☐ |

**6 Complete the text with adjectives from Exercise 4. Sometimes more than one answer is possible, but don't use each adjective more than once.**

> Last night, we went to a magic show. It was very good – in fact, it was absolutely [1]______ . The magician was really [2]______ – we couldn't stop laughing. In one trick, he had two hats: a really small one and an [3]______ one. But from the big hat he pulled out an absolutely [4]______ rabbit and from the small hat he pulled out a huge one. It was great fun and I left feeling really [5]______ .

→ workbook page 56

## LISTENING

**7** 6.04 **Listen to two people talking about a haircut. What is unusual about James' haircut?**

**8** 6.04 **Listen again. Tick (✓) the reasons why Mia is so upset about James's haircut.**

1 It was expensive. ☐
2 He'll spoil his sister's wedding photos. ☐
3 It looks silly. ☐
4 He missed his date with her. ☐
5 His parents will be angry. ☐
6 It was done badly. ☐

**9 Replace the underlined words or phrases with the words below from the dialogue.**

centre of attention | furious | a work of art | must be joking | a disaster

1 It's a brilliant creation.
2 It's extremely bad.
3 She should be the person everyone is looking at.
4 You can't be serious.
5 They will be very angry.

## GRAMMAR

### *have something done*

**10 Underline the subject in each sentence. Do we know who is performing the action? Then complete the rule with *us* and *someone*.**

1 I've had my hair cut.
2 I can have the lizard shaved off.
3 I'm going to have my arms tattooed.

**RULE:** We often use the structure ***have*** + object + past participle when we arrange for [4] ______ to do something for [5] ______ . In less formal contexts, *get* often replaces *have*.

**11 Complete the sentences. Use *have* + object + past participle.**

Lord Uppity doesn't do anything himself.

1 He never cooks. He ______ his meals ______ by chefs.
2 He and his wife never do any housework. They ______ it ______ by cleaners.
3 He never goes into shops. He ______ everything ______ by his assistant.
4 Neither he nor his wife drives. They ______ their car ______ by an ex-racing driver.
5 They never organise parties. They ______ them ______ by party organisers.
6 They don't look after their children. They ______ them ______ by a nanny.

Life is boring. There's simply nothing to do!

**12 Use the words to write questions.**

car | clean | ~~cut~~ | do | ~~hair~~ | make | repair | tattoo | teeth | wedding cake

0 *Where can you have your hair cut* ? At the To Dye For salon.
1 ______________________ ? At Derek's Bakery.
2 ______________________ ? At Bridge Street Mechanic's.
3 ______________________ ? At Body Art.
4 ______________________ ? At the Northgate Dental Surgery.

→ workbook page 54

## SPEAKING

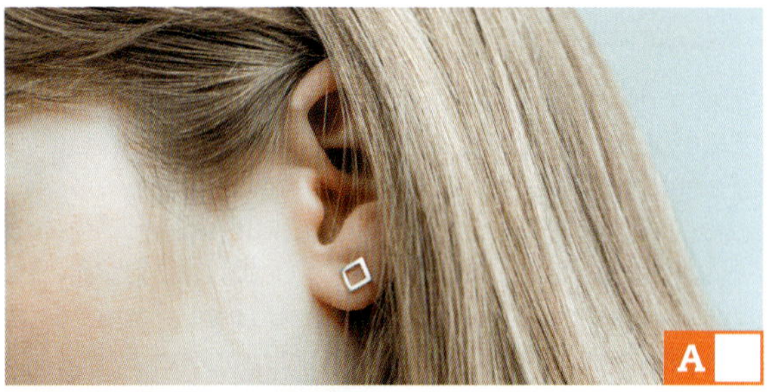

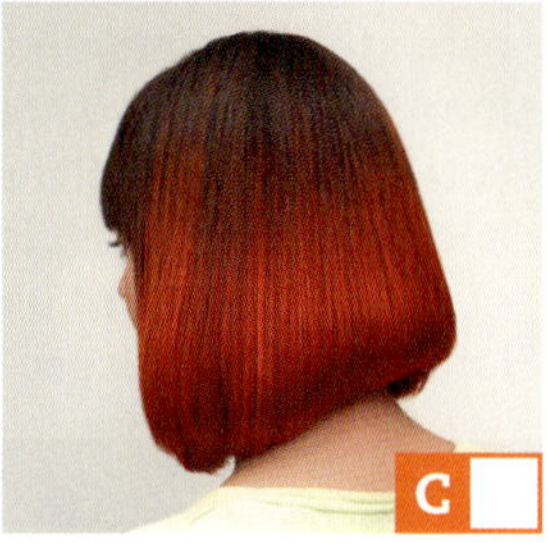


**13 Match the photos with 1–3.**

1 'My parents won't let me have my hair dyed.'
2 'Dad was right. What a bad idea it was to get a tattoo!'
3 'I'm not allowed to get my ears pierced.'

**14 Work in pairs. Think of possible reasons for these teenagers' parents' attitudes.**

**15 How do you feel about these issues? Tell your partner.**

## READING

**1** **Read the blog entry quickly and number the photos in the order they are mentioned 1–5.**

A

B

C

D

E

# BIG QUESTIONS BIGGER ANSWERS!

**I've just discovered a fantastic new show called *Big questions – bigger answers!* It's one of the best online series at the moment! The idea is simple: take a topic – like dolphins, for example – and then think of lots of little mysteries that can be explained. How do dolphins communicate? How do baby dolphins stay awake for a whole month? How can dolphins hear sounds that are so far away? That sort of thing. Then get two young, enthusiastic presenters to travel the world and find answers to these questions, add some cool graphics to explain the rest and there's your show. Get the idea?**

Each episode looks at a different subject. As well as *Dolphins*, topics that have already been covered include *Famous buildings*, *The body*, *Around the house*, *Natural wonders* and *Magic* – my favourite so far. Still to come are *Sport* and *Travel*. But back to dolphins. I really learnt a lot of fascinating facts about them. Here's one I liked: how can dolphins look in two different directions at the same time? The answer: one eye looks in front and the other looks behind – amazing! And what about this? Dolphins replace their skin every two hours. Yes, every two hours! Also, did you know that dolphins can dive 550 metres under water and hold their breath for 12 minutes? These are just a few of the things I learnt on this great new show. And yes, I think you've guessed that I love dolphins!

What I like best about the show is that it's fun and you learn something at the same time, so you don't feel guilty about spending 60 minutes in front of a screen. We've been shown how birds make their way back to exactly the same place each summer (they use the stars), and how a touchscreen works (that one didn't really make much sense to me). We haven't been shown how to eat chocolate without putting on weight yet, but I'm still hoping they might include that!

In future episodes, secrets like how top athletes can run so fast and why elephants can't jump will be revealed. The one I'm personally looking forward to the most is how frogs can freeze without dying.

So if you aren't already watching *Big questions – bigger answers!*, I strongly recommend that you make time to. It gives you facts that you can use to pretend that you're actually quite intelligent for a while – as long as you can remember them, of course. Why not log in and watch this week's show now or download the box set at the end of the series? Many fascinating questions will be answered. So get watching and start learning!

**2** 6.05 **Read and listen to the blog again. Answer the questions.**

1 What do presenters on the programme do?
2 How many different topics are mentioned?
3 How can dolphins see in two different directions?
4 Why couldn't the writer tell you how a touchscreen works?
5 What amazing thing can frogs do?
6 How can watching this programme make you more knowledgeable?

**3** **In which episode are these questions probably answered?**

1 Why do we sneeze?
2 Why is the Eiffel Tower 15 cm taller in the summer?
3 How can solar heating work when it's raining?
4 How does Aurora Borealis (the Northern Lights) work?
5 How do you make a rabbit come out of a hat?

**4** SPEAKING **Work in pairs. Choose four of the episodes from the text and think of a question you would like to see answered in each episode.**

# GRAMMAR

## Future and present perfect passive (review)

**5 Complete the sentences from the blog on page 60 with the words in the list. Then complete the rule with past participle (x2), *be* and present perfect.**

been shown | been covered
be answered | be revealed

1 ... topics that have already ________________ include *Famous buildings* ...
2 We haven't ________________ how to eat chocolate without putting on weight yet ...
3 In future episodes, secrets like how top athletes can run so fast ... will ________________ .
4 Many fascinating questions will ________________ .

**RULE:**
- To make the **future passive**, we use *will* + [5]______ + the [6]______ .
- To make the **present perfect passive**, we use the [7]______ form of *to be* and the [8]______ .

**6 Rewrite the sentences using the passive.**

1 They will show the match live on TV.
2 They will choose the next Olympic city in April.
3 People all over the world will watch the match.
4 They have already sold all the tickets for the show.
5 They have already made the decision.
6 Someone has already spent that money.

**7 Complete the text with the future passive form of the verbs.**

### Good news for fans of *How Do They Do That?*

A new series [1]______ (film) over the next three months and the new episodes [2]______ (show) in the new year. They [3]______ (present) by Helen, but she [4]______ (not join) by Liam this time. A new presenter [5]______ (choose) in the next few weeks – watch this space! The presenters [6]______ also ______ (join) by Spike the robot dog, but we aren't sure exactly what he'll do. Topics that [7]______ (cover) include *Buildings*, *Space* and *Food*. There'll also be a new time for the show. It [8]______ (not show) at the old time of 9 pm on Tuesdays. It [9]______ (move) to Sunday afternoons at 3 pm and the producers are hoping it [10]______ (watch) by a bigger audience. I know one person who will be watching for sure – me!

**8 Look at the list and write sentences. Use positive and negative present perfect passive forms and *already* or *yet*.**

### Mum and Dad's anniversary party – things to do

| | |
|---|---|
| arrange a date for the party | ✓ |
| buy decorations | ✗ |
| find a place for the party | ✓ |
| send invitations | ✓ |
| buy drinks | ✗ |
| prepare food | ✗ |
| hire a DJ | ✓ |
| choose music | ✗ |

*A date has already been arranged for the party.*
*The decorations haven't been bought yet.*

→ workbook page 55

# VOCABULARY

## *make* and *do*

**9 Write the words in the correct columns. Use page 60 to help you.**

an experiment | housework | money
sense | time | well | your way

| make | do |
|---|---|
| | |

**10 Complete the sentences with the correct form of *make* or *do*.**

0 I really need to *do* well in this test. I'm going to study hard tonight.
1 I've been ______ housework all day. I'm exhausted.
2 It's a really good exhibition. You should ______ time to see it.
3 Sorry I can't meet you at the station, but I'm sure you can ______ your own way to my house.
4 Don't go in there. They're ______ a dangerous experiment.
5 The film is very long, so it ______ sense to have something to eat first.
6 He ______ a lot of money in banking and retired when he was 50.

→ workbook page 56

# Fiction

1 What is a 'mind map'? What do people use them for?

2 6.06 Read and listen to the extract. What two things surprise Lucho very much?

# THE MIND MAP

BY DAVID MORRISON

Lucho and Eva are classmates at a school in Salvador. Their teacher tells them to make a mind map together. Lucho starts one at home, around the word *guaca*, which are special gold objects made by South American tribes. At home Lucho has a gold pendant that his grandmother gave him. Here, Lucho and Eva go to a computer to find more information for the mind map Lucho started.

Eva typed 'Kogi' and pressed Enter. [...] Soon [she] had found the web page she was looking for.

'OK.' Eva started reading. 'The Sierra Nevada mountains are home to the Kogi tribe. The ancestors of the Kogi were the brave Tairona ...,' she continued. 'Like their ancestors, the Kogi still make things from gold.'

'Should I write this down?' asked Lucho.

'Of course, or we will forget it,' Eva answered.

Lucho put his notebook on the table next to the computer and looked at the screen, where there was a photograph of a Kogi chief. The chief was wearing a jaguar skin and he had jaguar teeth on a piece of gold string round his neck. He seemed to be looking straight at Lucho from the screen. [...]

'What are you waiting for, Lucho? Write these things on your mind map!' Eva said.

[Lucho] opened his notebook and turned to the page where he had drawn his mind map, but when he saw what had happened, he almost fell off his chair.

'Eva, something's wrong!' Lucho shouted.

'Shh!' said Eva. 'We're in the library!'

'The mind map has changed, Eva. Look!'

He showed her the mind map. There were words now in the four circles he had drawn with the pendant. The words were, 'Nebtashi', 'Hotel Continental', 'Esmeralda' and 'Ichua'.

'I don't even write like that, Eva!'

'Lucho,' said Eva, 'this is not the time for silly jokes. We don't have much time before the next class.'

'Eva, I promise. All I did last night was to draw the circles and the lines and write "guaca" in the centre circle. Something amazing has happened!'

Eva stood up.

'I'm sorry, Lucho.' Her voice was very serious now. 'I don't think you're a bad person, but you are a little strange. I will do the mind map alone. You can tell your story to Mr Parra on Monday.'

Eva walked out of the library. Lucho didn't know what to think. How had the words appeared on the mind map? Something strange, something very strange, was happening.

Quickly, he typed 'Ichua' into the computer, but couldn't find any information. He now knew that 'Nebtashi' meant 'jaguar', and 'Esmeralda' was his grandmother's name. He looked for information about the 'Hotel Continental', but could only find pages about hotels in places he had never heard of.

'I must show Eva that I'm not lying!' he said to himself as he put his notebook and pen into his bag and stood up. Suddenly he sat down again. Big red letters had started to appear on the computer screen and slowly the letters became words, three words:

'TAKE IT BACK.'

Lucho could not believe his eyes.

**3** **Read the extract again. Answer the questions.**

1. What do the Kogi people still do now that they did in the past?
2. Why does Lucho open his notebook?
3. Why does Lucho almost fall off his chair?
4. Why does Eva leave the library?
5. What does Lucho look for after Eva leaves?
6. What does Lucho want to prove to Eva?

**4** SPEAKING **Work in pairs and answer the questions.**

1. What do you think 'it' could be in the message on Lucho's screen?
2. What might the words in the mind map mean?
3. Why has he been told to 'take it back'?

## FUNCTIONS
### Talking about sequence

**5** SPEAKING **Work in pairs. In what order do these things happen when an aeroplane takes off? Number the boxes. Discuss your ideas.**

*First, I think ...*

*After that, ...*

*Next, ...*

*Finally, ...*

*The engine is powered up.*

*The brakes are taken off.*

*The wheels are pulled up.*

*The plane is turned around in the air.*

*The nose is lifted into the air.*

*The plane is lined up on the runway.*

## WRITING
### Explaining how things are done

**1** INPUT **Read the explanation and check your answers to the last exercise.**

## HOW DO PLANES TAKE OFF?

To get an aeroplane into the air, you need the correct airspeed. Airspeed is not the speed of the plane, but how fast the air is moving over it. If the plane is facing a strong wind, the airspeed is already quite high. That's why planes are usually lined up to take off facing into the wind.

The engines are turned up to a certain power. Then the brakes are taken off and the plane speeds down the runway. As it does this, air passes over the wings. The wings are curved on the top, so the air has further to travel over the wings than under the wings, and has to travel faster. This creates a force that pushes upwards. When that force is big enough, the nose of the plane is pushed into the air and when the correct airspeed is reached, the whole plane takes off.

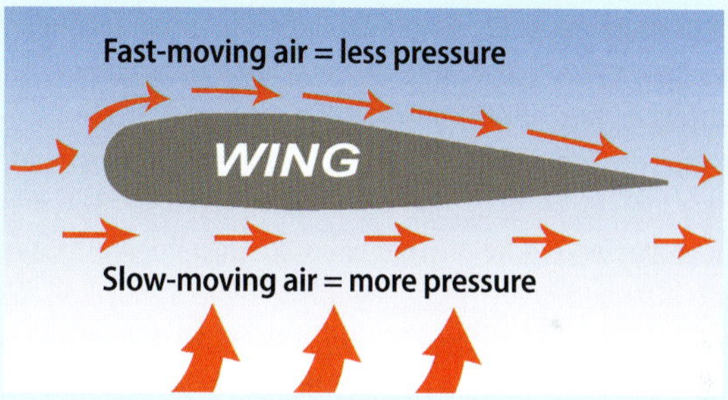


When the plane is high enough in the air, the wheels are pulled up and the plane is turned around, leaving space for the next one to take off.

**2** ANALYSE **Read the explanation again. Then make two lists for ...**

- the procedure (what happens and in what order).
- the theories (explanations of why things happen).

**3** PRODUCE **Choose an activity from the list or your own idea. Write an explanation of how to do it (150 words).**

- how to play the guitar
- how to play your favourite computer game
- how to do a headstand

**Think about:**

- the procedure and the sequence.
- whether you need to explain any theories.
- how to explain any difficult vocabulary.

## READING AND USE OF ENGLISH
### Multiple choice

→ workbook page 61

**1 You are going to read a text about urban legends. For questions 1–4, choose the answer (A, B, C or D) which you think fits best according to the text.**

People have been telling stories for as long as they have been walking the Earth. And from cave paintings to Shakespeare's Globe Theatre to Hollywood blockbusters, the methods of telling them have got more and more sophisticated.

In the 1960s, a new storytelling art form emerged – the urban legend. Even if you've never heard the term, you've certainly heard an urban legend. What about the story of the unwanted pet alligators that were flushed down the toilet and are now living in the sewers of New York City? Or the man who woke up in a bathtub full of ice and saw a note informing him that one of his kidneys had been taken out?

One of the key features of the urban legend is its lack of an author. The stories appear mysteriously and are then passed on by word of mouth. And although we know these mini-tales of horror, humour and embarrassment are almost certainly not true, part of us wants to believe them.

Then the internet, which is packed with fiction (everything from jokes to the latest releases from top-selling authors), helped create and spread urban legends. Before the internet, urban legends went around quite slowly. They took time to reach a larger audience. The internet changed all that almost overnight.

The internet is the perfect vehicle for the urban legend, for it not only allows the stories to spread much faster but also allows for greater anonymity, too – a lot of what we read online doesn't have an author's name attached to it. This anonymity adds to the overall mystery.

Of course, the internet also allows you to check the truth of a story more easily. Over time, a number of sites have appeared which collect stories, investigate their origins and report the results. Often there isn't any truth to the story at all. But sometimes the urban legend grew from something that did actually happen. Thanks to the internet, learning about the origins of an urban legend can be as interesting and entertaining as the story itself.

1 What do we learn about stories from the first paragraph?
  - A They've never been as popular as they are now.
  - B They have their origins in the days of Shakespeare.
  - C They were much longer in the past.
  - D Ways of telling them have changed over time.

2 What does the author suggest about urban legends?
  - A Everyone knows the term 'urban legend'.
  - B Everyone knows an example of one.
  - C They appeared at the same time as the internet.
  - D They're always about horrific events.

3 What does the author mean when he says 'the internet ... is packed with fiction'?
  - A You can find every story written online.
  - B You can get most fiction for free online.
  - C There are lots of stories on the internet.
  - D There are too many stories on the internet.

4 What does the author suggest about urban legends in the last paragraph?
  - A They're generally mystery stories.
  - B They're usually short.
  - C Nowadays it's easier to discover if they're true or not.
  - D Some include the author's name.

## VOCABULARY

**1 Complete the sentences with the words in the list. There are four extra words.**

character | delighted | ending | enormous | fascinating | freezing
hero | hilarious | opening | plot | setting | terrible | tiny | villain

1 The __________ of the film is an amazing doctor who can travel through time and save people.
2 The show that we saw in the theatre last night was __________ . I couldn't stop laughing.
3 I've just read the last page of the book, and I don't like the __________ .
4 I couldn't read all the words very well because the letters were __________ .
5 He dived into the __________ water.
6 There is one __________ in the film who is really funny. He makes everybody laugh.
7 I haven't done my homework. I had a __________ headache last night.
8 I can't put this book down – it's __________ . I'm learning so much!
9 I'm __________ that you can come and see the show. The other actors will be happy, too.
10 The __________ of the story is an evil vampire.

/10

## GRAMMAR

**2 Complete the sentences with the words/phrases in the list. There are two extra words/phrases.**

are used | have it removed | have been taken | whose | where | who | that | are pulled

1 It's a story __________ has been passed down from generation to generation.
2 Hundreds of photos of the magician __________ .
3 She's an actor __________ has a great talent for storytelling.
4 Jack had a tattoo done a few years ago, and now he wants to __________ .
5 Two rabbits __________ out of a hat in this trick.
6 He still lives in the city __________ he was born.

**3 Find and correct the mistake in each sentence.**

1 The decision will be done by the judges tonight.
2 I didn't make very well in the test.
3 The marathon will have shown live on TV.
4 I won a medal for swimming last term, what made me feel proud.
5 I'm not allowed have my hair dyed.
6 Mrs Jones, who son I went to school with, is my piano teacher.

/12

## FUNCTIONAL LANGUAGE

**4 Choose the correct words.**

1 A You'll never *know* / *believe* what happened just now.
B *What* / *Really*?
A I guessed all the answers in the TV quiz show correctly. What are the *chances* / *opportunities* of that?
2 A What's that song you keep singing?
B That's the *annoying* / *angry* thing! I can't remember what it's called or who sings it.
3 A How does this machine work, then?
B First, the engine *is* / *was* turned on. After *it* / *that*, the handbrake is released.
4 A My dyed hair is a work of art!
B A work of art? You must be *laughing* / *joking*.

/8

**MY SCORE** /30

22–30 | 10–21 | 0–9

# PRONUNCIATION

## UNIT 1
### Linking words with *up*

1 1.04 **Read and listen to the dialogue.**

**Steve** What's up, Jenny?
**Jenny** I'm tired! I'm up late every night studying.
**Steve** You need your sleep! Can't you get up later?
**Jenny** Not really. I've taken up the flute this year. I practise in the mornings.
**Steve** Well, it's up to you, but I'd give that up!
**Jenny** Hmmm … I wish I hadn't signed up for the school orchestra now!

2 **What happens to the words in blue? Choose the correct word to complete the rule:**

A word ending in a *consonant* / *vowel* sound links with the following word when it begins with a *consonant* / *vowel* sound.

3 1.05 **Listen, repeat and practise.**

## UNIT 2
### Initial consonant clusters with /s/

1 2.02 **Read and listen to the tongue twisters.**

Strong winds spread the sparks through the streets.
Stella's got straight hair and stripes on her skirt.
Stewart sprayed his phone with a special screen cleaner.

2 **Say the words with blue letters in them.**

3 2.03 **Listen, repeat and practise.**

## UNIT 3
### Strong and weak forms: /ɒv/ and /əv/

1 3.05 **Read and listen to the dialogue.**

**Julia** What do you always buy the same brand of?
**Jack** I always buy the same brand of trainers. They're called Ace. I bought a pair of green ones last week.
**Julia** Ace? What are they made of?
**Jack** They're made of fabric and rubber. They put a lot of effort into the design and quality of them.
**Julia** And into the marketing of them, too!

2 3.05 **Listen again and make a note of each of which is stressed and each of which is unstressed.**

3 3.06 **Listen, repeat and practise.**

## UNIT 4
### Consonant–vowel word linking

1 4.05 **Read and listen to the dialogue.**

**Lisa** I was only joking, but I wish I hadn't said it. I think she hates me.
**Henry** Well, it was unkind of you to say you didn't like her new haircut.
**Lisa** I know! I can't believe I said that she looked like a boy! It just came out. What should I do?
**Henry** First, I'd apologise. Then I'd admit that I prefer it long. Actually, I think she looks amazing!

2 4.05 **Find examples of linking in the dialogue. Then listen and check.**

3 4.06 **Listen, repeat and practise.**

## UNIT 5
### The schwa /ə/ in word endings

1 5.06 **Read and listen to the tongue twisters.**

Ireland's a nation with famous traditions.
My neighbour's a brilliant classical musician.
The monster's a villain who frightens the children.

2 5.06 **Listen again and focus on the syllables in blue. Are they stressed or unstressed? They all have the same short vowel sound. What is it?**

3 5.07 **Listen, repeat and practise.**

## UNIT 6
### The /ʒ/ phoneme

1 6.02 **Read and listen to the interview.**

**Helen** Welcome to *Film Night Television*. Our guest is Tom Potts, who stars in an unusual thriller called *Asian Treasure*. Why did you decide to take on this role?
**Tom** It was a difficult decision, Helen. I play the part of an amazing illusionist.
**Helen** There are so many collisions and explosions in the film that I thought you would never find that treasure.
**Tom** It's true! Occasionally I was frightened for my own life!

2 6.02 **How is each 's' in blue pronounced?**

3 6.03 **Listen, repeat and practise.**

# GET IT RIGHT!

## UNIT 1
### Present simple vs. present continuous

**It's common to confuse the present simple and present continuous.**

**We use the present simple to describe facts, routine activities and opinions.**

✓ *I **usually go** there on foot.*

✗ *~~I'm usually going~~ there on foot.*

**We use the present continuous to describe events that are happening now or around now.**

✓ ***I'm sending** you a photo of my new bike.*

✗ *I ~~send~~ you a photo of my new bike.*

**Find the error in each of these sentences. Rewrite the sentences correctly.**

0 I know how hard you try to get on the team.
*I know how hard you are trying to get on the team.*

1 I think I am the person you look for.

______________________________

2 I'm playing tennis on Tuesdays.

______________________________

3 At the moment I write a letter to a friend.

______________________________

4 I like what you wear today.

______________________________

5 I know what you mean and are appreciating your help.

______________________________

6 We are playing football during most school breaks.

______________________________

## UNIT 2
### Present perfect vs. past simple

**Students often confuse the present perfect and past simple tenses.**

**We use the past simple when we include a past time expression to say when in the past an event took place.**

✓ *Yesterday I **ate** rice.*

✗ *Yesterday I ~~have eaten~~ rice.*

**We use the present perfect to talk about past events when we don't say exactly when they took place and with expressions such as *yet, before, ever* and *never*.**

✓ ***I've** never **been** to London before.*

✗ *I ~~didn't go~~ to London before.*

**Make sentences using the prompts below.**

0 we / see / the advertisement at the bus stop / yesterday
*We saw the advertisement at the bus stop yesterday.*

1 I / not see / the new Hobbit film / yet

______________________________

2 you / ever / go / to Spain?

______________________________

3 John / take / his exam / last week

______________________________

4 Nina / get / here / a few minutes ago

______________________________

5 they / not eat / at this restaurant / before

______________________________

6 I / not eat / breakfast / so I'm really hungry and it's two hours till lunchtime!

______________________________

## Past continuous vs. past simple

**Learners sometimes confuse the past continuous with the past simple.**

✓ *I was happy when I* ***came*** *first in the race.*

✗ *I was happy when I ~~was coming~~ first in the race.*

**Which of these sentences are correct and which are incorrect? Rewrite the incorrect ones.**

0 Last time I was visiting the library, I couldn't find the book I was looking for.
*Last time I visited the library, I couldn't find the book I was looking for.*

1 When she arrived, I cooked dinner so I was a bit distracted.

2 After that, I watched TV for about an hour.

3 As usual, we were arriving at about 6 pm; then we had dinner.

4 My teacher came to see how our project went.

5 I'll never forget the time I was spending in Nepal.

6 The police saw the men and asked them what they did there.

# UNIT 3

## *have to* vs. *had to*

**Learners sometimes confuse *have to* and *had to*.**
**We use *have to* to talk about an obligation in the present, and *had to* to talk about an obligation in the past.**

✓ *Shopping is stressful, especially if you* ***have to*** *find a particular item of clothing.*

✗ *Shopping is stressful, especially if you ~~had to~~ find a particular item of clothing.*

**Which of these sentences are correct and which are incorrect? Rewrite the incorrect ones.**

0 The trains were fully booked so we have to forget about that trip.
*The trains were fully booked so we had to forget about that trip.*

1 I'm sorry I can't attend class tomorrow because I had to go to the doctor.

2 My dad was going to work for another company so we have to move house.

3 If you want a drink after swimming, you have to go somewhere else.

4 If I have to choose between going to a small school or a large one, I would choose a large one.

5 Do we have to bring any money for the trip next week?

6 Yesterday we had to write an essay about Barack Obama.

## *don't have to* vs. *mustn't*

**Learners sometimes make errors with *don't have to* and *mustn't*.**
**Although *have to* and *must* both mean something is necessary, *don't have to* means that something is not necessary, whereas *mustn't* means that something is prohibited.**

✓ *I* ***don't have to*** *work tonight, as I've already finished everything.*

✗ *I ~~mustn't~~ work tonight, as I've already finished everything.*

✓ *I* ***mustn't*** *fail my exam, or I'll have to retake it.*

**Write the sentences with *mustn't* or *don't have to*.**

0 You / stay out late or you'll be really tired tomorrow.
*You mustn't stay out late or you'll be really tired tomorrow.*

1 You / finish your essay now. Mr Jenkins said that we can hand it in next Friday.

2 You / bring anything to the party – just bring yourself!

3 You / eat food in class – it's against the rules.

4 You / talk during exams.

5 You / revise every unit. The exam only includes Units 1 to 3.

6 You / use your phone in class. It'll be confiscated.

## UNIT 4
### *if* vs. *when*

**Learners often confuse *if* with *when*.**
**We use *if* to indicate possible actions or events.**
✓ *It'll be best for us **if** everyone goes by bicycle. Car parking facilities are limited.*
✗ *It'll be best for us ~~when~~ everyone goes by bicycle. Car parking facilities are limited.*

**We use *when* to indicate events which have happened in the past or are going to happen in the future.**
✓ *I can pass on your message. I'll tell him **when** I see him tomorrow.*
✗ *I can pass on your message. I'll tell him ~~if~~ I see him tomorrow.*

**Complete these sentences with *if* or *when*.**

0 I was very pleased ___*when*___ I read your letter.
1 I had a great time ____________ I went to New York.
2 Would it be OK ____________ I invited my friend?
3 I'll call you ____________ I get home tonight.
4 Do you mind ____________ we meet at 5 pm instead of 4 pm?
5 ____________ you're free on Saturday, come to the cinema with us!
6 He went to Africa ____________ he was 21 because of his job.
7 How much would it cost ____________ we were a group of ten?

## UNIT 5
### Relative pronouns

**Learners sometimes confuse *who* and *which*.**
**We use *who* to refer to people and *which* to refer to things.**
✓ *Next week I'm going to visit my Uncle Joe, **who** lives in Manchester.*
✗ *Next week I'm going to visit my Uncle Joe, ~~which~~ lives in Manchester.*

**Complete the sentences with *who* or *which*.**

0 There are several problems ___*which*___ can't wait any longer.
1 My friend Paul, ____________ I've known since primary school, is coming.
2 Animals ____________ can protect themselves shouldn't be kept in a zoo.
3 My dad works for a company ____________ sells dental products.
4 It's a great film but it's really sad. It's about a soldier ____________ goes to war.
5 She was the only one ____________ talked to me.
6 He's currently working for a charity ____________ helps elderly people.

## UNIT 6
### *absolutely* vs. *very*

**A common mistake is using intensifiers like *absolutely* and *very* with the wrong types of adjectives.**

**We use *absolutely* to modify non-gradable adjectives or adjectives with a strong or extreme meaning.**
✓ *It's **absolutely** delicious.*
✗ *It's ~~very~~ delicious.*

**We use *very* to modify gradable adjectives.**
✓ *I was **very** disappointed with it.*
✗ *I was ~~absolutely~~ disappointed with it.*

**Complete the sentences with *absolutely* or *very*.**

0 In my opinion, the countryside is ___*very*___ relaxing.
1 This museum is ____________ fascinating.
2 The view from the top was ____________ amazing.
3 I thought the documentary was ____________ interesting.
4 I was ____________ thrilled to get an 'A' on that assignment.
5 This food is ____________ tasty.
6 She's a ____________ good singer.

This page is intentionally left blank.

# STUDENT A

## UNIT 1, PAGE 18

**Student A**

You aren't very happy with your brother or sister. He/She plays loud music that you don't like when you're trying to work. He/She doesn't even keep the door closed. What else upsets you about this? You have decided to talk to him/her about it. Try and use the expressions in Exercise 5.

*Excuse me, [name], I need a word …*

# STUDENT B

## UNIT 1, PAGE 18

**Student B**

You aren't very happy with your brother or sister. He/She keeps taking your clothes without asking you. He/She makes a real mess when he/she takes them from your wardrobe. What else upsets you about this? You have decided to talk to him/her about it. Try and use the expressions in Exercise 5.

***Excuse me, [name], I need a word …***

**Acknowledgements**

The authors and publishers acknowledge the following sources of copyright material and are grateful for the permissions granted. While every effort has been made, it has not always been possible to identify the sources of all the material used, or to trace all copyright holders. If any omissions are brought to our notice, we will be happy to include the appropriate acknowledgements on reprinting and in the next update to the digital edition, as applicable.

Key: W= Welcome; U = Unit.

**Text**

**U3:** Cambridge University Press for the text from *How I Met Myself by* David A. Hill. Copyright ©

2006 Cambridge University Press. Reproduced with permission; **U6:** Cambridge University Press for the text from *The Mind Map* by David Morrison. Copyright © 2009, 2010 Cambridge University Press. Reproduced with permission;

**Photography**

All the photographs are sourced from Getty Images.

**W:** SDI Productions/E+; Ben Hider/Getty Images Entertainment; BrianAJackson/iStock/Getty Images Plus; Dennis K. Johnson/Lonely Planet Images/Getty Images Plus; JoyceMarrero/iStock/Getty Images Plus; CircleEyes/iStock/Getty Images Plus; Henglein and Steets/Cultura; Hemant Mehta; Frederic J. Brown/AFP; iconeer/DigitalVision Vectors; Pakorn Kumruen/EyeEm; UmbertoPantalone/iStock/Getty Images Plus; **U1:** Westend61; caiaimage; Maskot; BJI/Blue Jean Images; xavierarnau/E+; AaronAmat/iStock/Getty Images Plus; stock_colors/E+; Luxx Images/DigitalVision; Tim Robberts/DigitalVision; Jason LaVeris/FilmMagic; Cory Disbrow/Moment; Atlantide Phototravel/Corbis Documentary; Graiki/Moment; Chanokporn Sudthinon/EyeEm; AntonioGuillem/iStock/Getty Images Plus; **U2:** AFP; Print Collector/Hulton Archive; Stefano Bianchetti/Corbis Historical; Bettmann; jenjen42/iStock/Getty Images Plus; Nastasic/DigitalVision Vectors; Universal Images Group/Hulton Fine Art/Hulton Fine Art Collection; DEA/G. Dagli Orti/De Agostini; ilbusca/DigitalVision Vectors; Heritage Images/Hulton Archive; magnetcreative/E+; FamVeld/iStock/Getty Images Plus; Martinelli73/E+; John Seaton Callahan/Moment; Tony Nguyen/Moment; Fine Art/Corbis Historical; Hero Images; **U3:** Chaay_Tee/iStock/Getty Images Plus; Doug Cheeseman/Photodisc; Highwaystarz-Photography/iStock/Getty Images Plus; Johner Images; Xuanyu Han/Moment; drbimages/E+; Rudy Sulgan/Corbis Documentary; Morsa Images/DigitalVision; **U4:** CiydemImages/iStock/Getty Images Plus; FatCamera/E+; kali9/E+; skynesher/E+; **U5:** adventtr/E+; kali9/E+; Capuski/E+; stock-eye/E+; Ronald Dumont/Hulton Archive; Yuri_Arcurs/E+; FotoDuets/iStock/Getty Images Plus; Ian Ross Pettigrew/Moment; Alankrit Sarmah/EyeEm; WilliamSherman/iStock/Getty Images Plus; cinoby/iStock/Getty Images Plus; **U6:** View Stock; Eetum/iStock/Getty Images Plus; FXQuadro/iStock/Getty Images Plus; Don Arnold/WireImage; Kevin Winter/ACM2009/Getty Images Entertainment; Sean Gladwell/Moment; chuwy/DigitalVision Vectors; Kateryna Shcherban/EyeEm; Brandi Thompson/EyeEm; stock_colors/iStock/Getty Images Plus; Towfiqu Photography/Moment; PeopleImages/E+; Donhype/iStock/Getty Images Plus; Burazin/Photographer's Choice/Getty Images Plus; Viviane Hofmann/EyeEm; Constantine Johnny/Moment; metamorworks/iStock/Getty Images Plus;

The following images are sourced from other sources/libraries.

**U2:** Naveen Macro/Shutterstock; **U3:** © Swatch; © Jaguar; © WhatsApp; © Pret A Manger; **U4:** Image Source/Alamy Stock Photo; **U5:** Scholastic Limited for the cover image of *The Hunger Games* by Suzanne Collins, Copyright © 2008 Suzanne Collins. Reproduced with permission of Scholastic Ltd; Cambridge University Press for the front cover image of *Berlin Express* by Michael Austin. Reproduced with permission of Cambridge University Press; Cambridge University Press for the front cover image of *Love in the Lakes* by Penny Hancock. Reproduced with permission of Cambridge University Press; Cambridge University Press for the front cover image of *Darwin* edited by William Brown & Andrew C. Fabian. Reproduced with permission of Cambridge University Press; Cambridge University Press for the front cover image of *Tales of Terror* by Edgar Allen Poe and others. Reproduced with permission of Cambridge University Press; Cambridge University Press for the front cover image of *Running Wild* by Margaret Johnson. Reproduced with permission of Cambridge University Press; Cambridge University Press for the front cover image of *The University Murders, An Inspector Logan Story* by Richard MacAndrew. Reproduced with permission of Cambridge University Press; Cambridge University Press for the front cover image of *The War of the Worlds* by HG Wells. Reproduced with permission of Cambridge University Press;

**Illustrations**

Martin Sanders (Beehive Illustration) pp. 10; Daniella Geremia pp. 17, 35, 55; Ben Scruton (Meiklejohn) pp. 31, 38, 42; Mark Ruffle pp. 43; Fausto Bianchi p. 48; Dan Lewis p. 51; Martin Sanders p. 59; Ricardo Ortiz p. 62; Graham Kennedy pp. 63.

**Documentary video stills**

All the stills are sourced from Getty Images.

**U1:** wojteKolakowski; **U2:** BlackLight Films-Louie Schwartzberg/Image Bank Film; Worldpicture/Creatas Video+/Getty Images Plus; **U3:** Mikhail Spaskov/Creatas Video+/Getty Images Plus; **U4:** Stephen Marks Inc./Photolibrary Video; **U5:** mith_67/Creatas Video; christine schmitthenner/Moment Video RF; **U6:** SKA/Image Bank Film: Signature

Vlog & Grammar Rap video stills: Silversun Media Group.

Full video acknowledgements can be found in the online Teacher's Resources.

Audio Production: Leon Chambers.

This page is intentionally left blank.

WORKBOOK
COMBO A 3

CEFR B1+

# TH!NK

SECOND EDITION

**Herbert Puchta,**
**Jeff Stranks &**
**Peter Lewis-Jones**
with Clare Kennedy

CAMBRIDGE
UNIVERSITY PRESS

This page is intentionally left blank.

# CONTENTS

# WELCOME

## A THAT'S ENTERTAINMENT

### *let* and *allow*

**1 Rewrite the sentences using the words in brackets.**

House rules: what my parents let or don't let me do.

0 My parents don't let me play loud music in my bedroom. (allowed)
*I'm not allowed to play loud music in my bedroom.*

1 My parents let me stay up late at the weekend. (allowed)
______________________

2 I'm allowed to practise my electric guitar in the garage. (let)
______________________

3 I'm not allowed to go out on school nights. (let)
______________________

4 My parents let me have parties at home. (allowed)
______________________

5 I'm not allowed to go to concerts on my own. (let)
______________________

### Music

**2 Unscramble the words and write them in the correct list. Add two more items to each list.**

inapo | jzaz | laslacsic | oilniv
opp | par | srumd | tagriu

| Musical instruments | Types of music |
|---|---|
| 1 ________ | 7 ________ |
| 2 ________ | 8 ________ |
| 3 ________ | 9 ________ |
| 4 ________ | 10 ________ |
| 5 ________ | 11 ________ |
| 6 ________ | 12 ________ |

**3 Complete the sentences so that they are true for you.**

1 I really like listening to ____________
2 I never listen to ____________
3 I play ____________
4 I'd love to play ____________

### Verbs of perception

**4 Complete the sentences.**

feel | looks | smells | tastes

1 I love your new haircut. It ________ fantastic!
2 Your hands ________ very cold. Are you OK?
3 This fruit juice ________ disgusting! I don't want any more.
4 Lunch ________ really good. Let's eat now!

**5 Complete the sentences with the correct form of the verbs in brackets.**

1 Why ________ you ________ (smell) the milk? Is it bad?
2 What's for dinner? It ________ (smell) great.
3 What ________ you ________ (look) at?
4 You ________ (not look) great. What's the matter?
5 This sandwich ________ (taste) awful. What's in it?
6 Why ________ you ________ (taste) the soup again?
7 A Why ________ you ________ my scarf (feel)?
B I love it! It's just so soft.
8 Leah's gone home because she ________ (not feel) well.

### The big screen

**6 Complete the word puzzle and find the name of one of the *Avengers* films.**

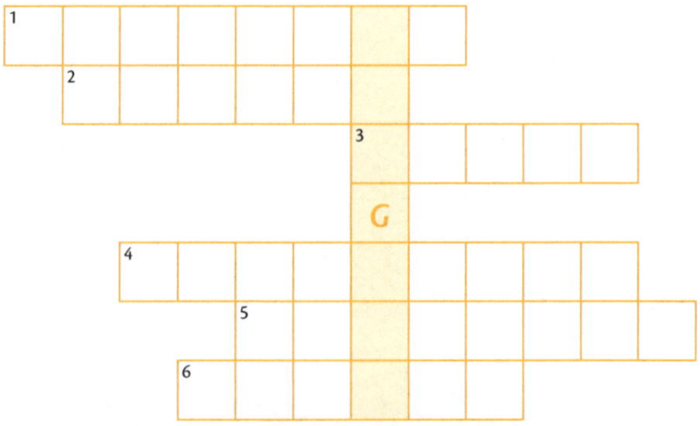


1 a serious film with lots of exciting moments
2 a film with a lot of explosions and car chases
3 a serious story with realistic characters
4 a cartoon-style film, usually for children
5 a ________ comedy is a love story that makes you laugh, and maybe cry
6 a film that makes you laugh

## Present perfect tenses

**7 Circle the correct options.**

1 I haven't *watched* / *been watching* TV for more than a week.
2 We've *seen* / *been seeing* this film before.
3 The cinema has *shown* / *been showing* the same film for weeks now.
4 If you've *lost* / *been losing* your ticket, you can't come in.
5 They've *waited* / *been waiting* in the cinema queue for three hours.
6 You've *read* / *been playing* that game for an hour. Can I have a go now?

## TV programmes

**8 Match the parts to make types of TV programme.**

| | |
|---|---|
| 0 chat | com |
| 1 game | programme |
| 2 drama | show |
| 3 sit | news |
| 4 sports | show |
| 5 the | series |

# SUMMING UP

**9 Complete the dialogue with the words and phrases in the list. There are three you don't need.**

're watching | let | 've been watching | the news | jazz | allowed to | watch | to watch | watched | 've watched | guitar | drama series

**Logan** Max, it's my turn [1]__________ TV.
**Max** Just give me 20 more minutes.
**Logan** But you [2]__________ TV for more than two hours now. You're not even [3]__________ watch so much TV. Does Mum know?
**Max** Yes, she does. Anyway, I'm almost finished.
**Logan** Yes but I want to watch [4]__________ and it starts in five minutes.
**Max** You can [5]__________ it later. I really need to see the end of this.
**Logan** What is it that you [6]__________, anyway?
**Max** *Crime Wave.*
**Logan** What, the American [7]__________ ?
**Max** Yes, that's right. This is the last episode in the series. I can't miss it. I [8]__________ all the others. I want to know how it ends.
**Logan** I'll tell you how it ends. The police officer is the murderer. Now [9]__________ me watch my show.

# B TIME TO ACT

## Our endangered planet

**1 W.01 Complete the sentences with the words in the list. Then listen and check.**

climate change | flooding | fumes | litter | pollution | smog

1 With the Earth's temperature rising each year, many scientists now believe __________ is the biggest threat to our planet.
2 __________ from factories and cars are creating huge __________ problems and many of the world's largest cities are permanently covered by thick __________ .
3 There has been serious __________ across the area and many people have had to leave their homes.
4 I get so angry when I see people dropping __________ in the streets. Why can't they use the bins?

## Question tags

**2 Match the sentences with the question tags.**

1 You don't care about the environment, ☐
2 Helen campaigns for the environment, ☐
3 Global warming is getting serious, ☐
4 The world isn't going to end tomorrow, ☐
5 Your friends didn't go on the protest march, ☐
6 Mark threw the rubbish in the bin, ☐
7 The Earth can't take much more, ☐
8 Science can find a solution, ☐

a isn't it?
b did they?
c can it?
d can't it?
e didn't he?
f do you?
g is it?
h doesn't she?

**3 Complete the sentences with question tags.**

1 You're from Argentina, __________ ?
2 This is pretty easy, __________ ?
3 You know him, __________ ?
4 They played really well, __________ ?
5 Qi and Bo don't speak English, __________ ?
6 She's working in London now, __________ ?
7 He can't sing, __________ ?
8 Tom won't be late, __________ ?
9 You've been to Canada, __________ ?
10 I shouldn't have said that, __________ ?

## Party time

**4 Match the parts of the sentences.**

Am I ready for the party? Well, so far …

1 I haven't found anywhere ☐
2 I haven't got permission ☐
3 I haven't drawn up ☐
4 So clearly I haven't sent out ☐
5 I haven't hired ☐
6 Or even got the money to pay ☐
7 I haven't decorated ☐
8 And I haven't organised ☐

a the guest list.
b the food.
c a DJ.
d the deposit for one.
e the room.
f from Mum and Dad.
g to have the party.
h any invitations.

## Indefinite pronouns

**5 Complete the sentences with the words in the list.**

anyone | everyone | everything | no one | nothing | nowhere | something | somewhere

The party was terrible.

1 I didn't know __________ .
2 __________ I tried to speak to just ignored me.
3 There was __________ to eat at all.
4 You had to pay for your drinks and __________ on the list was really expensive.
5 We wanted to leave our coats __________ but there was no cloakroom.
6 It was so crowded, there was __________ to sit.
7 Sally wanted __________ to do so we went to the dance floor.
8 But __________ was dancing. We were the only ones!

## Arranging a party

**6 Complete the dialogue with the words in the list. There are two you don't need.**

anyone | anything | decorating | everyone | everything | everywhere | get | hiring | nowhere | organising | sent out | something

**Sonya** So, Rory, is [1]__________ ready for the party tomorrow?
**Rory** I think so. I've just finished [2]__________ the room and [3]__________ the food.
**Sonya** So there will be [4]__________ to eat?
**Rory** Yes, and to drink.
**Sonya** So who's coming? [5]__________ I know?
**Rory** There'll be loads of people you know. I [6]__________ about 30 invitations.
**Sonya** That's a lot of people. Did you have to [7]__________ permission from your parents?
**Rory** Of course, I'm having the party at our house.
**Sonya** Is there [8]__________ I can do?
**Rory** Well, you could bring some music with you. I'm not [9]__________ a DJ.
**Sonya** OK, I'll bring some music that will get [10]__________ dancing.

## SUMMING UP

**7 W.02 Put the dialogue in order. Listen and check.**

☐ **Rob** Of course there is. I'm organising a protest march for Sunday. Do you want to join me?
☐ **Rob** That's a shame. But you could donate a bit of money, couldn't you?
☐ **Rob** Yes, and I don't think the government will do anything about it.
☐ **Rob** So that is why I think we should do something about it.
1 **Rob** I think the pollution in our city is getting worse each year.
☐ **Mia** I'm afraid I left my wallet at home. Sorry.
☐ **Mia** So do I. It's a real problem, isn't it?
☐ **Mia** Neither do I. They never do.
☐ **Mia** But there's nothing we can do, is there?
☐ **Mia** I'd love to but I can't. I'm busy.

# C IN MY OPINION, ...

## Feeling under the weather

**1 Match the parts of the sentences.**

1 Take this medicine and you'll feel
2 I always get
3 Dad's going to hospital to have
4 Can you phone the doctor and make
5 Why don't you see
6 You need to take more

a sick when I travel by car.
b an appointment for me?
c a doctor about your headaches?
d exercise to lose some weight.
e better in half an hour.
f an operation next week.

**2 Complete the sentences with the correct form of the phrases in the list.**

take some exercise | feel sick | have an operation
make an appointment | get better | see a doctor

1 I hope you ______________ soon.

2 He's ______________ .

3 That cat needs to ______________ .

4 Hello, I'd like to ______________ with Dr Hill.

5 I think you need to ______________ .

6 I ______________ !

## Giving advice

**3 Complete each piece of advice with one word.**

*I get really tired when I have to run.*

1 You __________ take more exercise.
2 You __________ better see a doctor.
3 You __________ to lose some weight.
4 You should __________ eat so much.
5 You had __________ be careful.
6 You ought __________ join a gym.

**4 Write one piece of advice for each of these people.**

1 'I can't do my homework.'

______________________________

2 'I'm bored.'

______________________________

3 'I haven't got any money.'

______________________________

4 'I'm new at school and I don't know anyone.'

______________________________

## Comparisons

5 **Complete the sentences with the words in brackets and any other necessary words.**

1 The Oscars are ________________ (important) award ceremony in the film industry.
2 The host wasn't ________________ (funny) the guy who did it last year.
3 The ceremony was a lot ________________ (long).
4 The best actor's speech was ________________ (bad) I can remember.
5 However, I think the actors were dressed ________________ (beautiful) than usual.
6 Apparently one actress was wearing ________________ (expensive) dress in the world.

6 **Rewrite the sentences so that they mean the same thing.**

1 It's hotter today than it was yesterday.
Yesterday wasn't ________________
2 I've never seen a more boring film in my life.
That was ________________
3 She's the kindest person I know.
I don't know anyone as ________________
4 I used to remember things more easily when I was younger.
I don't ________________
5 Martin and Simon play tennis equally as well.
Simon plays tennis ________________
6 It's the most expensive car in the world.
There isn't a car as ________________

## SUMMING UP

7 W.03 **Put the dialogue in order. Listen and check.**

☐ **Brody** I'm going to. I've made an appointment.
☐ **Brody** I'm not sure. Every day I wake up more tired than the day before.
☐ **Brody** I know. I'm not sure I can wait that long.
1 **Brody** I've been feeling really sick recently.
☐ **Brody** The problem is the appointment's for next Thursday. They didn't have one any earlier.
☐ **Verity** Oh dear. What's wrong?
☐ **Verity** You'd better call them and tell them it's an emergency.
☐ **Verity** What! That's a week from now.
☐ **Verity** Sick and tired. You should see a doctor.
☐ **Verity** Well, hopefully, he'll be able to help you get better.

# D HELP!

## Reported speech

1 **Report the conversation.**

0 **Amy** I need help.
1 **Jen** What's the matter?
2 **Amy** I can't find my key.
3 **Jen** Check inside your pocket.
4 **Amy** I've already done that.
5 **Jen** Have you checked the door?
6 **Amy** Why do you want me to do that?
7 **Jen** That's where you always leave them.

0 Amy said that *she needed help.*
1 Jen asked Amy ________________
2 Amy said that ________________
3 Jen told Amy ________________
4 Amy said ________________
5 Jen asked Amy ________________
6 Amy asked Jen ________________
7 Jen said ________________

## Sequencing words

2 **Unscramble the sequencing words.**

1 rafte ________
2 hent ________
3 yanllif ________
4 ta rifts ________

3 **Complete the story with words from Exercise 2.**

1 ________ we thought we'd never get out. The door just wouldn't open.
2 ________ five minutes of kicking the door, we were exhausted.
3 ________ Dad found the key in his pocket.
4 ________ we got the door open.

## Asking for and offering help

4 **Complete the words.**

1 Have you got a f________ m________?
2 C________ I help you?
3 Can you l________ me a h________?
4 Could you h________ me with something?
5 Do you n________ any help?

**5 Put the dialogue in order.**

- [ ] **Mimi** I said that I was going to tidy it after I'd done my homework.
- [ ] **Mimi** What deal?
- [ ] **Mimi** Could you help me with my homework?
- [ ] **Mimi** That's the same deal we had before!
- [ ] **Mimi** But you said you'd help me.
- [1] **Mimi** Dad, have you got a few minutes?
- [ ] **Dad** Tidy your room and then I'll lend you a hand with your homework.
- [ ] **Dad** And you said you'd tidy your room – remember?
- [ ] **Dad** That depends. What do you want?
- [ ] **Dad** I'm sorry, but I'm a bit busy.
- [ ] **Dad** So, I'll make you a deal.

## IT vocabulary

**6 Match the parts of the sentences.**

1 Have you seen that Matt has posted [ ]
2 Before you start you have to key [ ]
3 I'm having a problem installing [ ]
4 Send me the photo – you can attach [ ]
5 I'm going to upload [ ]
6 I'm sorry – I deleted your [ ]
7 I'm not sure how to activate [ ]
8 It's taking ages to download [ ]

a all my holiday photos online.
b message. Can you send it again?
c flight mode on this tablet.
d this program. Can you help?
e this file. It's really big.
f another photo on the school website?
g it to an email.
h in your password.

## Passive tenses

**7 Rewrite the sentences in the passive.**

1 Five people have posted new messages on my website.
Five new messages ________________________
________________________________________

2 Someone uploaded the video onto YouTube.
The video ________________________
________________________________________

3 Someone had already keyed in my password.
My password ________________________
________________________________________

4 Two million people have downloaded this video.
This video ________________________
________________________________________

5 The teacher sent the email to all the students.
All the students ________________________
________________________________________

6 The program is attaching the file to the message.
The file ________________________
________________________________________

## SUMMING UP

**8 Complete the dialogue with words and phrases in the list.**

files | said I | buy | has accessed
said he | passwords | has been
delete | installed | is being | then

**Loris** My computer [1]________________ hacked.
**Anne** What do you mean, 'hacked'?
**Loris** Someone [2]________________ my computer from another computer.
**Anne** Really? How do you know?
**Loris** A program has been [3]________________ that has deleted loads of my [4]________________ .
**Anne** That's terrible.
**Loris** And all my [5]________________ have been stolen, too.
**Anne** So what are you going to do?
**Loris** My computer [6]________________ looked at by an expert at the moment. He [7]________________ could hopefully [8]________________ the program.
**Anne** And if he can't?
**Loris** He [9]________________'d have to buy a new computer.
**Anne** Well, if you do, remember to [10]________________ better anti-virus software.
**Loris** Yes, and [11]________________ create some new passwords!

# 1 BIG DECISIONS

Grammar rap!

## GRAMMAR

### Present tenses (review)

→ SB p.14

**1** ★☆☆ **For each sentence, choose the correct tense. Write PS (present simple), PC (present continuous), PPS (present perfect simple) or PPC (present perfect continuous).**

0 I <u>haven't decided</u> what I want to do yet. _PPS_
1 I always <u>do</u> my homework when I get home from school. ______
2 Liam <u>hasn't been doing</u> well at school for a few months. ______
3 My sister<u>'s always talking</u> on her phone. ______
4 They<u>'ve been thinking</u> about buying a new house for more than a year now. ______
5 Lewis <u>has forgotten</u> to do his homework again. ______
6 Stella <u>doesn't want</u> to go to university next year. ______
7 It's the last week of term, so we <u>aren't doing</u> very much at school. ______

**2** ★★☆ **Complete the sentences with the words in the list.**

've been writing | don't write | 've played | 's playing | hasn't been playing | plays | haven't written | 'm writing

1 No, he isn't busy. He ______________ a game on the computer.
2 I ______________ my party invitations. Who should I invite?
3 Most people ______________ letters any more, just emails.
4 I ______________ all morning. My hand's tired.
5 My cousin usually ______________ tennis twice a day. He loves it.
6 I ______________ to thank my aunt for my present yet. I must do it tonight.
7 We ______________ all of these games. Have you got any others?
8 Celia isn't very good at the piano. She ______________ for very long.

**3** ★★☆ **Circle the correct options.**

We [1]*do / 're doing* some really important exams at school over the next few weeks, so I [2]*spend / 'm spending* most of my free time studying for them at the moment. Normally, the two things I [3]*like / 'm liking* most in life are TV and computer games, but I [4]*don't watch / 'm not watching* any TV and I [5]*don't play / 'm not playing* computer games while I've got exams. I usually [6]*help / am helping* my dad in his shop at the weekends. He [7]*doesn't pay / isn't paying* me a lot, but I [8]*like / 'm liking* getting the money. I [9]*don't work / 'm not working* for a while, though. I [10]*need / 'm needing* the time for revision.

**4** ★★☆ **Complete the dialogues. Use the present perfect simple or continuous.**

1 **A** You look tired, Paula.
**B** I am. I ______________ very well lately. (not sleep)

2 **A** ______________ your homework? (finish)
**B** Nearly.

3 **A** Where's Eddie?
**B** I don't know. I ______________ him for a few hours. (not see)

4 **A** You're dirty. What ______________? (do)
**B** Helping Mum in the garden.

**5** ★★★ **Complete the dialogue with the verbs in brackets. Use the present simple, present continuous, present perfect simple or present perfect continuous.**

**Jules** [0] _Have_ you _seen_ (see) Elena recently? I [1]______________ (not see) her for weeks.
**Dylan** No, but she [2]______________ (text) me most days.
**Jules** So what [3]______________ (she/do) these days?
**Dylan** Well, she [4]______________ (train) really hard for the past month.
**Jules** Training? For what?
**Dylan** She [5]______________ (want) to be a professional footballer. Chelsea Football Club [6]______________ (invite) her to train with them. She starts with them on Monday.

## Future tenses (review)

→ SB p.15

**6** ★★☆ **Look at Greta's diary and write sentences about her plans for next week. Use the present continuous.**

| DIARY | | |
|---|---|---|
| **Monday** | **am:** | fly to Madrid |
| | **pm:** | have meeting with Pablo |
| **Tuesday** | **am:** | take train to Barcelona |
| | **pm:** | watch football match at Camp Nou stadium |
| **Wednesday** | **am:** | fly back to London |

0 On Monday morning, _she's flying to Madrid_ .
1 On Monday afternoon, ________________ .
2 On Tuesday morning, ________________ .
3 On Tuesday afternoon, ________________ .
4 On Wednesday morning, ________________ .

**7** ★★☆ **Complete the sentences. Use a verb from the list and the correct form of *going to*. Then match the sentences with the pictures.**

make | move | not ski
not visit | ~~see~~ | study

0 We _'re going to see_ a play tonight. I've got the tickets.
1 The car's broken down. We ________________ Grandma today.
2 I ________________ a curry tonight. I've just bought all the ingredients.
3 Fiona ________________ Maths at Bristol University in September.
4 Penny has hurt her leg. She ________________ today.
5 They're selling their house. They ________________ to London.

A 0

B

C

D

E

F

**8** ★★☆ **Read the sentences. Mark them P (prediction), I (intention), or A (arrangement).**

0 I've got a tennis lesson at ten o'clock. [A]
1 I phoned the dentist and made an appointment to see him this afternoon. [ ]
2 People living on the moon one day? Yes, definitely. [ ]
3 We've decided where to stay in London – the Ritz hotel. [ ]
4 I've decided what to do next year – travel around the world. [ ]
5 My mum, let me go to the party? No way! [ ]

**9** ★★★ **Rewrite the sentences in Exercise 8 using the correct future tense.**

0 _I'm playing tennis at ten o'clock._
1 ________________
2 ________________
3 ________________
4 ________________
5 ________________

**10** ★★★ **What do you think your life will be like when you are 30?**

1 (work as a)
________________
2 (have children)
________________
3 (live in a different country)
________________

## GET IT RIGHT!

### *will* vs. present continuous

**Learners often use *will* + infinitive where the present continuous is needed.**

✓ ***I'm seeing*** *the dentist because my tooth is hurting.*
✗ *I'll see the dentist because my tooth is hurting.*
✓ *I'm not sure we'll **get** it done in time.*
✗ *I'm not sure we're getting it done in time.*

**Complete the sentences with the correct form of a verb from the list.**

~~come~~ | go | have (x2) | not go | see | win

0 It's good that you _are coming_ to see me in Brazil!
1 We ____________ a party next weekend – do you want to come?
2 I think Real Madrid ____________ tonight.
3 My brother ____________ to university next week. He's packing at the moment.
4 I ____________ to Nina's party later because I have to study for tomorrow's exam.
5 We think you ____________ a great time on holiday.
6 Maybe I ____________ you there.

# VOCABULARY

## Making changes

SB p.14

**1 ★☆☆ Match the parts of the sentences.**

1 I've decided not to make ☐
2 Noemi's trying to give ☐
3 Jason's on a diet and doing ☐
4 I'm trying to get fitter, but I'm struggling ☐
5 We needed a new hobby, so we've taken ☐
6 You must take this chance ☐
7 It's good for kids to get into ☐
8 My dad needs to eat better, but he's never going to change ☐

a really well. He's lost 5 kg already.
b with getting myself to the gym every day.
c the habit of doing some exercise every day.
d his ways.
e up photography.
f up eating chocolate, but she's finding it really difficult.
g any New Year's resolutions this year.
h to study in Australia! It won't happen again!

**2 ★★★ Write down examples that are true for you.**

1 A resolution you'd like to make for next year:
____________________
2 Something you'd like to give up:
____________________
3 A school subject you do well in:
____________________
4 A school subject you struggle with:
____________________
5 A new hobby you'd like to take up:
____________________
6 A good habit you should get into:
____________________

## Life plans

SB p.17

**3 ★★☆ Read the definitions and complete the phrases.**

1 t________ t________ w________ : go out and see other countries
2 g________ p________ : be given a better job (usually in the same company)
3 l________ s________ : finish compulsory education
4 r________ : finish your professional life
5 g________ a d________ : graduate from university
6 s________ d________ : have a steady job, buy a house with a partner, etc.
7 s________ a f________ : have children
8 s________ a c________ : begin your professional life

**4 ★★☆ Complete the sentences with phrases from Exercise 3.**

1 My brother just loves being free. I can't see him ever wanting to ____________________ .
2 It isn't easy to ____________________ a new ____________________ when you're 50.
3 The government wants to raise the age that you can ____________________ to 18.
4 We certainly want to ____________________ one day. We'd like at least three children.
5 Katy wants to take a few years off work and ____________________ . She'd love to spend some time in Asia.
6 These days, many people can't afford to ____________________ before they're 70.
7 George ____________________ from university, but he's never really used it in his professional life.
8 If you work hard, you might ____________________ to junior manager next year.

## WordWise: Phrases with *up*

SB p.17

**5 ★★☆ Put the sentences in the correct order.**

☐ **Lisa** Hi, Andy. What are you <u>up to</u>?
☐ **Lisa** So, what's the problem?
☐ **Lisa** Is the game <u>almost up</u>?
☐ **Lisa** But you love video games. So, <u>what's up</u>?
☐ **Andy** I'm playing a new video game with my dad – unfortunately.
☐ **Andy** No, but it isn't <u>up to me</u>. Dad wants to finish it all.
☐ **Andy** Well, he isn't very good, so he can't pass the difficult levels – he just isn't <u>up to it</u>.
☐ **Andy** We've been playing for hours and I want to go out.

**6 ★★☆ Match the <u>underlined</u> phrases in Exercise 5 with their meanings.**

1 doing ________________
2 capable of ________________
3 nearly finished ________________
4 what's the matter ________________
5 my decision/choice ________________

**PRONUNCIATION**
Linking words with *up* Go to page 118.

# REFERENCE

## MAKING CHANGES

change your ways
do well
get into the habit (of doing something)
give (something) up
make a resolution
struggle with (something)
take (something) up
take a/the chance (to do something)

## LIFE PLANS

| | |
|---|---|
| get a degree | start a career |
| get promoted | start a family |
| leave school | settle down |
| retire | travel the world |

## PHRASES WITH *UP*

**up to (an hour, etc.)**
*It can take **up to** 8 weeks to get a new passport.*

**be up to something**
*What **are** you and your friends **up to** on Saturday?*

**What's up?**
***What's up**, Simon? Are you OK?*

**(time) is up**
*Stop! The time's **up**. Stop writing and give me your test papers.*

**be up to somebody**
*If you don't enjoy your job, it's **up to you** to find a new one.*

**be up to something**
*I'd like to invite Lucy onto the project, but I'm not sure she's **up to it**.*

# VOCABULARY *EXTRA*

**1 Match the phrases (1–6) with the definitions (a–f).**

1 get rid of
2 jump into
3 let something go
4 make a decision
5 put an end to
6 take charge of

a decide
b move suddenly and quickly
c make something finish
d throw away
e take control
f stop holding something

**2 Complete the sentences with the correct verb.**

1 It isn't easy to ______________________ a decision about your future career.
2 Little Maisie ______________________ go of the balloon and it flew up into the sky.
3 When the teacher arrived, he ______________________ an end to the game.
4 It was late, so we ______________________ into the car and drove off.
5 Sally's decided to ______________________ rid of her old clothes.
6 George ______________________ charge of organising the trip.

**3 Answer the questions so that they are true for you.**

1 How do you get rid of your old clothes and toys?
______________________________________________

2 What sort of decisions are the most difficult for you to make?
______________________________________________

3 If we want to make the world a better place, what things must we put an end to?
______________________________________________

# SMART GOALS

It's that time of the year again that we all look forward to so much. Exams! I'm joking, of course! Well, this year I'm not afraid because I'm going to change my ways: I'm going to use SMART goals to make sure I do well. I read an article about SMART goals. They're what all successful people in life use, apparently.

So what are SMART goals exactly and how are they going to change my life (hopefully)?

Well SMART goals are Specific, Measurable, Attainable, Relevant and Timely. See how they get their names? No? Look at the first letter of each of the words. That's what you call an acronym.

**SPECIFIC** – because they are detailed. It isn't good enough to simply say, 'I'm going to revise for my exams.' That plan's too general. A specific goal is something like: 'I'm going to spend at least 20 hours revising for each subject and make a timetable to show exactly how I'm going to do this.' That is a 'Specific' goal.

**MEASURABLE** – because you should be able to measure your goals and ask yourself questions like: 'How much have I done?'; 'How much have I still got to do?'; 'How much time do I still need?'; 'Is this nightmare ever going to end?' Well, maybe the last one isn't such a great example, but you get the idea!

**ATTAINABLE** – because your goal should be something that you can actually do. If your goal is, for example, to raise £1 million for charity, write a novel, climb Mount Everest and revise for your exams, then you might want to ask yourself if you really can do all this. Maybe you should get rid of one or two of them.

**RELEVANT** – because all your plans should help you work towards your final goal. So, for example, a plan to help your mum and dad with all the cooking, washing-up and helping out with housework might make you the most popular child in your house, but it isn't really going to help you with the revision, is it?

**TIMELY** – Your goal must have a time frame. In other words, it must have a start and a finish. There isn't much point if you're planning to finish revising a couple of weeks after your exams are over. That really doesn't make much sense.

Likewise, you need to think about when would be a good time to start. And, as they say, there's no time like the present, so I guess it might be a good idea to stop writing about SMART goals and start getting into the habit of using them!

## READING

1 **Read the blog. How do SMART goals get their name?**

______________________________________________

2 **Read the blog again. Mark the sentences T (true) or F (false). Then correct the false sentences.**

1 The writer enjoys doing exams. ☐
2 SMART is an example of an acronym. ☐
3 SMART goals encourage people to do more than they can. ☐
4 You don't need to think about when to start your SMART goals. ☐

3 **Read the goal. Then follow the instructions.**

'My goal this year is to be healthier.'

1 Make this goal more specific.
2 Write down what you can measure about this goal.
3 Write an example of an attainable plan and an unattainable plan for it.
4 Write an example of a relevant and an irrelevant plan for it.
5 Make a time frame for the plan.

4 CRITICAL THINKING **For each adjective in the acronym SMART, the writer gives an example of how a goal is not SMART and how a goal is SMART. Read the blog again and complete the table.**

| Goals | Not SMART | SMART |
|---|---|---|
| 1 Specific | | |
| 2 Measurable | | |
| 3 Attainable | | |
| 4 Relevant | | |
| 5 Timely | | |

5 **Think of a goal you have and write a short paragraph about it. Is it a SMART goal?**

# DEVELOPING *Writing*

## An email about a problem

**1** INPUT **Read the email and answer the questions.**

Who is …

1 Connor? ____________

2 Damon? ____________

3 Josh? ____________

**2** ANALYSE **Read the email again and answer the questions.**

1 What specific problems does Josh have with Connor?

____________

____________

2 Underline the expressions that show you he isn't happy with these things.

____________

____________

3 What plans has he made to resolve the situation?

____________

____________

**3** **Circle the language which introduces each of Connor's plans.**

**4** **Match the content (A–D) with the paragraphs (1–4).**

A Josh describes the problem. ☐

B He says what he'll do if his plan isn't successful. ☐

C He explains his plan. ☐

D He says why he hasn't written recently. ☐

Josh
joshyB@thinkemail.com

Hi Damon,

1 Sorry for not writing back sooner, but I've been pretty busy with school and basketball. Next week, we're in the championship final – very exciting! Here's a photo of us at basketball training last week.

2 I've been having a few problems at school recently with a new kid called Connor. The teacher asked me to look out for him and I was happy to do that. The problem is that he's now decided I'm his best friend. He's always sending me messages and wanting to hang out with me. He's nice enough, but I'm getting a bit tired of him following me everywhere. He also gets really jealous of my friends and says some really mean things about them. That really annoys me.

3 I know it isn't easy changing school and getting to know new people, so I'm going to help him – and I hope it'll help me, too! Next week, I'm having a welcome party for him so that he can meet some other people and make friends. I've also told him about the youth club and I think he's going to join it. The best thing is that I can't go to youth club for the next few weeks because of basketball training, so he'll have to get to know some other people.

4 That's my plan and if it doesn't work, I'll find him some friends myself! I'll write and let you know how it goes.

See you,

Josh

**5** PLAN **Think of a person, real or imaginary. Write down three complaints about him / her and think of two ways to resolve the problem.**

| The problem | The solution |
| --- | --- |
| 1 He's / She's always … | |
| 2 The problem is … | |
| 3 I'm not happy with … | |

**6** PRODUCE **Write an email to a friend explaining your problems and what you're going to do about them (250 words). Use your plan from Exercise 5. Make sure you include all the points in the checklist.**

### CHECKLIST

- ☐ Introduction
- ☐ Describe the problem(s)
- ☐ Explain your ideas for solutions
- ☐ Say goodbye
- ☐ Use informal language

## LISTENING

**1** 1.03 **Listen to three dialogues and complete the sentences.**

1 Laura and Jodie are doing ________________ .
2 Jodie can't help with it because ________________ .
3 Laura's never ________________ again.
4 Maddie asks Shaun about ________________ .
5 Shaun feels ________________ .
6 Lily wants to speak to her dad about ________________ .
7 The new teacher always ________________ .
8 Lily's going to join ________________ .

**2** 1.03 **Listen again and complete the dialogues.**

1 **Laura** She's [1]__________ things like this.
**Charlie** She needs to [2]__________ . Next time why don't you …?

2 **Maddie** Where have you [3]__________ ?
**Shaun** Er, nowhere. Well, er, you know how it is. I [4]__________ really hard at school.
**Maddie** [5]__________ ! You've got to relax sometimes.
**Shaun** Well, [6]__________ Maddie, I do.

3 **Dad** Now [7]__________ it, I haven't heard you playing much recently.
**Lily** The [8]__________ , I'm not happy with the new teacher.

## DIALOGUE

**3 Put the lines in order to make three short dialogues. Write them in the correct spaces.**

1 Making arrangements
A *Are you doing anything after school, Tina?*
B ________________
A ________________
B ________________

2 Talking about future intentions
C *When do you leave school, Wang?*
D ________________
C ________________
D ________________

3 Making personal predictions
E *Do you think you'll have children one day?*
F ________________
E ________________
F ________________

1 I'm going to study medicine at Cambridge University.
2 One or two.
3 Probably. I hope so.
4 I'd love to, thanks.
5 Toby and I are going swimming. Do you want to come?
6 Next year in July.
7 How many do you think you'll have?
8 And what are you going to do next?
9 No, I've got nothing planned.

## PHRASES FOR FLUENCY

SB p.18

**4 Put the words in order to make phrases.**

0 silly / be / don't *Don't be silly* .
1 go / we / here __________ .
2 you're / star / a __________ .
3 hiding / have / been / where / you __________ ?
4 start / where / I / shall __________ ?
5 mention / you / now / it … __________ ,

**5 Complete the dialogues with phrases in Exercise 4.**

0 A Shall we invite Nathan to the game with us?
B *Don't be silly* . He doesn't like football.

1 A You look busy. Have you got a lot to do?
B Busy? ________________ I've got exams all week, I've got to organise Susanna's birthday, buy her a present …

2 A Can I make you something to eat?
B Thanks. I'm starving. ________________ , Julio.

3 A I haven't seen you for weeks, Philip. ________________
B Nowhere. I've just been really busy.

4 A I know you've got to study for your exams, but would you like to come for a quick bike ride?
B Well, I am busy but ________________ , it might be a good idea to get out for a while.

5 A Boys, get in here, you're 10 minutes late!
B ________________ . We're in trouble now.

# TOWARDS B2 First for Schools

## READING AND USE OF ENGLISH

### Multiple-choice cloze

### EXAM GUIDE

**You will read a short text with eight gaps in it. For each gap, you have to choose one of four options. This part tests your knowledge of vocabulary, including phrasal verbs, collocations and the difference between words with similar meanings.**

- Read through the text quickly to get a general understanding.
- Look at the instructions and the example to make sure you understand exactly what you have to do.
- Start with gap 1. Re-read the whole sentence and pay particular attention to the words that come just *before* and *after* the gap, because they can help you choose the correct word.
- Look carefully at options A, B, C and D. Eliminate any that you are sure are wrong and focus on the others.
- For words with similar meanings, it may help to think about the context of the text to choose the right one.

For phrasal verbs, you will have one of the words and will have to choose the other.

For collocations and idioms, you may have to think about the word that sounds best.

For some gaps, you have to use your knowledge of grammar to make the right choice.

**1 For questions 1–2, read the text below and decide which answer (A, B, C or D) best fits each gap. There is an example at the beginning (0).**

TEENAGE RESOLUTIONS

According to a recent survey, more than 75% of 16-year-olds [0] __A__ at least one resolution at the beginning of each New Year. The most popular ones are [1] ______ better at school and being nicer to family members. Other common resolutions include spending less time watching TV and giving [2] ______ playing computer games altogether.

| | A | B | C | D |
|---|---|---|---|---|
| 0 | (A) make | do | form | find |
| 1 | studying | making | revising | doing |
| 2 | in | over | out | up |

**2 For questions 1–8, read the text below and decide which answer (A, B, C or D) best fits each gap. There is an example at the beginning (0).**

DECISIONS

Although I'm in my final year at school, I still haven't [0] __A__ what to do next. Everyone else in my family has gone to university, so I think my parents [1] ______ me to go, too. Of course, it's up to me to decide, but the [2] ______ is, I'm not sure what to study.

What's more, when my parents were young, they didn't have to pay anything to get a [3] ______ . Whereas university is going to [4] ______ me up to £40,000 for the course and living away from home for three years. This means I need to be absolutely certain about the course before I start. Starting a course and then [5] ______ it up would be a waste of time and money.

If I'm [6] ______ , I'd like to take a few years out to do some work and maybe [7] ______ the world. Perhaps with a little more life experience, I'll be able to make a better decision before I have to start my [8] ______ .

| | A | B | C | D |
|---|---|---|---|---|
| 0 | (A) decided | thought | settled | fixed |
| 1 | expect | hope | accept | wait |
| 2 | matter | question | problem | decision |
| 3 | examination | degree | grade | career |
| 4 | spend | pay | cost | save |
| 5 | making | being | doing | giving |
| 6 | reliable | certain | true | honest |
| 7 | travel | tour | move | discover |
| 8 | work | career | progress | activity |

# 2 A HARD LIFE

Grammar rap! ▶05

## GRAMMAR

### Narrative tenses (review)

→ SB p.22

1 ★☆☆ Circle the correct options.

1 Joey *was* / *had been* tired because he *had run* / *had been running*.
2 My mum *was* / *was being* angry because I *was watching* / *had been watching* TV all afternoon.
3 My friends *played* / *had been playing* football for hours when I *arrived* / *was arriving*.
4 We *had been waiting* / *were waiting* for the concert to start for half an hour, when they *made* / *were making* the announcement.
5 My sister *was learning* / *had been learning* French for six years before she *went* / *was going* to France.
6 They *swam* / *had been swimming* for about an hour when it *started* / *had started* to rain.

2 ★★☆ Complete the sentences. Use the past simple and the past continuous once in each sentence.

0 While Amelia Earhart *was working* (work) one day, Captain Railey *asked* (ask) her to fly to the UK from the US.
1 It ______ (sail) across the Atlantic Ocean when it ______ (hit) an iceberg.
2 People ______ (dance) in the streets after they ______ (hear) he was finally free.
3 The world ______ (watch) on TV when Neil Armstrong ______ (step) onto the moon.
4 A science student ______ (make) a medicine when he ______ (see) a new colour.
5 A plane ______ (crash) while it ______ (take off) from LaGuardia airport in New York. All the passengers survived thanks to the pilot's skill.
6 A group of young boys ______ (become) trapped while they ______ (explore) a cave. They were all rescued.

3 ★★☆ Match the sentences in Exercise 2 with the events in world history (A–G).

☐ A the Hudson River air accident (2009)
☐ B first person on the moon (1969)
☐ C freedom for Nelson Mandela (1990)
☐ D Thai cave rescue (2018)
☐ E sinking of the *Titanic* (1912)
0 F the first woman to fly across the Atlantic (1928)
☐ G the discovery of purple (1856)

4 ★★☆ Complete the sentences. Use the past perfect and the past simple once in each sentence.

Yesterday afternoon I had a guitar lesson.

0 When I *had finished* (finish) my guitar lesson, I *walked* (walk) home.
1 We ______ (have) dinner after I ______ (arrive) home.
2 I ______ (do) the washing-up after we ______ (eat) dinner.
3 When I ______ (finish) the washing-up, I ______ (call) my friend Tina.
4 I ______ (do) my homework after I ______ (speak) to Tina.
5 When I ______ (finish) my homework, I ______ (watch) a film.

5 ★★★ What did you do yesterday? Write similar sentences to the ones in Exercise 4 using the past perfect and the past simple.

1 Yesterday afternoon I ______
2 When ______
3 ______
4 ______
5 ______

## *would* and *used to*

SB p.25

**6 ★☆☆ Complete the sentences with the verbs in the list.**

be (x2) | have | have to | make | play | take

Life in the 1960s was very different from now …

1 There used to ___________ public telephones in the streets.
2 Children used to ___________ outside in the streets with their friends.
3 Cars didn't use to ___________ seat belts.
4 TV didn't use to ___________ in colour, only in black and white.
5 People didn't use to ___________ many photos, just on special occasions.
6 Parents used to ___________ a lot of their children's clothes.
7 You used to ___________ go to a cinema to see a film.

**7 ★★☆ Complete the sentences about yourself with *used to* or *didn't use to*.**

When I was five, …

1 I ________________ go to a different school.
2 my mum ________________ wake me up at 7 am.
3 I ________________ eat cereal for breakfast.
4 I ________________ walk to school.
5 I ________________ have a lot of homework.
6 my dad ________________ read me a bedtime story every night.

**8 ★★★ Antonio is asking Elsa about her primary school. Write the questions. Then match them with the answers.**

0 Which / school / go / to
*Which school did you use to go to?* [d]
1 wear / school uniform
________________________________ [ ]
2 have / a lot of homework
________________________________ [ ]
3 learn / English
________________________________ [ ]
4 learn / any other languages
________________________________ [ ]
5 What / favourite / subject
________________________________ [ ]

a It used to be Maths.
b Yes, I used to learn French.
c Yes, I used to be really good at it.
d I used to go to Middleham Primary School.
e No, I used to wear my ordinary clothes.
f No. Our teacher didn't use to give us much.

**9 ★★☆ In three of the sentences, you can use *would* or *wouldn't*. Tick them and rewrite them using *would*.**

1 I used to have curly hair. [ ]
________________________________
________________________________
2 I used to play in the park every day after school. [ ]
________________________________
________________________________
3 I didn't use to like cheese but now I do. [ ]
________________________________
________________________________
4 I used to eat vegetables with each meal. [ ]
________________________________
________________________________
5 I used to be very good at English. [ ]
________________________________
________________________________
6 I used to go for a long bike ride every weekend. [ ]
________________________________
________________________________

### GET IT RIGHT!

#### *used to* and *usually*

**Learners sometimes confuse *used to* and *usually*. We use *used to* to refer to events which happened regularly in the past.**

✓ *When I was at college, I **used to** work in a clothes shop.*

**We use *usually* to refer to events which happen regularly in the present. We do not use *used to* for this.**

✓ *I **usually** go to the cinema on Wednesdays because it's cheaper.*

✗ *I ~~used to~~ go to the cinema on Wednesdays because it's cheaper.*

**Complete the sentences with *used to* or *usually* and the correct form of the verb in brackets.**

0 I *used to live* (live) in a really small village and I really liked it.
1 We ________________ (sing) in shows together when we were younger.
2 These days I ________________ (go) to bed early.
3 They ________________ (watch) TV on Wednesday evenings because that's when their favourite programme is on.
4 Could you give us the 10% discount that we ________________ (get) in the past?
5 Rex is more attractive than he ________________ (be).
6 Do you ________________ (wear) that funny hat?

# VOCABULARY
## Descriptive verbs

→ SB p.22

**1 ★☆☆ Unscramble the words to make descriptive verbs.**

1 cefro ______
2 ssmha ______
3 ketris ______
4 gnreea ______
5 okhsc ______
6 ebg ______
7 osdliemh ______

**2 ★★☆ Complete the sentences with the correct form of verbs from Exercise 1.**

0 Passengers were *enraged* by the 90-minute delay to their flight.
1 The man ______ the window to rescue the boy from the fire.
2 The building was unsafe after the fire, so the council ______ it.
3 The young man ______ the woman not to leave him.
4 Our neighbours were ______ to find a burglar in their flat.
5 The police ______ the door open to enter the house.
6 Some cars were ______ by the falling tree.

**3 ★★☆ Complete the crossword with synonyms of the underlined words.**

ACROSS
1 Don't push the window so hard. You'll break it!
7 They knocked down the old cinema and built a car park.

DOWN
2 The football fans were really angry when their team lost.
3 We asked him again and again to tell us the secret, but he refused.
4 No! We've broken the window!
5 It was lucky the ball didn't hit you on the head!
6 This news is going to be a bad surprise for everyone.

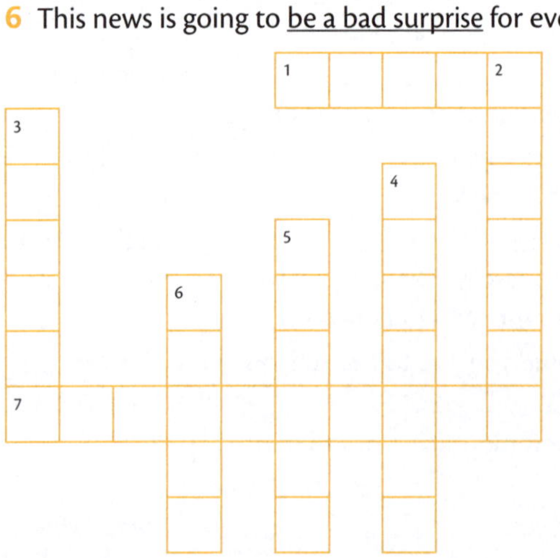

**4 ★★★ Complete the information about a robbery with the correct form of the verbs from Exercise 1. Then number the events in the order they happened.**

☐ A The two men tried to [1]______ the horse into the van. They pushed and pulled but it refused to go in.
☐ B First, Fred went to get the horse. He was [2]______ when he saw it because it was much bigger than he had thought. But he got on it and rode nervously out of the field.
☐ C Just then, a car appeared. A woman got out and [3]______ the men to stop. The horse recognised its owner immediately and waited quietly while she phoned the police.
☐ *1* D It was a champion racehorse. Charlie and Fred had a brilliant plan: steal it and ask a million pounds for its return!
☐ E The horse was walking slowly down the road, but when it saw Charlie and the van, it started to run very fast. Fred [4]______ his head on a tree and nearly fell off.
☐ F The horse became so [5]______ that it [6]______ a window and nearly [7]______ the van!

**PRONUNCIATION**
Initial consonant clusters with /s/
Go to page 118.

## Time periods

→ SB p.25

**5 ★★☆ Match the parts of the sentences.**

1 In this day and age, ☐
2 A decade ago, ☐
3 In the last century, ☐
4 In medieval times, ☐
5 From 1837 until 1901, ☐

a not many people had electric cars.
b there were two world wars.
c there was no electricity.
d most people have a smartphone.
e Queen Victoria was on the throne.

**6 ★★★ Write your own sentences using the time phrases.**

1 In this day and age, ______
2 A decade ago, ______
3 In the last century, ______
4 Nowadays, ______
5 Not so long ago, ______
6 In medieval times, ______

## REFERENCE

**Time periods**

- a long, long time ago in history
  - in the last century
  - in the olden days
  - in medieval times
- the recent past
  - not so long ago
  - a decade ago
  - from 2000 until 2020
- the present
  - these days
  - in this day and age
  - nowadays

### DESCRIPTIVE VERBS

beg

demolish

enrage

force

shock

smash

strike

## VOCABULARY *EXTRA*

**1 Match the parts of the sentences.**

1 A strong hurricane **destroyed**
2 Iona **endured** weeks
3 Two prisoners **escaped**
4 Firefighters **fought**
5 Oscar **screamed**
6 Everyone in the town **suffered**

a 'Help!'
b to save the old building.
c of pain after her accident.
d after the earthquake.
e the town.
f during the night.

**2 Complete the table with the verbs in bold in Exercise 1.**

| Verbs to describe ... |
|---|
| people's feelings |
| |
| |
| |
| actions |
| |
| |
| |

**3 Complete the sentences. Choose the correct pairs of verbs in the list and write them in the correct form.**

destroy / suffer | endure / fight | escape / scream

1 The boys ______ for help while they ______ from the fire.
2 While the doctors ______ to save the boy's life, he ______ a lot of pain.
3 Many people ______ after their homes were ______ in the storm.

**4 Complete the sentences with your own ideas.**

1 I screamed when ______ .
2 I endured terrible pain when ______ .
3 In history, people suffered hardship when ______ .

# BAD TIMES, GOOD TIMES

My name is Henry Ackroyd. I was born in 1845 in Bradford, a town in the north of England. Bradford was well known for its wool cloth. Business was good, but industry polluted the town with smoke and industrial waste. Thick black smoke would pour out of hundreds of tall chimneys day and night, seven days a week. The town's drinking water came from a river full of industrial waste. Unsurprisingly, the people of the town suffered from bad health. Thousands of people used to die every year from diseases such as typhoid and cholera.

Like most other people, my parents moved to Bradford from the countryside to find work. These workers needed somewhere to live, so houses were built very quickly. They were close together with few windows and no heating. Families like mine would live in one small room with just one water tap at the end of the street. I remember the streets were full of rubbish and there were pigs and rats eating it. My parents endured long working hours in the factory – 12–15 hours a day – for very low pay.

Life was extremely hard until the day my father changed his job. He went to work in a factory that was owned by Mr Titus Salt. Soon after, Mr Salt, who owned four more factories, moved his business out of Bradford and built one enormous, modern factory on the River Aire. Nearby, he built 824 houses for his workers and their families. We were lucky enough to move to Saltaire! Can you see where the name came from?

Mr Salt was one of the few factory owners who understood that happy, healthy workers were good for business: they worked harder and produced more.

Life suddenly got better! My father, like all Mr Salt's workers, only used to work ten hours a day. We lived in a new house with bedrooms, a kitchen, a living room, a bathroom and a vegetable garden. Workers used to pay a rent of 12 percent of their weekly pay. The village also had shops, a wash-house, a library, clubs, a small hospital and an evening school for adults. Mr Salt believed in education and encouraged his workers to study and improve themselves. My sisters and I went to the village school – all the children had to go to school until they were 12. That was one of Saltaire's rules. Another one was that if workers lost their job, they lost their house, too. My parents were always telling us how lucky we were to live in Saltaire. Mr Salt wasn't the only factory owner with new ideas, but he certainly changed the lives of people like me and my family for the better. We were very fortunate!

## BRADFORD
### AND THE INDUSTRIAL REVOLUTION

**POPULATION**
**1801:** 13,000 **1851:** 104,000

**INDUSTRY:** WOOL FACTORIES
**1851:** 200 factories

**FAMOUS FOR:** wool cloth and pollution
Bradford was the most polluted town in England.

## READING

**1 Read the article quickly. Why were Henry Ackroyd and his family fortunate?**

**2 Read the article again and answer the questions.**

1 Why was Bradford so polluted?

______________________

2 What were the living conditions of most workers like?

______________________

3 How did Henry Ackroyd's life change?

______________________

4 In what ways was Titus Salt different from other factory owners at the time?

______________________

**3** CRITICAL THINKING **Put the sentences in order according to the text.**

- [ ] **A** Mr Salt built one large factory in the countryside near the town.
- [ ] **B** Living and working conditions for Mr Salt's workers improved.
- [ ] **C** Bradford grew into a big industrial town with many problems.
- [ ] **D** Mr Salt's workers lived in a village near the factory.
- [ ] **E** Bradford was an ordinary small town.
- [ ] **F** Mr Salt had a number of cloth factories in Bradford.

**4 What do you think life was like for teenagers in these places? Choose either Bradford or Saltaire, and imagine you were living there in the 19th century. Write a paragraph describing your life.**

# DEVELOPING Writing

## A newspaper article

1 INPUT Read the article and complete the fact file.

**FACT FILE**

**THE ISLE OF LEWIS CHESSMEN**

**Found:** (place) [1] ______________
**Found:** (date) [2] ______________
**Material:** [3] ______________
**Made:** (date) [4] ______________
**Made:** (place) [5] ______________

1 *Lost for* **200 YEARS**

2 **Imagine discovering that an old object in your house is in fact a valuable treasure! That is exactly what happened recently to a family in Edinburgh.**

3 A small statue of a man that the family had had for years was, in fact, one of the Isle of Lewis chessmen. Ninety-three chessmen had been found, buried on a beach on the Isle of Lewis, Scotland, in 1831. Five of the chessmen had been lost and this funny little statue was one of them! The chess set was probably made in the 12th century in Norway from the teeth of whales and walruses. It is now one of the most popular displays at the British Museum, London.

4 The chessman had belonged to the family since their grandfather gave it to them. His daughter loved the statue and she used to keep it in a special bag. From time to time, she would take it out and look at it because she liked the funny little man.

5 The family realised that the statue was very old and had often wondered what it was and where it had come from. Not long ago, they showed it to an antiques expert. As they were unwrapping it, the expert immediately recognised it as one of the missing chessmen from the Isle of Lewis in Scotland. But that wasn't the only shock. The expert told them the statue that their grandfather had bought for £5 in 1964 is now worth about a million pounds!

2 ANALYSE **Match the parts of the article (1–5) with the descriptions (A–E).**

A The lead sentence – a short introduction ☐
B The discovery – what's happening to the chessmen now ☐
C The headline ☐
D The story of how the family got the chessman ☐
E Background information about the chessmen ☐

3 PLAN **Think about an interesting discovery in your town or country. It can be real or imaginary. Make a plan using these questions.**

- What was discovered? ______________
- Where was it discovered? ______________
- Why is it important? ______________
- How was it discovered? ______________
- What's happening to the object now? ______________

4 PRODUCE **Write an article for your school newspaper about an interesting discovery in your town (200–250 words). Use your plan from Exercise 3. Make sure you include all the points in the checklist.**

**CHECKLIST**

- Think of an eye-catching headline.
- Use past tenses appropriately.
- Check spelling and punctuation.

## LISTENING

**1** 🔊 2.02 **Listen to a conversation about schools in the 19th century. Which subjects did children use to have to study?**

A Maths, Reading and Writing
B Maths, Chemistry and Physics
C Reading, Writing and Geography

**2** 🔊 2.02 **Listen again and match the parts of the sentences.**

1 Before 1870, only boys [ ]
2 After 1870, all children [ ]
3 They used to have separate [ ]
4 They didn't use to have any [ ]
5 In the olden days, not many men [ ]
6 They didn't use to have Geography [ ]
7 They used to finish school [ ]
8 They used to have a two-hour lunch break [ ]

a playgrounds for boys and girls.
b at 5 pm.
c posters on the walls.
d used to go to school.
e so they could walk home for lunch.
f used to become teachers.
g aged 5–13 used to go to school.
h lessons at school.

## DIALOGUE

**3** **Put the sentences in order to make a conversation between a mother and her son.**

[ ] **Mum** No, the Millennium Bridge didn't use to be here either.
[ ] **Mum** Yes, it did. It used to be an old power station.
[1] **Mum** I used to walk along here every afternoon after school.
[ ] **Mum** It's completely changed. The Globe Theatre didn't use to be here.
[ ] **Mum** That's the Tate Modern. It's a big modern art gallery.
[ ] **Son** And what's that huge building over there?
[ ] **Son** Did it always use to look like that?
[ ] **Son** Didn't it? What about this bridge?
[ ] **Son** Lucky you, Mum! Has much changed?

**4** **Complete the dialogues with the phrases in the list.**

in those days | school dinners
the other children | use to watch
would play football | your favourite meal

**1**

**Tanya** What did you use to do after school?
**Dad** I would meet up with ______________ in the neighbourhood. If it was raining, we would play board games indoors. When the weather was nice, we ______________ in the park.

**2**

**Ricky** What kind of programmes did you ______________, Grandma?
**Grandma** I liked programmes about pop music. ______________, there used to be a show every Saturday with the new songs of the week. They'd often have the band in the studio playing their song. That was my favourite!

**3**

**Tim** Did you use to take a packed lunch to school, Mum?
**Mum** No, I didn't. We used to get ______________. The menu was the same every week or every two weeks. I can still remember every single meal.

**4**

**Carlos** What was ______________?
**Mum** Well, I can tell you my least favourite meal – a slice of beef, cabbage and mashed potato.

# TOWARDS B2 First for Schools

## SPEAKING
### Interview

### EXAM GUIDE

**For this part of the test, there will be two examiners and two candidates in the room. You will talk to one of the examiners (the interlocutor). The other examiner (the assessor) will just listen. The examiner will ask you short questions about your everyday life and personal experiences. Candidates interact individually with the examiner. The examiner speaks to the candidates alternately.**

- Give a short but complete answer to each question.
- If you don't hear or don't understand the question, ask the examiner to repeat it.

First, the examiner will say:

*Good morning / afternoon / evening.*

*My name is ... and this is my colleague ... .*

*And your names are?*

*Where are you from?*

*First, we'd like to know something about you.*

Then the examiner will ask you two or three questions on topics such as:

- family
- holidays
- future plans.

**1 Match the questions with the topics above.**

1 Are you going to do anything exciting soon? ___________
2 Who are you most like in your family? Tell me about him / her. ___________
3 What's the best holiday you've ever been on? ___________
4 Tell us about a person in your family that you enjoy spending time with. ___________
5 What do you think you will be doing in 10 years' time? ___________
6 How do you like to spend time with your family? ___________
7 Do you think English will be useful in your future work? ___________
8 Tell us about a holiday you've really enjoyed. ___________
9 Where would you like to go for your next holiday? Why? ___________

**2** 2.03 **Listen to an interview with two candidates and write the question numbers.**

1 Katya answered questions ______ and ______ .
2 Alexei answered questions ______ and ______ .

**3** 2.03 **How well did they do? Listen again and grade the candidates' performance.**

* = quite good ** = good *** = very good

| | Katya | Alexei |
|---|---|---|
| 1 easy to understand | | |
| 2 answered the questions | | |
| 3 good vocabulary | | |

**4 Imagine you are an exam candidate. Answer the questions in Exercise 1.**

# CONSOLIDATION

## LISTENING

1 2.04 **Listen and circle the correct option: A, B or C.**

1 How does Isabel feel about her future?
 A frightened
 B confident
 C optimistic

2 What do Jack and Isabel agree about?
 A They're looking forward to university.
 B It's easy to start a career nowadays.
 C There's a wide range of university courses.

3 Jack and Isabel think their parents had
 A very little careers advice at their schools.
 B a lot of help preparing for their future careers.
 C the opportunity to study interesting subjects.

2 2.04 **Listen again and answer the questions.**

1 What is Jack looking forward to?

______________________________

2 What's Isabel's main problem?

______________________________

3 Why does Jack think life was easier for their parents?

______________________________

4 What is a careers advisor?

______________________________

5 What advice does Jack give Isabel?

______________________________

## GRAMMAR

3 **Circle the correct options.**

1 I *go* / *'m going* for a walk in the park every weekend.
2 Max and I *go* / *are going* for a walk tomorrow morning.
3 When I arrived, the place was empty – everyone *went* / *had gone* home.
4 I used to *going* / *go* and play by the river every day.
5 In the future, life *is being* / *will be* very different from today.
6 The film finished, so then I *had gone* / *went* to bed.
7 Tomorrow I*'m meeting* / *meet* my friends in town.
8 Many years ago, my family *would* / *used to* live in a very small flat.

## VOCABULARY

4 **Complete each sentence with one word.**

1 In this ____________ and age, almost everyone knows how to use a computer.
2 I've ____________ a resolution to never eat chocolate again.
3 She only started work here last month, but she's already got ____________ .
4 I want to travel – I don't want to get married and settle ____________ .
5 Is this film from 2014 or 2015? Well, it's from about a ____________ ago, anyway.
6 He went to university and got a ____________ in Mathematics.
7 Look! There's a broken window. Who ____________ the glass?
8 As you get older, it becomes harder to ____________ your ways.
9 The house was old and dangerous, so the city council ____________ it.
10 The post office said it could take ____________ to two weeks to deliver the package.

5 **Match the parts of the sentences.**

1 When he reached the age of 63, ☐
2 We'd forgotten our keys, ☐
3 They were shocked ☐
4 When she stopped working, ☐
5 They're only 20 but they've decided ☐
6 She decided to start a career ☐
7 It isn't a good idea to get into ☐
8 My friend didn't do very ☐
9 It's up to you – ☐
10 People don't write many letters ☐

a by the monsters in the horror film.
b well in the exam, unfortunately.
c in banking.
d nowadays.
e he decided to retire from his job.
f she took up photography.
g you decide.
h the habit of eating a lot of fast food.
i so we smashed the window and climbed in.
j to settle down and start a family.

## DIALOGUE

**6** 2.05 **Complete the dialogue with the phrases in the list.**

don't be silly | where shall I start
now you mention it | you're a star
stuff like that | here we go
where have you been hiding | what's up

**Johnny** Hi, Sofia! I haven't seen you for ages. [1]________________ ?

**Sofia** Hi, Johnny. Yes, I'm sorry. I've just had so much to do lately.

**Johnny** Oh, [2]________________ with the excuses. Like what?

**Sofia** Oh, well, [3]________________ ? Like, revising for exams, taking care of my brother ... [4]________________ .

**Johnny** Your brother? [5]________________ with him?

**Sofia** Didn't you hear? He had a pretty bad accident a few weeks ago. He was in hospital for over two weeks. He's home now. I have to look after him in the afternoon when I get back from school.

**Johnny** Wow, Sofia. I'm sorry to hear that. [6]________________ . I don't know how you manage to look after someone who's ill.

**Sofia** Oh, [7]________________ . There isn't much to manage really – but he can't move around much, so I just have to get food and things, help him get dressed, stuff like that. Anyway, he's my brother, so I want to help him. I'm sure you've helped people in your family, too.

**Johnny** Well, [8]________________ , I helped to look after my dad when he was ill a few years ago.

**Sofia** See? We all do things when we have to. And that's what I'm doing. It is tiring, though.

## READING

**7** **Read the article and mark the sentences T (true) or F (false). Then correct the false sentences.**

### *Charles Dickens and* 'Hard Times'

Charles Dickens was one of the most famous and successful writers in England during the 19th century. He became very wealthy and travelled to the US twice to give talks. His books are still popular today and many have been made into films – *Great Expectations*, *Oliver Twist* and *A Christmas Carol* are perhaps the best-known examples.

But Dickens' life was not always an easy one, especially when he was a small boy. His parents had serious money problems. When disaster struck, Charles had only just turned 12 years old. He had to leave school to start work to earn enough money for his family to live on. He got a job in a factory where he had to stick labels onto bottles full of 'blacking', a polish for cleaning shoes. He was paid six shillings a week – that's about £12.50 a week in today's money. He hated the factory and the work, but the experience changed his life and inspired his career as a writer.

A short time later, his father was sent to prison because he owed money – this happened to many people at that time. Then the family house was sold, and Charles' mother, brothers and sisters went to live in the prison, too. Charles never forgot this period of his life. As an adult, he wanted people to know about the terrible conditions that children often had to work in. And when he started writing, his stories were full of people who suffered the things that he had gone through himself. In fact, one of his novels is called *Hard Times*.

1 Charles Dickens' work is mostly forgotten today. ☐
2 Charles had to go to work to help his family. ☐
3 Charles was almost 13 when he went to work in the factory. ☐
4 Charles' job was to polish shoes. ☐
5 The whole Dickens family was sent to prison. ☐
6 In his later life, Charles wanted to help improve the situation for children. ☐

## WRITING

**8** **Write a short description (150–200 words). Imagine you are 12-year-old Charles Dickens, working in the factory. Say what your work is like and how you feel.**

# 3 WHAT'S IN A NAME?

Grammar rap!

## GRAMMAR

### *(don't) have to / ought to / should(n't) / must*

SB p.32

**1 ★☆☆ Look at the pictures and complete the sentences with the phrases in the list.**

ask someone | be so shy | buy a hairbrush | go and see it
go to bed so late | wear something warmer

1 You should ________________ .

2 He shouldn't ________________ .

3 I must ________________ .

4 I shouldn't ________________ .

5 We ought to ________________ .

6 We must ________________ .

**2 ★★☆ Circle the correct options.**

1 It's a holiday tomorrow. We *have to / don't have to* go to school.
2 Well, it's your party. You *have to / don't have to* invite people you don't like.
3 Coffee isn't free here. You *have to / don't have to* pay for it.
4 Just your first name is OK. You *have to / don't have to* write your full name.
5 Well, those are the rules – you *have to / don't have to* be 16 to be allowed in.

**3 ★★☆ Complete the conversation with *have to / has to / don't have to / doesn't have to*.**

**Joe** Why do I [1] ________________ go to bed now? Helen [2] ________________ , and she's only two years older than me.

**Dad** That's right. But Helen [3] ________________ get up at seven o'clock to go to school. You do.

**Joe** Only because you say so. It only takes me 15 minutes to get dressed and have breakfast.

**Mum** But you [4] ________________ have a shower, too, remember.

**Joe** OK, 20 minutes. But I [5] ________________ leave the house until 7.50. So, I could get up at 7.30. And so, I [6] ________________ go to bed now.

**Mum** All right, but remember – it's me who [7] ________________ deal with you when you're tired and irritable in the morning!

**4 ★★★ Complete the sentences with the correct form of *have to* and a suitable verb.**

1 I'm going to a wedding tomorrow, so no T-shirt for me! I ________________ a suit and tie.
2 Rory, if you're going skateboarding, you ________________ in the park and not go on the road.
3 Lucy can't come out with us tonight – she ________________ her baby sister.
4 In some countries, you can eat with your hands – you ________________ with a knife and fork.
5 Lottie's got a well-paid job, so she ________________ about money.
6 Well, if you want better grades, you ________________ more.
7 We ________________ the dishes – we can put them all in the dishwasher.
8 My sister and I have each got a laptop now, so we ________________ one any more.

## *had better (not)*

→ SB p.33

**5 ★☆☆ Match the parts of the sentences.**

1 We mustn't be late, so ☐
2 This food isn't very fresh, so ☐
3 You've already spent a lot of money, so ☐
4 It's probably going to be cold, so ☐
5 My eyes are getting tired, so ☐
6 The children didn't understand the rules, so ☐
7 I don't think the water in that bottle is clean, so ☐
8 I hate it when you call me names, so ☐

a I'd better wear a jumper.
b we'd better leave now.
c you'd better explain them again.
d we'd better not drink it.
e you'd better throw it away.
f you'd better not do it again.
g you'd better not buy anything else.
h I'd better not look at a screen any more.

**6 ★★☆ Complete each dialogue with *'d better / 'd better not* and a verb from the list.**

apologise | call | eat | stay
study | tell | turn | wear

1 A We've got a test tomorrow.
B Well, you ______________________ , tonight, then.

2 A My parents get worried if I get home late.
B OK, we ______________________ too long at the party, then.

3 A I think he's quite upset about what I said.
B You ______________________ , then.

4 A I've got tickets for the concert tonight.
B Well, you ______________________ Harry. He couldn't get one, so he'd be envious.

5 A I don't feel too well.
B Well, you ______________________ any more crisps, then.

6 A Look! That man's fallen over. I think he's ill.
B We ______________________ an ambulance right away.

7 A The neighbours are complaining about the noise.
B Oh, OK. We ______________________ the music down a bit.

8 A It's a very special party tomorrow night.
B Yes, I know. We ______________________ something nice.

## *can('t) / must(n't)*

→ SB p.35

**7 ★☆☆ Complete the meaning of each sign. Use *can / can't* or *mustn't* and a verb, where necessary.**

1 You ________________ turn right.

4 You ________________ take photos here.

2 You ________________ park here.

5 You ________________ here.

3 You ________________ go in here.

6 You ________________ your phone here.

## GET IT RIGHT!

### Confusion between *could* and *should*

**We use *should* to indicate that something is a good idea or that something will happen under normal circumstances.**

**We use *could* to indicate that something may be true or possible.**

✓ *If you want, you **could** bring some drinks.*
✗ *If you want, you ~~should~~ bring some drinks.*

**Circle the correct modal verb.**

0 Two hours (*should*) / *could* be enough to do everything. That's how long it normally takes.
1 I would like to ask if I *should* / *could* have another month to finish the project.
2 If you want to get healthier, you *should* / *could* eat balanced meals.
3 On the other hand, there *should* / *could* be risks with that plan.
4 *Should* / *Could* you please consider my application and look at my case?
5 I think that we *should* / *could* take the route around Lake Frene.
6 Martha did not know whether she *should* / *could* tell the police or not.

# VOCABULARY

## Making and selling

→ SB p.32

**1 ★★☆ Complete the phrases.**

advertisement | brand | chain
consumer | image | logo
manufacturer | product

1 a ______________ of shops
2 a ______________ of doors and windows
3 the ______________ that a company makes
4 an ______________ in a magazine or on TV
5 the ______________ that people prefer to buy
6 the ______________ that a company uses to identify its products
7 an ______________ that a company creates in consumers' minds
8 a ______________ who buys goods or services

**2 ★★☆ Circle the correct words.**

1 This shop is one of a *brand* / *chain* – there are over 30 in this country.
2 I love that company's new TV *logo* / *advertisement*.
3 Some of the best-known car *manufacturers* / *products* are Korean.
4 The marketing department designed a new *image* / *logo* to put on their products.
5 Our company is launching a new *brand* / *product* next week.
6 Many companies support a charity – it improves their *consumer* / *image*.

**PRONUNCIATION**
Strong and weak forms: /ɒv/ and /əv/
Go to page 118.

## Expressions with *name*

→ SB p.35

**3 ★★☆ Complete the sentences with expressions with *name*.**

1 I eat everything – ______________ , and I'll eat it!
2 Nobody knew Petra Tomes ten years ago, but she soon ______________ for herself as an athlete.
3 They're engaged to be married, but they haven't ______________ yet.
4 You've probably never heard of Peter Gene Hernandez, but his ______________ is Bruno Mars.
5 Go and talk to that boy – um, ______________ , you know, the new guy.
6 Well, if you want to be successful, you have to work hard – sorry, but that's ______________ .
7 It's so childish, I think, when kids at school ______________ other kids ______________ .
8 Everyone knows who Lilian Rainey is – she's a ______________ in this country!

**4 ★★☆ Find eight words in the wordsearch. Then use them to complete the sentences.**

| E | B | S | K | Q | U | R | W |
|---|---|---|---|---|---|---|---|
| K | I | T | D | B | W | E | Y |
| A | G | A | M | E | A | L | Q |
| M | I | G | R | F | D | H | M |
| P | O | E | L | L | A | C | E |
| W | H | A | T | X | Y | U | R |
| T | S | O | Y | L | P | A | J |

1 My cousin's got loads of video games. You name ______________ , he's got it!
2 Tallulah's a great singer. She's sure to ______________ a name for herself in music.
3 We don't know when the party is. We're waiting for Kelly to name the ______________ .
4 Oh! I've just seen ______________'s-her-name. I can never remember what she's called!
5 Say sorry. It isn't nice to ______________ people names.
6 Elvis Cool isn't his real name. It's only his ______________ name.
7 It's my favourite brand and it's a ______________ name in sportswear.
8 You have to train hard if you want to be in the team. It's the name of the ______________ .

**5 ★★★ Answer the questions about yourself.**

1 Which brand logos do you like? Why?
______________
2 What is your favourite brand of clothes? Why?
______________
3 What is your favourite advertisement? Why?
______________
4 Who has made a name for themselves in your country recently and why?
______________
5 Who is the biggest name in sport in your country?
______________
6 What are the most popular chains of shops in your country?
______________

## REFERENCE

### Making and selling

advertisement, brand, chain, consumer, image, logo, manufacturer, product

### Expressions with name

**a big name**
*Microsoft is **a big name** in the IT world.*

**stage name**
*Her real name is Rachel Dean, but her **stage name** is Little D.*

**the name of the game**
*Training every day is **the name of the game** if you want to be an athlete.*

**to call someone names**
*It's upsetting when kids **call each other names** on social media.*

**you name it**
*There's plenty to do here – hiking, swimming, surfing, **you name it**!*

**to name the day**
*I hear Olivia and Dan are getting married. Have they **named the day** yet?*

**what's-his/her-name**
*Look, it's that actor – you know, **what's-his-name** … Paul Peters!*

**to make a name for yourself**
*My dad **made a name for himself** by becoming the best in the business.*

## VOCABULARY *EXTRA*

1 Circle the correct words.

1 A *competitor / consumer* is another business that makes or sells the same products as your company.
2 Washing machines, fridges and televisions are examples of electrical *manufacturers / goods*.
3 A house is usually the biggest *purchase / product* a person makes in their life.
4 You can save money if you wait to buy things in a *chain / sale*.
5 There's a weekly market with hundreds of different *shops / stalls*.

2 Complete the mind map with words from Exercise 1 and the Reference section. Sometimes several answers are possible.

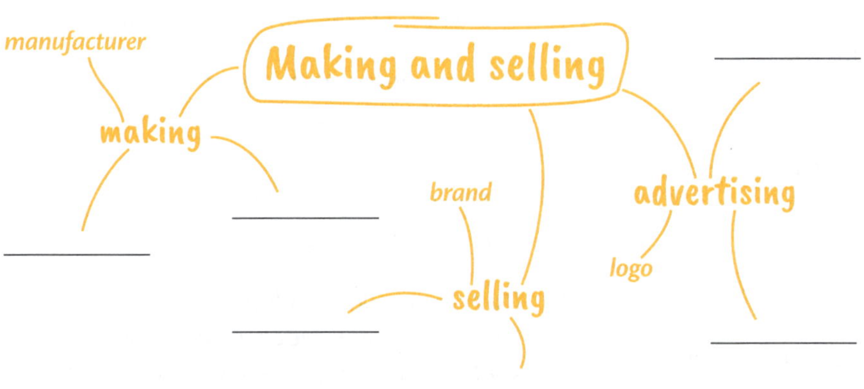


3 Write examples of shops, products and brands that you know.

1 Manufacturers:
______
______
2 Electrical goods:
______
______
3 Chains:
______
______
4 Your favourite market and its stalls:
______
______

# IT STARTED AS A BRAND

I've got it on my memory stick.

Watch this new trick I can do with my yo-yo!

I'd love to ride on a Jet Ski!

**What have these phrases all got in common? They all contain words that are brand names. Can you spot them?**

Some brands have become so successful that their names are now part of our language. However, we shouldn't really use these names, because they belong to the manufacturers. Every time we use a brand name, we are advertising a product. It's also a question of law: a brand name is owned by a company and must not be used without permission, and often requires payment!

So, why have so many brand names entered our everyday vocabulary? They are created by advertisers to make a product appear attractive – it's all part of its image. A successful brand name sounds cool and is easy to say. We like it, so we use it!

Some brand names are used by everyone to include all types of the same product, such as [1]__________ for all cola drinks. In the same way, inline skates are generally called [2]__________ and a ballpoint pen is often known as a [3]__________ . By the way, this name wasn't created, it's the surname of its inventor!

Sometimes, producers need a better name for their product. In the 1960s, New Zealand farmers wanted to increase sales of a fruit called a Chinese Gooseberry, but they had to find a shorter name for it. They chose the name [4]__________ because it's the nickname for New Zealanders and the name of their national bird.

Also, where would we be without hook and loop fasteners? You probably know them better as [5]__________ as it's so much quicker to say. You won't be surprised to know that it was invented by a Swiss engineer after he noticed how bits of sticks and leaves stuck to his dog's fur during walks in the forest!

What about all the new inventions that haven't already got a name? A new product appears and because it's the first one in existence, people only know it by its brand name. This is what happened for the first moving staircase or [6]__________ and many toys and games, such as the [7]__________ ! So, we shouldn't call every flying plastic disc by this name. Interestingly, this game was invented by a group of American students using a metal pie plate – ouch!

## READING

**1** **Read the article quickly and write the name of the products under the photos.**

**2** **Complete the article with the brand names in the list.**

biro | coke | escalator | frisbee
kiwi | rollerblades | velcro

**3** **Read the article again. Choose the correct words.**

1 If you want to use a brand name, you should *ask* / *tell* the owner of the brand.

2 The brand name is an important part of a product's *advertisement* / *image*.

3 We use brand names in everyday language because we like the *words* / *products*.

**4** CRITICAL THINKING **Choose the best option (A, B or C).**

1 What is the purpose of the text?

A to advertise certain products

B to explain the origins of words

C to explain the laws of brand names

**5** **Tick the sentences that are true for you.**

- I learned something new. ☐
- The text was interesting. ☐
- This information could be useful. ☐
- I can apply this to other situations. ☐

**6** **Do some research to find other brand names that have become part of everyday vocabulary in English and in your language. Write a short paragraph about one of them.**

## An email reply

1 INPUT **Read the email. What does Zehra want to know?** ____________________

**Zehra**
FloraH@mailme.com
Re: Exchange visit!

Hi Flora!

My name's Zehra and I'm coming to your school on an exchange visit next month. I'm really excited about it – hope you are, too!

Why am I writing this right now? The thing is, I really don't want to do the wrong thing while I'm there, especially at school. So I'm wondering if you could tell me a bit about it, like, what are the rules? About phones, clothes, talking in class, food … you know what I mean, don't you?

Could you send me a quick email to tell me?

Take care and hope to hear from you soon.

Zehra

**Flora**
ZehraP@mailme.com
Re: Exchange visit!

Hi there, Zehra!

Thanks for your email – great to hear from you. Yes, I'm looking forward to the exchange, too!

Anyway, about the rules. The school here isn't very strict about most things, but there are a few things you should know. First of all – clothes. We haven't got a uniform, so you can wear what you want, but we can't wear jeans with holes in them or anything like that, or T-shirts with writing on them. You should wear things that are comfortable. Oh, and it'll be kind of cold when you're here, so you'd better bring some warm clothes, OK?

The school's pretty strict about phones. Of course, you can bring them, but you have to switch them off in lessons – you can't just put them on silent. You can bring food to school, but you must eat it outside during the break – except if it's raining. Then, you can eat in the classroom (but not in the corridors!).

Not much else to say – I mean, it's a normal school and the teachers are mostly kind of normal, too – so no stress! You really don't have to worry about anything else.

Hope this helps. Write again soon and tell me if there's anything else you need to know.

Love,

Flora

2 **Read Flora's reply and mark the sentences T (true) or F (false). Then correct the false sentences.**

1 Flora gives all the information Zehra asked for. ☐
2 Students don't have to wear a uniform at Flora's school. ☐
3 Students can wear any clothes they like. ☐
4 Students must not take their phones into class. ☐

3 ANALYSE **Answer the questions about informal language in the emails.**

Flora writes: '… you'd better bring some warm clothes, OK?'

1 She uses the word 'OK' to *check for understanding* / *show disagreement*.
2 What does Zehra use instead of 'OK' to do this?
____________________

Flora writes: 'it'll be kind of cold when you're here.'

3 'kind of' means *very* / *a bit*.
4 Find and underline another time when Flora writes 'kind of' in her email.

Flora writes: '… great to hear from you.'

5 She has left out the words *This is* / *It is*.
6 Find two other times when she leaves words out. What are the missing words? ____________________

4 PLAN **Imagine that Zehra wrote her email to you. Plan your reply to her.**

Think about the rules in your school and the things Zehra asks. Make notes about:

- clothes
- food
- phones
- talking in class
- other rules Zehra should know about

5 PRODUCE **Write your reply to Zehra (200–250 words). Use your plan from Exercise 4. Make sure you include all the points in the checklist.**

### ✓ CHECKLIST

Start with a friendly greeting.

Answer all Zehra's questions and tell her about any other rules.

Use an informal style with short sentences, short forms of verbs (*it's, I'm, that's*), direct questions and short phrases, such as *you know, right? OK, Yeah.*

End the email in a friendly way and offer to give Zehra more information if she needs it.

## LISTENING

**1** 3.02 **Listen to a conversation between Annie, Ben and the new girl. Choose the correct answer (A, B or C).**

1 The new girl's name is …
 A Maureen. B Morgan. C Morwenna.
2 She is from …
 A Cornwall. B Wales. C London.
3 She says that in Cornwall …
 A there is nothing to do.
 B some names have strange pronunciations.
 C the beaches aren't very nice.

**2** 3.02 **Listen again and mark the statements T (true) or F (false).**

1 Annie asks Morwenna to repeat her name. ☐
2 The name Morwenna is Welsh. ☐
3 Part of Morwenna's family lives in Cornwall. ☐
4 Morwenna says Newquay is a good place for surfing. ☐
5 The water in Newquay is warm. ☐
6 Ben pronounces Mousehole correctly. ☐
7 People in Cornwall don't mind if names are pronounced wrongly. ☐
8 Annie gets Morwenna's name wrong again. ☐

**3** 3.02 **Listen again. Complete the parts of the conversation.**

1

**Annie** I've never been there. Cornwall, I mean, but I'd really like to go.
**Morwenna** Oh, [1]________________. It's really nice. We go quite often – my mum's got family down there. In Penzance.
**Ben** Anything to do there?
**Morwenna** Sure – there are nice beaches and if you like surfing, [2]________________ Newquay.
**Annie** But isn't the water really cold?
**Morwenna** Well, yes! So if you go surfing, [3]________________ a wetsuit to keep warm in the water.

2

**Morwenna** Yeah, really. If you go to Cornwall, [4]________________ how to pronounce the names. Local people don't like it when tourists say the names wrong.
**Annie** I guess not.
**Ben** I think Annie's right – [5]________________ a new brain.
**Morwenna** Sorry?
**Ben** Listen, [6]________________ back. The next lesson starts in a few minutes.

## DIALOGUE

**4** **Complete the dialogues.**

'd better learn | 'd better take
should know | should visit

1

**A** You live in Vancouver, don't you? I've always wanted to go there.
**B** That's right. And if you ever go there, you [1]________________ Stanley Park. It's beautiful!
**A** Is the weather nice there?
**B** Well, it can be OK in summer – but it rains quite a lot, so you [2]________________ an umbrella!

2

**A** You live in Hamburg, right? I've always wanted to go there.
**B** Yes, I do. If you come, you should go and see the Miniature Wonderland. It's fantastic.
**A** Do you think I [3]________________ German before I go?
**B** Well, you [4]________________ a few words, I guess – but lots of people speak English, so you don't have to worry too much.

**5** **Write a dialogue between you and a friend.**

The friend begins: *'You live in (name of your town / city), right? I've always wanted to go there.'*
Give the friend some advice about where to go, what to see and what to do.
Use the dialogues in Exercise 4 to help you.

# TOWARDS B2 First for Schools

## LISTENING
### Multiple choice

### EXAM GUIDE

**You will listen to eight different recordings. The eight recordings are a mix of short monologues and dialogues. For each one, there is a three-option multiple-choice question to answer. The questions tend to focus on gist, detail, purpose, attitude and opinion. You hear each recording twice.**

- Before you listen, read the context sentence (the question and the three options, A, B and C). This will give you a general idea of what you will hear.
- Listen carefully. Remember, you will not hear the same words as in the options, so listen for synonyms, paraphrases and expressions with a similar meaning.
- When the question asks you to understand a speaker's attitude or opinion, you need to form an impression by listening to the whole recording.

1 3.03 **You will hear people talking in eight different situations. For questions 1–8, choose the best answer (A, B or C).**

1 You hear a conversation in a shop. What is the problem with the shoes?
A His wife doesn't like them.
B He doesn't think they're right for him.
C They're too small for him.

2 You hear a girl talking about puzzles. What does she say about them?
A The puzzles are always easy to do.
B She always solves the puzzles.
C They develop her thinking abilities.

3 You hear a man telling a friend about a trip he made to China. What does he say about Shanghai?
A It was amazing.
B He spent seven days there.
C He didn't see it.

4 You hear a woman telling a friend about her journey to work. How does she usually travel?
A by car
B by bike
C by bus

5 You hear two teenagers talking about school. Why did the girl change schools?
A Her old school was too far away.
B She wanted to work harder.
C Her parents decided for her.

6 You hear part of a radio interview with a man. What does the man do?
A He writes poetry.
B He's a singer in a band.
C He writes the words for songs.

7 You hear a woman talking about her hobby. How does she feel while she is birdwatching?
A tired
B hopeful
C excited

8 You hear a boy who wants to be a chef. How did he first become interested in cooking?
A He tasted some excellent food in a restaurant.
B He enjoyed cooking dinner for himself.
C His mum cooked him a special birthday dinner.

# 4 WHAT WOULD YOU DO?

Grammar rap!

## GRAMMAR

### First and second conditional (review)

→ SB p.40

**1** ★☆☆ **Match the sentences with the pictures.**

1 If we lose this game, I won't be happy.
2 If we lost this game, I'd be very surprised.
3 If it snows tomorrow, we won't have to go to school.
4 If it snowed here, it would be very strange.

**2** ★★☆ **Complete the sentences with the correct form of the verbs in brackets to make first or second conditional sentences.**

0 I ___will tell___ (tell) you my secret if you ___promise___ (promise) not to tell anyone.
1 Be careful. The cat ___________ (bite) you if you ___________ (touch) it.
2 If Nils ___________ (be) taller, he ___________ (be) a really good basketball player.
3 If you ___________ (meet) the president, ___________ (you / ask) her to do something about climate change?
4 Hurry up, Molly! If we ___________ (not leave) now, you ___________ (miss) the train.
5 If I ___________ (know) the answer, I still ___________ (not tell) you.
6 If those students ___________ (not stop) talking now, the teacher ___________ (get) angry with the whole class.
7 ___________ (you / be) scared if we ___________ (meet) a bear in the woods?
8 Our team is the best. I ___________ (be) very surprised if we ___________ (not win).

**3** ★★☆ **Complete the sentences with the correct form of the verbs in brackets to make second conditional sentences.**

What [1]_______________ you _______________ (do) if you found an envelope full of money in the street? [2]_______________ you _______________ (take) it to the police station? Or [3]_______________ you _______________ (keep) it and buy yourself something you really wanted? [4]_______________ you _______________ (buy) your mum and dad a present? If you [5]_______________ (buy) them a present, they [6]_______________ (want) to know where you got the money from. If you [7]_______________ (tell) them the truth, maybe they [8]_______________ (not be) so happy. And if you [9]_______________ (not tell) them the truth, you [10]_______________ (feel) really bad. You know what, I hope I never find an envelope full of money in the street!

### Time conjunctions

→ SB p.40

**4** ★☆☆ **Circle the correct options.**

1 Grace is going to get a new computer *when* / *unless* she has enough money.
2 I'll phone you *until* / *as soon as* she leaves.
3 We'll start the meeting *until* / *when* Mr Benson arrives.
4 *If* / *Until* I don't pass my English test, I'll take it again.
5 You won't pass your driving test *if* / *unless* you practise more.
6 We'll watch the game *as soon as* / *until* half time.

**5** ★★☆ **Complete the sentences with *if*, *unless*, *until* or *as soon as*.**

1 ___________ we hurry up, we'll be late for the party.
2 Jeremy's got the tickets, so we'll have to wait ___________ he gets there before we can get in.
3 What will you do ___________ we don't get any homework this weekend?
4 Maxine can't talk because she's in the shower. She'll call you ___________ she gets out.
5 I'm seeing Shaun tonight, so I'll ask him ___________ I see him.
6 ___________ we can't get tickets, we can just watch the match on TV at my house.
7 I've got to go to the shops. Can you look after the baby ___________ I get back?
8 I can't go to the party ___________ I finish my project by Friday.

## *wish* and *if only*

→ SB p.41

**6** ★☆☆ **Circle the correct words.**

1 My mum wishes she *has* / *had* more time.
2 Rose wishes she *can* / *could* go to the theatre tonight.
3 If only the neighbour's dog *won't* / *wouldn't* bark all day.
4 The teacher wishes her students *weren't* / *aren't* so noisy.
5 If only I *am* / *was* taller.
6 Logan wishes Kirsty *will* / *would* talk to him.
7 If only we *could* / *can* play the piano.

**7** ★★☆ **Read the sentences. Write Julia's wishes.**

0 'My sister keeps taking my clothes.'
I wish *my sister wouldn't keep taking my clothes.*
1 'I don't understand Maths.'
If only ____________________
2 'The girls in my class are so childish.'
I wish ____________________
3 'I can't find my phone. Where is it?'
I wish ____________________
4 'I can't afford to buy those new shoes.'
If only ____________________
5 'We want to go to the concert, but the tickets are sold out'
I wish ____________________
6 'We've got too much homework this weekend.'
If only ____________________

## Third conditional (review)

→ SB p.42

**8** ★☆☆ **Match the parts of the sentences.**

1 We wouldn't have watched the film ☐
2 I would have got a much better mark ☐
3 We would have saved a lot of money ☐
4 She would have got completely lost ☐
5 If you hadn't kicked the ball so hard, ☐
6 If Teresa had apologised, ☐
7 If I had had Finley's number, ☐
8 If the children had been a bit quieter, ☐

a if I'd studied harder.
b if she hadn't used the map on her phone.
c it wouldn't have knocked my glasses off.
d I would have sent him a message.
e if we had known it was so long and slow.
f they wouldn't have woken the baby.
g I would have forgiven her.
h if we'd eaten at home.

**9** ★★☆ **Read the story. Then complete the sentences with the correct form of the verbs in brackets.**

My friend Nathan threw a pen by mistake and it hit the teacher. The teacher was angry. Nathan didn't say anything. The teacher thought it was me and gave me detention. I went to detention and met a girl called Andrea. I asked her over to my place and she said yes. Now Andrea's my best friend.

0 If Nathan *hadn't thrown* a pen, it *wouldn't have hit* the teacher. (throw / hit)
1 If Nathan ____________ honest, he ____________ to detention. (be / go)
2 If I ____________ to detention, I ____________ Andrea. (go / meet)
3 If I ____________ Andrea, I ____________ invite her to my house. (meet / be able to)
4 If she ____________ no to my invitation, I ____________ at home alone. (say / stay)
5 If she ____________ to my place, we ____________ best friends. (come / become)

### GET IT RIGHT!

#### *would have* + past participle

**Learners sometimes underuse *would have* + past participle, or use it in the *if*-clause where the past perfect tense is required.**

✓ *After the musical, we **would have gone** to a restaurant, but we didn't have time.*
✗ *After the musical, we ~~would go~~ to a restaurant, but we didn't have time.*
✓ *We would have appreciated it if you **had contacted** us.*
✗ *We would have appreciated it if you ~~would have~~ contacted us.*

**Circle the correct options.**

1 If I *would have to* / *had to* choose between the cakes, I would choose the strawberry one.
2 We *would have liked* / *'d like* to visit the palace, but we didn't have the chance.
3 It would have been better if there *would have been* / *had been* more jobs available.
4 The food wasn't as tasty as I *would have liked* / *'d like*.
5 If I'd known about the risks, I *wouldn't have taken* / *wouldn't take* part in the race.
6 My class could have learned more if the facilities *would have been* / *had been* better.

## VOCABULARY
### Being honest

→ SB p.40

**1** ★★☆ **Match the parts of the sentences.**

1 Why don't you just own ☐
2 If I tell a ☐
3 I can be very open ☐
4 It's always best to tell ☐
5 It isn't always easy to do ☐
6 There's no point hiding the ☐
7 My sister believed me – I never thought I'd get ☐
8 Dylan's always trying to cheat ☐

a with my mum – we have a great relationship.
b truth – people always find out in the end.
c lie, my face just goes bright red.
d away with that lie.
e in exams – he tries to look at my paper.
f the right thing, so thank you for being honest.
g up and tell her you broke her phone?
h the truth because then people will trust you.

**2** ★★☆ **Complete the dialogue with the words in the list. There is one extra word.**

do | get | hide | lie | open | own | truth

**Moira** So what do you think we should do? ¹__________ up and tell the ²__________ ?

**Rebecca** No way. She'll be furious. I think we have to tell a ³__________ and say it wasn't us.

**Moira** We'll never ⁴__________ away with it. I think we have to ⁵__________ the right thing.

**Rebecca** Which is?

**Moira** Be ⁶__________ about it. Say we were hungry and there was nothing else to eat.

**Rebecca** But it was her birthday cake! She won't accept that as an excuse.

**Moira** So what do you think we should do?

**Rebecca** ⁷__________ the truth. Say the dog ate it.

**Moira** The dog? That's brilliant! Why didn't we think of that before?

### Making a decision

→ SB p.43

**3** ★★☆ **Match the phrases (1–6) with the definitions (a–f).**

1 first thought ☐
2 to think long and hard ☐
3 to change your mind ☐
4 to reconsider ☐
5 to make up your mind ☐
6 the wrong decision ☐

a to really consider something
b to think about your decision again
c to come to a decision
d not the right decision
e to come to a different decision
f original idea

**4** ★★★ **Answer these questions so they're true for you.**

1 What were your first thoughts when you met your best friend?

______________________________

2 What is the best decision you have ever made?

______________________________

3 When was the last time you made the wrong decision about something?

______________________________

4 When is it difficult to make up your mind?

______________________________

5 Can you remember when you changed your mind about something? What was it?

______________________________

6 What kind of things do you have to think long and hard about?

______________________________

### WordWise: Phrases with *now*

→ SB p.43

**5** ★★☆ **Rewrite the sentences so that they have *now* in the correct place.**

1 I go out dancing with my friends and again, but I'm not very keen.

______________________________

2 Zac left just, so if you run, you'll catch him.

______________________________

3 We hardly ever see Jason that he's got his own scooter.

______________________________

4 We've missed the last bus. What are we going to do?

______________________________

# REFERENCE

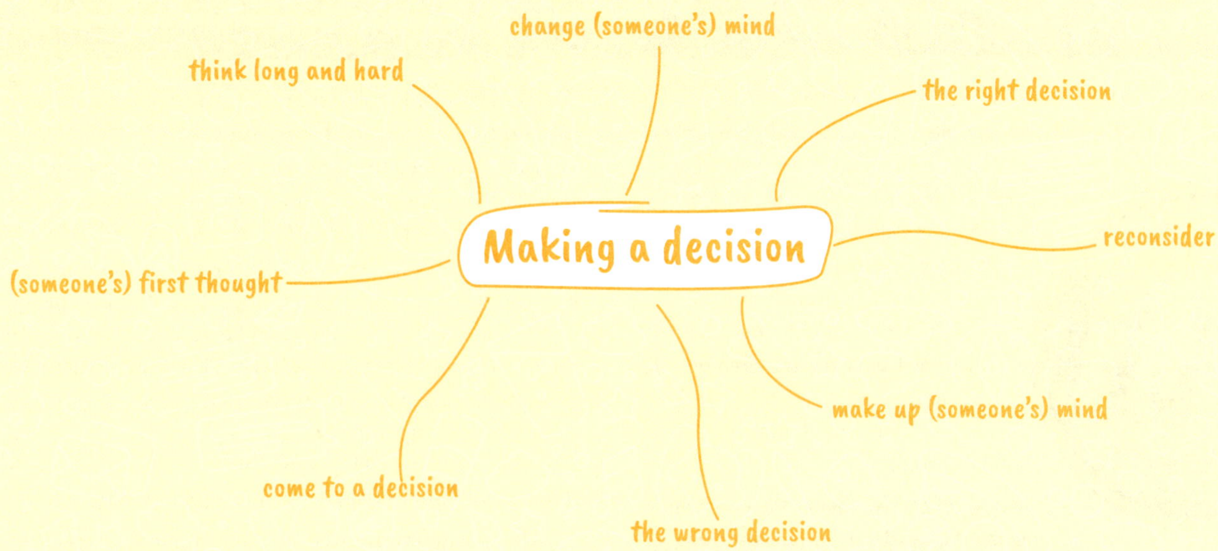


## BEING HONEST

| bad | good |
|---|---|
| cheat | be open about (something) |
| get away with (something) | do the right thing |
| hide the truth | own up (to something) |
| tell a lie | tell the truth |

## PHRASES WITH *NOW*

| | |
|---|---|
| now (= at this moment) | now (= in the near future) |
| now and again | just now |
| now that | |

# VOCABULARY *EXTRA*

**1 Match the phrases (1–6) with the sentences (a–f).**

1 take something seriously ☐
2 take someone's word for it ☐
3 keep a secret ☐
4 owe someone an apology ☐
5 as a matter of fact ☐
6 as far as I know ☐

a Nobody else must know.
b This is actually true.
c I believe what she says.
d I believe this is true.
e Pay attention – this is important.
f I made a mistake – I should say sorry.

**2 Complete the dialogue.**

a matter | an apology | far as | take me | to keep | your word

A You didn't [1]__________ seriously! You told Kate about the surprise.
B As [2]__________ of fact, she already knew about it.
A That doesn't matter. You owe me [3]__________ .
B Sorry. As [4]__________ I know, she doesn't know what the surprise is.
A OK, but she knows there is a surprise. You promised [5]__________ the secret and I took [6]__________ for it!

**3 Rewrite the sentences with the phrases in Exercise 1.**

1 My friend told me not to tell anyone her news.
______________________________
2 I'm sorry I took my brother's camera without asking.
______________________________
3 I know what my friend tells me is always true.
______________________________
4 We should all realise that climate change is a serious problem.
______________________________

# Golden balls

A few years ago, there was a game show on TV in which the contestants faced a really difficult dilemma. I can't really remember what happened in the show. I just remember how it finished. [1]At the end, there were two contestants and they had the chance to win some money. Depending on how successful they'd been during the show, the amount of money could be anything from a few hundred pounds to over £50,000. To get their hands on this money, they had to make one final decision.

In front of each of them were two balls. One had the word 'split' inside, the other had the word 'steal'. [2]If they wanted to share the money, they chose the 'split' ball. If they wanted to keep all the money for themselves, they chose the 'steal' ball. Each player chose a ball and then they showed it to each other at exactly the same time.

But it wasn't quite so simple. If they both chose the 'split' ball, then each contestant went home with half the money. If one player chose 'split' while the other chose 'steal', then the one who'd stolen won all the money, leaving the other player with nothing at all. However, if they both chose 'steal', then neither of them got any money.

Before they chose the ball, both players had a few minutes to explain to each other what they were going to do. Of course, they always promised they'd share, but they weren't always telling the truth. It wasn't cheating because those were the rules of the game. I remember always feeling really pleased when the two players kept their promises and they both won some of the prize money. [3]It's always good to see the best side of people. But unfortunately, it didn't always end that way. When one player stole from the other, it made me feel really bad, especially when there was a large amount of cash involved. [4]However, I think the best feeling I had was when two greedy players both stole. It was great to see the look of disappointment on their faces when they realised they'd both thrown away a great opportunity.

The programme showed all sides of human nature: the good and the ugly. As a matter of fact, social scientists watched it – for work, not fun! – to understand how contestants made up their minds to 'split' or 'steal'. On average, about half of the contestants were happy to share the prize. The main issues when deciding were the size of the prize and trust (for example, if the other player had lied in the earlier part of the game). As far as I know, [5]the show only lasted a few years before they stopped making it. I think that was probably the right thing to do.

## READING

**1** **Read the article. What was the dilemma the game show contestants faced?**

____________________________

**2** **Read the text again. Mark the sentences T (true) or F (false). Then correct the false sentences.**

1. If contestants played well in the first part of the show, the prize money would increase. ☐
2. Each player kept the word in their ball secret from the other player. ☐
3. Both players won some money in the end. ☐
4. The best result for the writer was when both players 'split'. ☐
5. There were often social scientists among the contestants on the show. ☐

**3** **Read the article again and answer the questions.**

There are two players, Emily and Jordan. There is a total prize money of £10,000.

How much does each player win in the situations below? How does the writer feel watching it?

1. They both choose the 'split' ball.
   Emily £________ Jordan £________ Writer feels ________
2. They both choose the 'steal' ball.
   Emily £________ Jordan £________ Writer feels ________
3. Jordan chooses 'split', Emily chooses 'steal'.
   Emily £________ Jordan £________ Writer feels ________
4. Jordan chooses 'steal', Emily chooses 'split'.
   Emily £________ Jordan £________ Writer feels ________

**4** CRITICAL THINKING **Read the underlined parts of the article. Decide if they express a fact (F) or an opinion (O).**

1 ____ 2 ____ 3 ____ 4 ____ 5 ____

**5** **Imagine you are a contestant in the show. There is a prize of £10,000. What would you do and why? Write a short paragraph.**

# DEVELOPING Writing

## A diary entry about a dilemma

1 INPUT **Read Zara's diary entry. What is her dilemma and what does she decide to do?**

_______________________________________________

**DIARY**

I haven't shown my best friend, Nell, the trust she deserves and I'm feeling really bad about it. It all started when she asked to borrow my phone to check her social-media messages. Of course, I let her use it. (A) The problem is that she forgot to log out of her account afterwards, so when I used it a few hours later, her messages were the first things I saw. I was just about to log into my account when I noticed a message with my name in the subject line. (B) There it was – a message from my brother to my best friend with my name in the first line! Why was my name there? Why were they writing about me? I thought [1] ________________ . I knew I should just close the page, but I couldn't help reading it. I knew it was the [2] ________________ to make but I opened the message. (C) As soon as I read it, I realised I'd made a horrible mistake. The message was all about arranging a surprise party for my birthday next week.

Now I've got a horrible dilemma. Should I [3] ________________ and [4] ________________ or say nothing and [5] ________________ from her? If I was braver, I'd tell her what I'd done. (D) I think that this time I won't say anything and pretend that the party is a surprise. But I know one thing – I'll never let anyone use my phone to check their messages again!

2 **Complete the diary entry with the phrases in the list. There is one extra phrase you won't need.**

hide the truth | long and hard | own up | tell a lie | tell her the truth | wrong decision

3 ANALYSE **Complete the sentences with the correct form of the verbs in brackets to make second or third conditionals. Then decide in which of the spaces (A–D) they go.**

1 If I ________________ (can turn) back time, I ________________ (close) the page without taking a look. ☐
2 If I ________________ (not see) it, I ________________ (never think) of reading any of her messages. ☐
3 If I ________________ (tell) her, she ________________ (never speak) to me again. ☐
4 If I ________________ just ________________ (say) no, I ________________ (not have) this dilemma. ☐

4 **Read the dilemmas. Then complete the conditional sentences.**

1 I broke my brother's games console.
   a If I'd been more careful,
   ________________________________ .
   b If he knew it was me,
   ________________________________ .

2 I saw my classmate cheating in an exam.
   a If I told the teacher,
   ________________________________ .
   b If she had studied harder,
   ________________________________ .

3 My friend wants to borrow £100 from me. It's all the money I've got.
   a If I gave it to him and he never paid me back, ________________________ .
   b If he had been more careful with his money, ________________________ .

5 PLAN **Choose one of the dilemmas in Exercise 4 or think of one of your own. Then make a plan for your diary entry.**

- explain the dilemma
- describe how it happened
- say what you should and shouldn't have done
- say what you have learned from the experience

6 PRODUCE **Write a diary entry about your dilemma (250 words). Use your notes from Exercise 5. Make sure you include all the points in the checklist.**

### CHECKLIST

- Use informal language.
- Imagine what would happen using second conditional sentences.
- Imagine what would have happened using third conditional sentences.
- Use some of the phrases about being honest and making decisions from page 39.

## LISTENING

**1** 4.01 **Listen to three dialogues. Match them with the pictures.**

**2** 4.01 **Listen again and match the sentences with the dialogues. There is one extra sentence.**

Dialogue 1 ☐
Dialogue 2 ☐
Dialogue 3 ☐

a Someone did the right thing.
b Someone cheated.
c Someone told a lie.
d Someone made a mistake.

**3** 4.01 **Listen again and complete these parts of the dialogues.**

**1**

A [1]________________ . I was going to send a message, but I forgot.
B I hope you were careful with them.
A [2]________________ . They're like new!

**2**

A Olivia, can you tell me what happened?
B I don't know what to say. [3]________________ .
A Thank you for owning up and speaking for the class, Olivia.
B It was a stupid thing to do. [4] ________________ .

**3**

A If you had looked where you were going, this [5]________________ !
B I'm sorry. [6]________________ .

## DIALOGUE

**4 Put the dialogue in order.**

[1] **Talia** Tell me it's not your birthday today.
☐ **Talia** It isn't fine. I'm going straight out and getting you something nice.
☐ **Talia** But I haven't got you a present or even a card. I feel awful about this.
☐ **Talia** What are you doing?
☐ **Talia** And tonight I'm taking you out for a meal. No argument.
[13] **Talia** Oh. I see.
☐ **Talia** And I've forgotten it. I'm so embarrassed.
☐ **Lena** Don't be so silly. It's easily done.
☐ **Lena** No seriously. You don't need to.
☐ **Lena** It is. It's the big one – 18.
☐ **Lena** No worries. It's fine.
☐ **Lena** But I can't. I've kind of got plans already.
☐ **Lena** Well, it's just me and a few friends going out dancing.

## PHRASES FOR FLUENCY

→ SB p.44

**5 Complete the phrases with the missing vowels.**

1 __r__ y__ __ __ __t __f y__ __r m__nd?
2 b__l__ __v__ __t __r n__t ...
3 b__tw__ __n y__ __ __nd m__ ...
4 __ w__s w__nd__r__ng __f ...
5 __ny ch__nc__ ...?
6 wh__t's w__th ...?

**6 Complete the dialogues with the phrases from Exercise 5.**

1 A ________________ the grumpy face, Brendan? Life isn't so bad, is it?
B No, I'm just a bit tired. I didn't get a lot of sleep last night.

2 A I think we should take a break and go and play some tennis.
B ________________ , I was thinking exactly the same thing!

3 A Um, Jenni, I don't know if you're busy tonight but ________________ you'd like to go to the cinema with me?
B Like to? I'd love to!

4 A We've got visitors and the living room's a mess. It needs tidying – Thomas, ________________ of doing that?
B Sorry, Mum, but I'm busy playing Minecraft.

5 A That cat's really cute. I think we should take it home with us.
B ________________ It probably belongs to someone.

6 A Are you going to Yolanda's party?
B ________________ , I don't really want to go so I think I might make up an excuse and give it a miss.

**PRONUNCIATION**
Consonant–vowel word linking
Go to page 119.

# TOWARDS B2 First for Schools

## WRITING
### A story

## EXAM GUIDE

**For this task, there is a choice of four questions. You have to choose one question to answer. The text types include: an article, a review, an essay, an email or letter or a story.**

- Before you start writing, think about what you want to write and make a brief plan.
- Organise your text into clear paragraphs and use linkers to connect ideas and show the sequence of events.
- Make sure you start with a brief introduction, and end with a conclusion.
- Use formal, informal or neutral language, according to the type of text you choose.
- Try to use a range of grammatical structures, vocabulary and verb forms.
- Keep within the word limit and remember that you have about 40 minutes for each of the texts.

**1 Look at the task. Underline the most important information in it.**

**WE ARE LOOKING FOR STORIES FOR A NEW WEBSITE FOR TEENAGERS.**

Your story must start with the following sentence:

*I opened the suitcase and could hardly believe my eyes – it was more money than I had ever seen in my life.*

Your story must include:
- a decision
- a police officer.

Write your story in 140–190 words.

**2 Read Nico's answer. Which part of the question does he fail to answer?**

I opened the suitcase and could hardly believe my eyes – it was more money than I had ever seen in my life. I closed it quickly and put the case back onto the seat. I was excited, but I was also very nervous. I sat down and thought about how this case had fallen into my hands.

The woman had seemed normal. We'd started chatting, first about the weather and then about where we were going. She was on her way to visit her aunt. When a man in a dark suit passed by, her mood suddenly changed. She seemed anxious and didn't want to talk. Then she got up and asked me to look after the case and left. Two hours later, the train had reached the station where I was getting off. What was I going to do? Leave the money on the train or take it with me?

I counted the money when I got home: £100,000 exactly. I used it to open a small shop. Now, more than 20 years later, I have a chain of 50 stores across the country. I wonder who that woman was.

**3 Look at the notes Nico made before writing. Use his story to answer the questions he asked himself.**

1 Where was I?

______________________

2 Why did I have this suitcase?

______________________

3 How did I feel when I saw the money?

______________________

4 What did I decide to do?

______________________

5 What were the consequences?

______________________

**4 Read the task. Plan and then write your answer.**

**WE ARE LOOKING FOR STORIES FOR AN ENGLISH LANGUAGE MAGAZINE FOR TEENAGERS.**

Your story must start with the following sentence:

*Should I stay or should I go? I had 30 seconds to decide.*

Your story must include:
- an animal
- a bike.

Write your story in 140–190 words.

**5 Ask a friend to read your story and complete the sentences about it.**

I really like the …

______________________

I thought the story was …

______________________

The language you used was …

______________________

You could improve it by …

______________________

# CONSOLIDATION

## LISTENING

1 4.04 **Listen to the dialogue. Choose the correct answer (A, B or C).**

1 The girl doesn't want the T-shirt because …
  A it's too big.
  B she doesn't like the colour.
  C she doesn't like the name on it.
2 The girl wants to exchange the T-shirt for …
  A a belt.
  B a different T-shirt.
  C two other T-shirts.
3 The man suggests that the girl could …
  A keep the T-shirt.
  B give the T-shirt to her brother.
  C give the T-shirt to someone else.

2 4.04 **Listen again and mark the sentences T (true) or F (false).**

1 The girl doesn't like clothes with the names of companies on. ☐
2 All the clothes in the shop have the company name on. ☐
3 The T-shirt was a present from the girl's brother. ☐
4 The shirt has a hole in it. ☐
5 The girl hasn't got the receipt. ☐
6 The belt is more expensive than the T-shirt. ☐
7 The girl is bigger than her friend Jenny. ☐
8 She decides to give the T-shirt to her friend. ☐

## VOCABULARY

3 **Match the sentences.**

1 Everyone knows who she is. ☐
2 She's travelled all over the world. ☐
3 She's totally honest. ☐
4 She just doesn't know what to do. ☐
5 She stuck with her original decision. ☐
6 She doesn't want to use her real name. ☐

a She can't make up her mind at all.
b So she's decided to use a stage name.
c She didn't want to change her mind.
d She's a big name in this country.
e I've never heard her tell a lie.
f You name it, she's been there!

4 **Circle the correct options.**

1 I haven't decided yet – I'm going to think long and *hard* / *strong* about it.
2 We don't go there very often – just *now that* / *now and again*.
3 Come on, tell us the *lie* / *truth* about what happened.
4 I know you did it. Come on, you should just *get away with it* / *own up to it*.
5 I really don't care if people *make me* / *call me* names.
6 I think you've made the wrong decision. If you want to *reconsider* / *come to a decision*, please call me.
7 I don't like the *logo* / *brand* of this company. It isn't very well designed.
8 He's the owner of a big *chain* / *brand* of shops in the north of the country.

## GRAMMAR

5 **Correct the sentences.**

1 I wish you are here.
______
2 I was happier if the weather was better.
______
3 If only I know the answer to this question.
______
4 We'd better to leave now, I think.
______
5 I'll phone you when I'll get home.
______
6 Do you think we should asking for some help?
______
7 He's a great guitar player – if only he can sing better.
______
8 If he'd left earlier, he hadn't missed the start of the film.
______
9 The bus ride there is free, so you have to pay for it.
______
10 Let's wait as soon as 5 pm to call them.
______

## DIALOGUE

**6** 4.05 **Complete the dialogue with the phrases in the list. Then listen and check.**

any chance | are you out of your mind
believe it or not | between you and me
had better | I was wondering
should have been | what's with

**Maya** Hey, Jonah. [1] ________________ if you're going to Laura's party later.

**Jonah** Yeah, I'm going. Why?

**Maya** [2] ________________ I can go with you? I just don't like arriving at parties on my own.

**Jonah** Sure, no problem.

**Maya** That's great. Thanks. Hey, you'll never guess what happened to me in a shop this morning.

**Jonah** Tell me. What happened?

**Maya** Well, I bought a really cool shirt for the party tonight. [3] ________________, it was £79.99! I can't believe I spent so much!

**Jonah** Wow, that's really expensive. But, so what?

**Maya** Well, you know, my parents gave me some money for my birthday, so I paid cash with two £50 notes. I put them on the counter, and, [4] ________________, the woman put the change on top of the notes! I picked it all up and left. So, I got the shirt and my money and the change! How cool is that?

**Jonah** Cool? [5] ________________? It's dishonest. Think about the poor shop assistant – she'll probably have to pay that money out of her own pocket. You [6] ________________ take it back and explain. Say it was a mistake.

**Maya** No way. She [7] ________________ more careful.

**Jonah** Whatever. I'm sure you wouldn't like it to happen to you.

**Maya** Oh, come on, Jonah. [8] ________________ you? Don't be so boring.

**Jonah** Boring? Maya, what you did was stealing, you know?

## READING

**SUZIE SHOPS**

**This week, I've been looking at bags – school bags and sports bags for your PE kit. There's a huge choice out there, so I've done the hard work and picked the best ones for you all.**

### BACKPACK: NORTHPACK 'COLLEGE': £30

**GOOD:** If you like backpacks, you must try this! It's available in ten colours – so there ought to be a colour you like! It doesn't look very big, but it's surprising how much you can fit in it. There's a special secure pocket for your laptop and two more pockets for books.

**BUT:** I wish it had an extra pocket because I have to carry loads of books.

**MY CHOICE:** because it's so comfortable to carry. If you get backache, I'd definitely recommend this backpack.

### MESSENGER BAG: COURIER 'DAILY' SPECIAL PRICE: £28

**GOOD:** Stylish, well-made bag from a top brand. It's specially designed for students, so there's plenty of space for everything. You don't have to worry about your things getting wet because it's waterproof.

**BUT:** If only there was a small pocket on the outside for a phone ...

**MY CHOICE:** because I love the design and the special price. If it hadn't been on special offer, it would have cost £40!

### SPORTS BAG: EACTIVE 'TOP KIT': £15

**GOOD:** This is a well-designed sports bag and ideal for your school PE kit. It's strong and it's got a special space for shoes, so you don't have to put them in a separate bag.

**BUT:** I wish it was a brighter colour ... but if it was a light colour, it wouldn't stay clean for long!

**MY CHOICE:** because it's light and excellent value for money. You wouldn't find this quality at a lower price!

**7** **Read the blog and answer the questions.**

1 What is the purpose of the blog?
________________________________________

2 What would Suzie like to change about the backpack?
________________________________________

3 How much can you save on the price of the messenger bag?
________________________________________

4 What does Suzie think about the quality of the sports bag?
________________________________________

5 What would be the disadvantage of a light colour sports bag?
________________________________________

## WRITING

**8** **Think of two products you know: one that you like the name of, and one that you don't like the name of. Write a short text (150–200 words). Include information about:**

- what the products are and what they do
- what their names are and why you like/dislike the names.

# 5 STORYTELLING

Grammar rap!

## GRAMMAR

### Relative pronouns

→ SB p.50

**1** ★☆☆ **Complete the sentences with *who, whose, where* or *which*.**

1. The book ________ I have just read is called *Clockwork Angel.*
2. It is a fantasy novel ________ was written by Cassandra Clare.
3. The name of the girl ________ is the heroine of the novel is Tessa Gray.
4. The story is set in London, ________ all the action takes place.
5. Tessa Gray is looking for her brother, ________ has disappeared.
6. Tessa gets help from two friends ________ names are Will and Jem.

### Defining and non-defining relative clauses

→ SB p.50

**2** ★★☆ **Combine the sentences about a famous vampire with *who, which, where* or *whose.***

0 Abhartach was a vampire. He came from Ireland.
*Abhartach was a vampire who came from Ireland.*

1 It was a legend. It inspired Bram Stoker to write *Dracula*.

________________________________________

________________________________________

2 Abhartach was an evil magician. He had very strong powers.

________________________________________

________________________________________

3 He lived in Derry. He ruled a small kingdom.

________________________________________

________________________________________

4 He was an evil ruler. His people were afraid of him.

________________________________________

________________________________________

5 *Dracula* comes from an Irish word. It means 'bad blood'.

________________________________________

________________________________________

**3** ★★☆ **Complete the dialogue with *which, who, that, where* or *whose.***

**Ella** What kind of books do you like reading?

**Beth** I like reading books [1] ________ are set in the olden days. My favourite book is one about a girl [2] ________ grandmother lives in a very old house. It's a fantasy novel about the people [3] ________ used to live in the house.

**Ella** Is it set in England?

**Beth** No, it's set in the US, [4] ________ Maryanne, the girl, is sent to spend the summer holidays with her grandmother. What about you? What kind of books do you like?

**Ella** I like historical novels. I'm reading one now [5] ________ is set in Victorian England. It's about a poor girl [6] ________ has to work. She works for a doctor [7] ________ main job is to look after his patients, but he's also a scientist. The girl helps him with his experiments.

**Beth** It sounds like the kind of book [8] ________ I'd like to read. Can I borrow it when you've finished?

**4** ★★☆ **Put the words in order to make sentences with non-defining relative clauses.**

1 aunt, / My / lives / in / Berlin, / who / an / author / is

________________________________________

________________________________________

2 film, / The / stars / Lucy Heyton, / which / out / in / cinemas / is / now

________________________________________

________________________________________

3 storyteller, / The / work / all / over / the / world, / whose / takes / him / in / Japan / is / at / moment / the

________________________________________

________________________________________

4 Prague, / where / boy / the / story / the / in / grew up, / my / hometown / is

________________________________________

________________________________________

5 heroine / story, / the / of / The / whose / father / French, / is / called / Sophie / is

________________________________________

________________________________________

**5** ★★☆ **Mark the relative clauses D (defining) or ND (non-defining).**

1 My favourite book, which is about a moon landing, has now been made into a film. ___
2 Leo, who had already read the book, liked the film. ___
3 The man who she's interviewing wrote the book. ___
4 I couldn't find any travel books on Morocco, where I'm going on holiday next month. ___
5 My aunt, who is a poet, lives in London. ___
6 The girl whose father was rescued in the story was Spanish. ___
7 The fairy story, which was written in the 19th century, is still read today. ___
8 I couldn't watch the horror film which was on TV last night. ___

**6** ★★★ **Rewrite the sentences with *who, which, where* or *whose* and the clauses in brackets.**

0 The girl had long red hair. (mother is the heroine of the story)
*The girl, whose mother is the heroine of the story, had long red hair.*
1 The city is my hometown. (all the action took place)
______________________________
______________________________
2 The park is the scene of the crime. (the stolen documents were found)
______________________________
______________________________
3 The story is very sad. (is set in a future world)
______________________________
______________________________
4 The villain was in fact a good man. (disappeared at the end of the story)
______________________________
______________________________
5 The meeting was the start of the adventure. (took place in a forest)
______________________________
______________________________

## Relative clauses with *which*

→ SB p.53

**7** ★★☆ **Read the sentence pairs. Write a new (third) sentence so that it has the same meaning as the sentence pair. Use *which*.**

0 My parents used to read lots of stories to me when I was a child. I enjoyed this a lot.
*My parents used to read lots of stories to me when I was a child, which I enjoyed a lot.*
1 Their train arrived four hours late. This meant they missed the show.
______________________________
2 None of the students had studied for the test. This made the teacher really angry.
______________________________
3 My friend Lia reads ten books a month. I find this amazing.
______________________________
4 Most of my friends don't like the new Avengers film. I can't understand this.
______________________________

**8** ★★★ **Complete the sentences so that they are true for you.**

1 One of my friends ______________, which is very good news.
2 Lots of people in my street ______________, which I find annoying.
3 Not many people want to ______________, which I find a great pity.

### GET IT RIGHT!

### *that* vs. *which* in relative clauses

**Learners sometimes mistakenly use *that* in non-defining relative clauses.**

**We can use *which* or *that* in defining relative clauses.**

✓ *This is the solution* ***that*** *you are looking for.*
✓ *This is the solution* ***which*** *you are looking for.*

**We only use *which* in non-defining relative clauses.**

✓ *I'm in Brazil,* ***which*** *is a beautiful country.*
✗ *I'm in Brazil, ~~that~~ is a beautiful country.*

**Tick (✓) the sentences which can use *that* or *which*. Cross (✗) the sentences where only *which* is possible.**

1 Jade spent £100 on accessories, (which / that) is too much. ☐
2 I'd love to have a sports car (which / that) can go fast. ☐
3 Pete has a very old computer (which / that) has one of the first video games on it. ☐
4 We should buy the one (which / that) is cheaper. ☐
5 I won't be there, (which / that) is a problem. ☐

# VOCABULARY

## Elements of a story

→ SB p.51

**1 ★★☆ Complete the dialogue.**

characters | ending | hero
setting | plot | villain

**Josh** OK, ask me questions and try to guess the book I'm thinking of.

**Micky** Right. Where does the action take place?

**Josh** The [1] __________ for the story is an island, a few hundred years ago.

**Micky** What's it about?

**Josh** The [2] __________ is about a man whose ship was destroyed in a storm. He was the only person who survived and it's about his experiences on the desert island. The [3] __________ of the book is this man.
There aren't many other [4] __________ in the story because the man thinks he's alone on the island until one day when he meets a young man who also lives there.

**Micky** Who's the bad character then? Who's the [5] __________ ?

**Josh** There isn't one.

**Micky** And does it have a happy [6] __________ ?

**Josh** Yes, it does.

**Micky** I think it's *Robinson Crusoe* by Daniel Defoe.

**Josh** Well guessed! You're right. Now your turn.

**2 ★★★ Use the words in Exercise 1 to complete this dialogue about a story (or a film) that you like.**

**Micky** Where does the action take place?

**Me** The __________________ for the story is __________________ .

**Micky** What's it about?

**Me** The __________________ .

**Micky** Who is the hero or heroine of the book?

**Me** __________________ .

**Micky** Who's the bad character then? Who's the __________________ ?

**Me** __________________ .

**Micky** And does it have a happy __________________ ?

**Me** __________________ .

**Micky** I think it's __________________ by __________________ .

**3 ★★☆ Complete the sentences with the words in the list.**

blockbuster | influential | tradition
romance | anecdotes | special effects

1. Nelson Mandela's __________ book *A Long Walk to Freedom* made people aware of the inequalities between people.
2. The two main characters fall in love, and the film follows their __________ .
3. My friend tells lots of funny __________ about her family.
4. The novel, which was very successful, was made into a __________ film.
5. It was a science fiction story, so the film had lots of amazing __________ .
6. Our family has a __________ of telling stories on Christmas Day.

## Types of story

→ SB p.53

**4 ★☆☆ Match the book descriptions (a–g) with the genres (1–7).**

1. horror story ☐
2. (auto)biography ☐
3. romantic novel ☐
4. historical novel ☐
5. crime novel ☐
6. science fiction novel ☐
7. fantasy novel ☐

a *War Horse* by Michael Morpurgo is set during the First World War. Albert's father sells his horse Joey to the army and he goes into battle in France.

b In *Noughts and Crosses* by Malorie Blackman, Sephy is a cross and Callum is a nought. They fall in love, but in their world, noughts and crosses shouldn't be friends. Like Romeo and Juliet, their love is forbidden.

c *Frankenstein* by Mary Shelley, which was published in 1818, is often considered to be the first book of its genre. It's the story about how a strange creature was created by a scientist.

d *Northern Lights* by Philip Pullman is the first of three stories about Lyra's journey through different worlds. Everyone in the story has an animal which represents their personality.

e *Haunted* by R. L. Stine is about a girl who is visited by a ghost from the future. Together they try to stop the death of a boy from happening. Sometimes it's quite scary.

f *The London Eye Mystery* by Siobhan Dowd. Ted and Kat's cousin Salim gets on the London Eye. He never gets off again. Ted and Kat follow the clues across London to help the police to find their cousin.

g *Boy: Tales of Childhood* by Roald Dahl is about the author's childhood in Wales and his time at an English boarding school.

## REFERENCE

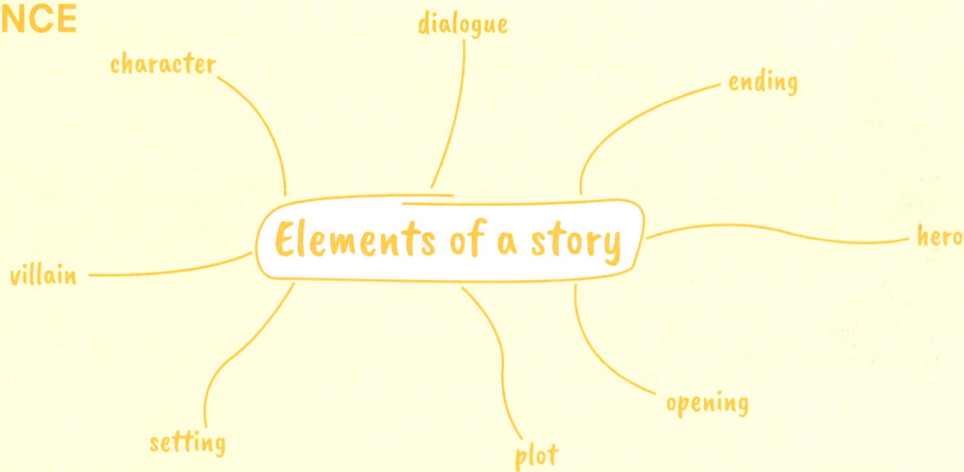

## VOCABULARY *EXTRA*

**1 Complete the mind map.**

chapter | essay | poetry | scene
short story | travel literature

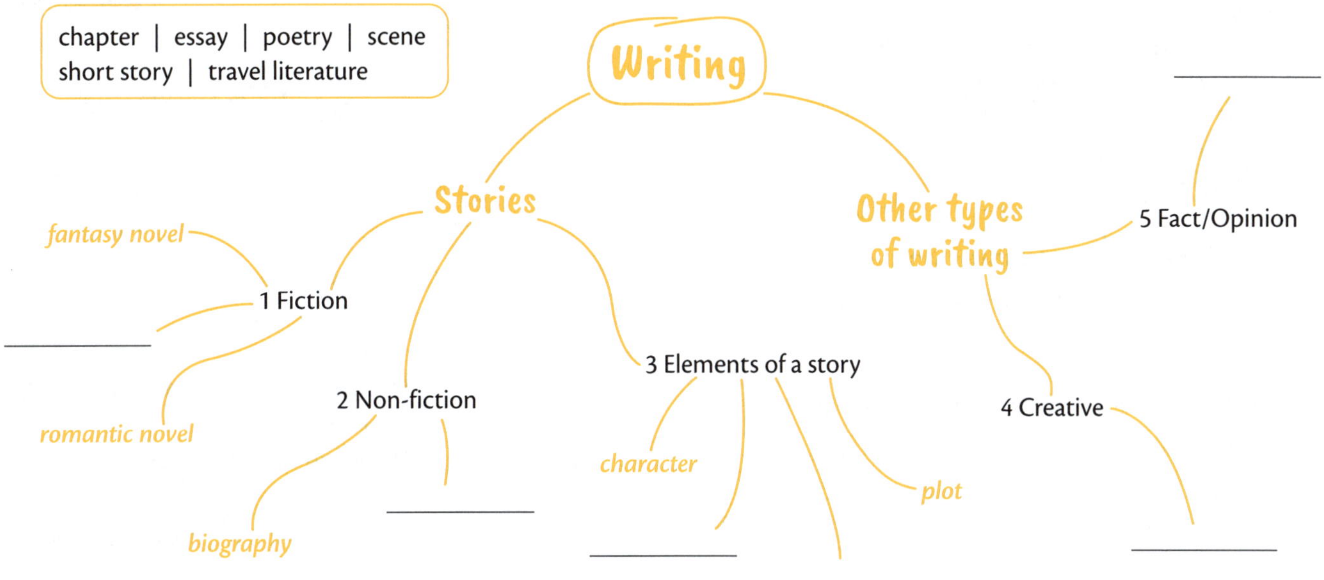


**2 Write an example that you know of each genre.**

1 short story: ________________
2 poetry: ________________
3 travel literature: ________________

**3 Complete the sentences with your own ideas.**

1 The last essay I wrote was about ________________ .
2 In my favourite book, the best scene is when ________________ .
3 I prefer books with *long* / *short* / *no* chapters because ________________ .

## MEET THE AUTHOR: JOHN GREEN

Today we're reading about … John Green! John, who is American, is one of the top authors of teenage literature in the world today. He's already won several book prizes and has a huge number of fans. Over 45 million of his print books have been sold worldwide and his stories have been translated into as many as 54 languages. Have you read any of his books? You might have seen *The Fault in Our Stars* (2014), which is the film version of one of his novels.

But that's not all! Oh, no! He is also well known for the online content which he creates and presents with his brother, Hank. *VlogBrothers*, which has been online since 2007, was their first YouTube channel. They post videos every week on a wide range of topics from comedy to serious world issues. They encourage their subscribers to join their community, and they are always creating new projects to bring teenagers together. *Crash Course*, which they started in 2011, is an educational channel whose aim is to teach topics in a way that is enjoyable and easy to understand.

## BIOGRAPHY

John Green was born in Indiana, but has lived in a number of different towns across the US. After studying Literature at university, he worked as a book reviewer in Chicago for a few years. His first book, *Looking for Alaska*, was published in 2005 and immediately won a prize for the best teen novel of the year. It is a romance set in a high school. He says that he was trying to remember his own experiences of bullying and feeling lonely while he was writing the story. Since then, he has written more novels and collections of short stories. He now combines writing with the online projects that he does with his brother.

## WHAT HIS READERS SAY

'His books are well written, his style is easy-going and he uses words that people my age use. At the same time, though, he also writes about world issues. That's why I love them.'

'I enjoy his books because the stories are believable and I can identify with the characters.'

'His novels are about normal young people – like me and my friends. People with good and bad sides to their personality. Nobody's perfect.'

'When I start a John Green book, I can't put it down until I've finished it! The story becomes part of my life. He's the best!'

'He understands what it's like to be young today. His stories are like real life and he writes how teenagers think.'

'John Green knows his readers are intelligent and that we can understand difficult stuff.'

## READING

**1 Read the article and answer the question.**

What two things is John Green well known for?

______________________________

**2 Read the article again and answer the questions.**

1 What kind of books does John Green write?

______________________________

2 How does he encourage teenagers to interact with each other?

______________________________

3 How successful was his first book? How do you know?

______________________________

4 What do readers say about the way he writes?

______________________________

5 What do readers like about the characters in his books?

______________________________

**3 CRITICAL THINKING Put the events from John Green's life in chronological order.**

- [ ] a A film of one of his books came out.
- [ ] b He began making videos to help students.
- [ ] c He had a bad time with people of his own age.
- [ ] d He published his first novel.
- [1] e He was born in Indiana, US.
- [ ] f He started working with his brother.
- [ ] g He wrote book reviews.
- [ ] h He went to university.

**4 Who is your favourite author? Write a short text to introduce the author and say why you like him/her.**

# DEVELOPING Writing

## A book review

1 INPUT **Look at the book cover and choose the genre you think it is. Then read the review and check.**

☐ horror story ☐ travel literature ☐ crime novel ☐ science fiction

1 *The Boy Who Biked the World* is a travel adventure. It was written by Alastair Humphreys, who completed a four-year bicycle ride around the world. In the story, the hero is a boy called Tom, who really wants to be an explorer. His favourite book is an atlas and he is more interested in adventurers than he is in footballers. One day, Tom finally sets off on his own adventure. He travels through Europe, the Middle East and Africa on his bicycle. The story is full of fascinating facts about the countries he travelled through, and the characters he meets.

2 One of my favourite parts was the opening of the book. Tom is caught daydreaming in his Maths class, which has happened to me, too. I loved Tom. My favourite thing about the book, however, was the funny illustrations and amusing little notes.

3 I would definitely recommend this book to anyone who loves geography and wants to go on an adventure. Although the book is for 8- to 12-year-olds, I think older kids will enjoy reading it, too, and it's perfect for students learning English. I give this book 4 out of 5 stars because it's very interesting.

★★★★☆

2 ANALYSE **Read the review again and answer the questions.**

Paragraph 1

1 What is the story about?

______________________________

______________________________

2 Where does the story take place?

______________________________

Paragraph 2

3 What happened to the main character that the writer of the review can identify with?

______________________________

______________________________

4 Did the writer of the review like the book? What was his/her favourite thing about it?

______________________________

Paragraph 3

5 Which age group does the writer of the review recommend the book for?

______________________________

6 How does the writer of the review rate the book? What are his/her reasons?

______________________________

3 **Match the paragraphs (1–3) with the content (a–c).**

Paragraph 1 ☐ Paragraph 2 ☐ Paragraph 3 ☐

a overall opinion and recommendations
b factual information and short summary of the plot
c the parts the reviewer enjoyed most

4 **Match the parts of the sentences.**

1 The **hero** or **heroine** of the book ☐
2 The **setting** ☐
3 The **opening sentence** ☐
4 It is very important to have a strong **ending** ☐
5 Some authors include jokes and amusing **dialogue** ☐
6 There may be several **characters** ☐

a should catch the reader's attention.
b which makes the story more entertaining.
c which satisfies the reader.
d is usually is the main character.
e is where the action takes place.
f who have different strong and weak points.

5 PLAN **Choose a book to review. Answer the questions in Exercise 2 about your book. Then use your answers to plan paragraphs, as in Exercise 3.**

6 PRODUCE **Write your book review (200–250 words). Use your plan from Exercise 5. Make sure you include all the points in the checklist.**

### ✓ CHECKLIST

☐ Arrange your ideas in paragraphs.
☐ Use some adjectives to make your review more interesting.
☐ Use long sentences with *which, who, whose* and *where.*

# LISTENING

**1** 5.01 **Read the sentences. Then listen and write the numbers of the conversations (1, 2 or 3).**

a He sees three footballers who play for his favourite football team. ☐
b She sees a famous actor whose name she has forgotten. ☐
c She sees a friend of a friend that she hasn't seen for months. ☐
d He was in a restaurant, where he was having a meal with his parents. ☐
e She was in a shop, where she was choosing a book. ☐
f She was shopping on Oxford Street. ☐

**2** 5.01 **Listen again and mark the sentences T (true) or F (false).**

1 Katie saw her best friend in the bookshop. ☐
2 Sometimes Amanda thinks about somebody and then they phone or text her. ☐
3 Jake's team won the football match on Saturday. ☐
4 Jake saw three Manchester United footballers in a restaurant. ☐
5 Sarah was shopping in Oxford Street when she saw the famous actor. ☐
6 The annoying thing was that Sarah can't remember the actor's address. ☐

# DIALOGUE

**3 Put the words in order to make sentences.**

1 never / what / believe / You'll / happened
______________________________?
2 strangest / me / to / happened / thing / The
______________________________.
3 me / finish / Let
______________________________.
4 the / That / annoying / thing / was
______________________________.
5 the / are / chances / What
______________________________?

**4 Put the dialogue in order.**

☐ **Matt** Well, I haven't seen her for ages, but yesterday I was thinking about her – and then this morning I saw her. What are the chances, eh?
☐ **Matt** Yes. And that's the annoying thing – you're always right!
☐ **Matt** The strangest thing happened to me this morning. I saw that girl Josie in town!
☐ **Matt** Yes, she does, but …
☐ **Iris** Let me finish. And she works in a shop in town, too. So, it isn't strange at all. Am I right?
☐ **Iris** You saw Josie? What's so strange about that?
☐ **Iris** The chances are really good, actually. I mean, she lives here, doesn't she? And …

**5 Complete the conversation with the words in the list. There is one extra word.**

annoying | believe | chances
finish | happened | strangest

**Lara** You'll never [1]______________ what happened last night. That film *Scared* was on TV! It was just the [2]______________ thing!
**Johnny** Why? What's so strange about that? They show *Scared* a lot on TV.
**Lara** Let me [3]______________. You see, I wanted to watch it on Sunday. I found the DVD at home, but the [4]______________ thing was that it didn't work any more.
**Johnny** Yes, I hate it when a DVD stops working properly.
**Lara** But then the next day, I switched the TV on – and there it was! What are the [5]______________ of that?
**Johnny** That is a little strange.

**PRONUNCIATION**
The schwa /ə/ in word endings
Go to page 119.

# TOWARDS B2 First for Schools

## READING AND USE OF ENGLISH
### Multiple choice

### EXAM GUIDE

**You will read a text followed by six multiple-choice questions with four options (A, B, C and D).**
**This part tests your detailed understanding of the text, including opinion, attitude, purpose, main ideas, details and gist. There are also questions to test your ability to understand meaning from context and follow the organisation of a text. The questions always follow the order of the text.**

- First, read the text for general meaning.
- Look at the first question and find the part of the text it refers to.
- Re-read the question and re-read the part of the text carefully.
- At this point, you may be able to eliminate at least two options.
- Continue to compare exactly what is written in the text with the options.
- Remember, you will never find the same words in the text and questions, so look out for words and phrases with a similar meaning.

1 **You are going to read a review of Jules Verne's classic novel *Around the World in 80 Days*. For questions 1–3, choose the answer (A, B, C or D) which you think fits best according to the text.**

HOME | REVIEWS | LATEST NEWS | BLOG

## Around the World in 80 Days

Jules Verne's novel *Around the World in 80 Days* has encouraged many people to travel around the world in unusual ways. It has also inspired several films, TV series, theatre productions and even board and video games.

So, where did Jules Verne get the idea from? Jules Verne told a reporter that he had been sitting in a café in Paris one day when he saw a newspaper advertisement for the first ever tourist trip around the world in 1872.

In Jules Verne's story, a wealthy English gentleman, Phileas Fogg, accepts a bet of £20,000 that he can travel round the world in 80 days. Phileas Fogg is a man who is very hard to please. For example, he fires his servant because he brings him some water to wash himself in that is 29°C instead of 30°C. He has a very strict routine and he follows it to the letter every day.

Fogg employs a new servant, Passepartout, and on Wednesday, 2 October 1872, they set off on their journey round the world. While he's in India, Fogg falls in love with an Indian girl, Aouda. The journey ends back in London with Fogg believing that he has arrived a day too late and that he has lost the bet. He tells Aouda that he cannot marry her now, as he's too poor. Passepartout learns that they have got the date wrong. The party travelled eastward, so they gained a day. Fogg hurries to his club and arrives there just in time to win the bet, and the story ends happily.

The story is an easy read. The amusing twists and turns of the plot keep readers entertained throughout. It is a romantic adventure story that I would strongly recommend to all my friends.

1 What gave Jules Verne the idea for the story?
- A He was looking for an unusual sort of holiday.
- B He had heard about a ship that had sailed around the world.
- C A man in a café in Paris mentioned the idea to him.
- D He had read about a round-the-world holiday.

2 What does the reviewer mean by: 'he follows it to the letter'?
- A He writes letters about what he does.
- B He never changes the order of his daily habits.
- C He writes notes to remind his servant what to do.
- D He writes all his appointments in a diary.

3 What does Passepartout do to help Phileas Fogg win the bet?
- A He introduces Aouda to Phileas Fogg.
- B He notices that Fogg has made a mistake.
- C He manages to reach London before Fogg.
- D He helps Fogg cheat so that he arrives in time.

# 6 THAT'S IMPOSSIBLE!

Grammar rap!

## GRAMMAR

### Present and past passive (review)

→ SB p.58

**1** ★☆☆ **Circle the correct options.**

1 The best sports cars *make* / *are made* in Italy.
2 The concert *showed* / *was shown* live on TV.
3 Lorna *posts* / *is posted* all her photos on social media.
4 The 2016 Olympics *held* / *were held* in Rio de Janeiro.
5 My dad *makes* / *is made* model trains as a hobby.
6 Letters *deliver* / *aren't delivered* on Sundays.
7 Jacob's really good at tennis. He *coaches* / *is coached* by his mum.
8 A girl in my class *won* / *was won* the talent show.

**2** ★★☆ **Complete the story with the past passive forms of the verbs in brackets.**

The school magic show was a complete success. All the tickets [0] *were sold* (sell) and some amazing tricks [1] ___________ (perform) by three very talented magicians. Here are some of my favourites. The headmaster [2] ___________ (saw) in half. A piece of paper [3] ___________ (turn) into hundreds of butterflies. Loads of gold coins [4] ___________ (find) behind the ears of Adam from 6E. And of course, a rabbit [5] ___________ (pull) out of a hat.

**3** ★★★ **Make questions in the present or past passive using the prompts.**

0 President Obama / elect
*When was President Obama elected* ?
1 America / discover by Columbus
When ___________________________?
2 The first electric car / build
When ___________________________?
3 BMW cars / make
Where ___________________________?
4 The Glastonbury music festival / hold
Where ___________________________?
5 2018 FIFA World Cup final / play
Where ___________________________?

**4** ★★★ **Write answers to the questions in Exercise 3. Use the clues in the list to help you.**

1492 | 2004 | ~~2008~~ | England
Germany | Moscow

0 *President Obama was elected in 2008.*
1 ___________________________
2 ___________________________
3 ___________________________
4 ___________________________
5 ___________________________

### *have something done*

→ SB p.59

**5** ★★☆ **Read about the hotel, then complete the letter.**

*Welcome to the*

**Ritz Carlton Hotel!**

**We have everything you need for the perfect weekend.**

0 We park your car on arrival.
1 We take your bags to your room.
2 A top chef cooks all your meals.
3 Room service brings your meals to your room.
4 We deliver tickets to top shows to your room.
5 We wash and iron all your clothes.
6 A top stylist cuts your hair for free.

*We had a wonderful weekend at the Ritz hotel.*

0 *We had our car parked for us when we arrived.*
1 ___________________________
2 ___________________________
3 ___________________________
4 ___________________________
5 ___________________________
6 ___________________________

6 ★★★ **What did these people have done yesterday? Write sentences.**

0 teeth / check

*He had his teeth checked.*

2 pizza / deliver

______________

______________

1 hair / dye

______________

______________

3 washing machine / fix

______________

______________

## Future and present perfect passive (review)

→ SB p.61

7 ★☆☆ **Complete the blog post.**

has been made | have been built
haven't been painted | haven't been widened
will be finished | will be put up
will be shown | will be sold

HOME | ABOUT | NEWS | CONTACT

It's only six months until the Olympic Games open here, but is the city ready? All of the stadiums [1] ______________ , but many of them [2] ______________ yet. The builders promise that they [3] ______________ before the opening day. The city airport [4] ______________ bigger to allow more planes to land here, but the roads from the airport into the city [5] ______________ and many people think the traffic will be a huge problem. Most of the tickets have been sold already and the organisers believe all of them [6] ______________ in the next few weeks. So if you're planning to come, make sure you get yours soon. Big screens [7] ______________ around the city and many events [8] ______________ live on them, so even if you can't get into the stadiums, you can enjoy the amazing Olympic atmosphere in this beautiful city.

8 ★★☆ **Complete the sentences with the present perfect passive form of the verbs in brackets.**

1 The windows are really dirty. They ______________ (not clean) for months.
2 Have you heard the news? The bank robbers ______________ (catch). They weren't happy!
3 The test ______________ (mark). You can find out your score online.
4 We've been waiting for an hour and our food still ______________ (not deliver).
5 Hey! Your bill ______________ (not pay) yet.

9 ★★★ **Rewrite the sentences using the passive.**

1 They'll play the final on Thursday.

______________________________

2 They won't pay me until next month.

______________________________

3 A famous actor will open the new shopping centre.

______________________________

4 They've closed the hospital.

______________________________

5 The earthquake has destroyed the whole city.

______________________________

6 No one has seen the mountain climbers for days.

______________________________

## GET IT RIGHT!

### Future passive

**Learners sometimes use the wrong tense where the future passive is needed, or use the future passive where it is not necessary.**

✓ *The changes will be introduced next year.*
✗ *The changes ~~will introduce~~ next year.*
✗ *The changes ~~are introduced~~ next year.*

**Correct the sentences.**

1 This money will use to develop the city.

______________________________

2 In the future the population will be increased.

______________________________

3 If the concert doesn't start soon, we are forced to leave.

______________________________

4 Please see the questionnaire which will be enclosed with this letter.

______________________________

5 The programme will show on Friday at 10 am.

______________________________

# VOCABULARY

## Extreme adjectives and modifiers

→ SB p.58

**1** ★☆☆ **Find ten extreme adjectives in the wordsearch. Then write them next to the non-extreme adjectives.**

| | | | | | | | | | | |
|---|---|---|---|---|---|---|---|---|---|---|
| G | R | E | A | T | T | L | U | F | W | A |
| N | P | G | B | E | N | I | B | V | W | D |
| I | Y | A | Q | R | A | K | C | G | J | E |
| T | T | E | F | R | I | O | O | K | E | L |
| A | V | T | C | I | L | P | E | P | N | I |
| N | W | U | O | B | L | N | L | B | O | G |
| I | G | N | I | L | I | O | B | C | R | H |
| C | R | I | I | E | R | F | O | P | M | T |
| S | U | M | N | I | B | E | F | K | O | E |
| A | A | B | L | I | H | Y | T | F | U | D |
| F | A | N | T | A | S | T | I | C | S | D |

interesting [1] ________________

happy [2] ________________

big [3] ________________

good (x3) [4] ________________, [5] ________________, [6] ________________

bad (x2) [7] ________________, [8] ________________

hot [9] ________________

small [10] ________________

**2** ★★☆ **Complete the sentences with extreme or ordinary adjectives.**

1 The play wasn't funny – it was absolutely h__________ .
2 Their new baby isn't s__________ – it's really tiny.
3 Our holiday wasn't just good – it was w__________ .
4 I wasn't s__________ – I was absolutely terrified.
5 Marcus isn't sad about his exam result – he's really m__________ .
6 It isn't c__________ outside – it's absolutely freezing.
7 The new airport isn't big – it's absolutely h__________ .
8 The rollercoaster ride wasn't just e__________ – it was thrilling.
9 The book wasn't just i__________ – it was fascinating.
10 Our trip wasn't just g__________ , it was amazing!

**3** ★★☆ **Circle the correct word, a or b. If both are possible, choose c (*both*).**

1 We spent our holiday in Mexico and it was ______ boiling.
   a very   b absolutely   c *both*
2 Have you seen their new house? It's ______ enormous!
   a very   b absolutely   c *both*
3 I enjoyed the film. I thought it was ______ funny.
   a very   b absolutely   c *both*
4 Put a jacket on. It's ______ cold outside.
   a very   b really   c *both*
5 I think the idea of time travel is ______ fascinating.
   a very   b absolutely   c *both*
6 She's an artist. Her paintings are ______ good.
   a very   b really   c *both*

## *make* and *do*

→ SB p.61

**4** ★☆☆ **Complete the sentences with *make* or *do*.**

1 It just doesn't __________ any sense to me.
2 There must be easier ways to __________ money.
3 Maybe it's time to __________ some housework.
4 Can you __________ your own way here? I'm a bit busy at the moment.
5 I don't usually __________ this kind of experiment, but I don't see what could go wrong.
6 Jack's been quite lonely since his best friend moved away. We should __________ time to see him this weekend.

**5** ★★☆ **Match the sentences in Exercise 4 with the pictures.**

## REFERENCE

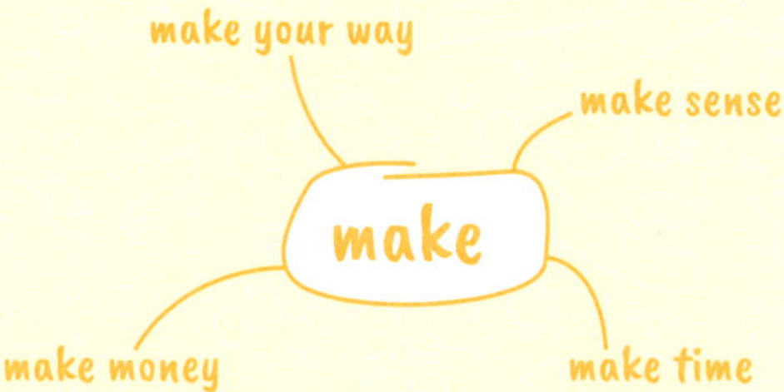


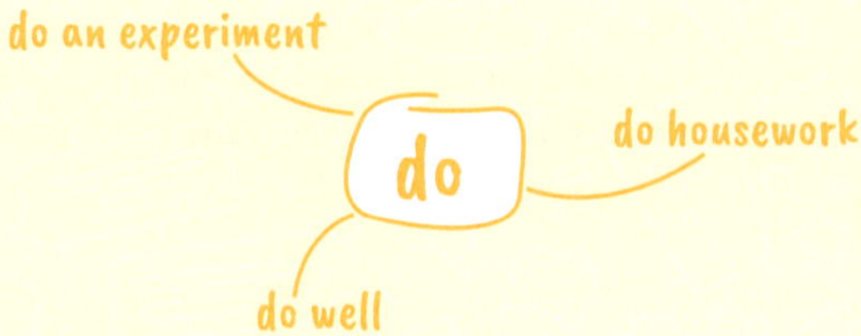


### MODIFIERS

absolutely really very

### EXTREME ADJECTIVES

| non-extreme | extreme |
|---|---|
| bad | awful, terrible |
| big | huge, enormous |
| cold | freezing |
| exciting | thrilling |
| funny | hilarious |
| good, great | fantastic, wonderful, brilliant, amazing |
| happy | delighted |
| hot | boiling |
| interesting | fascinating |
| sad | miserable |
| scared | terrified |
| small | tiny, minute |

## VOCABULARY *EXTRA*

**1 Look at the pictures and complete the phrases.**

fortune | mess | mistake

1 make a ___________

2 make a ___________

3 make a ___________

badly | best | research

4 do ___________

5 do ___________

6 do your ___________

**2 Complete the sentences with the phrases in Exercise 1. Use the correct form of *make* or *do*.**

1 Lexi's in the library. She ___________ for the Science project.
2 The Howard family worked hard at their business and they ___________ .
3 I ___________ such ___________ in the kitchen when I tried that new recipe!
4 Brady ___________ in the race. He came last.
5 The important thing is to ___________ even if you don't always get good marks.
6 I'm sorry, I ___________ . I thought you were someone else.

**3 Complete the sentences with your own ideas.**

1 If I made a fortune, I would ___________ .
2 In my family, ___________ makes the most mess because ___________ .
3 I'd like to do research into ___________ .
4 If I always did my best at school, ___________ .
5 The worst mistake I ever made was when ___________ .
6 When my favourite team plays badly, I ___________ .

# HOW DOES SHE DO IT?

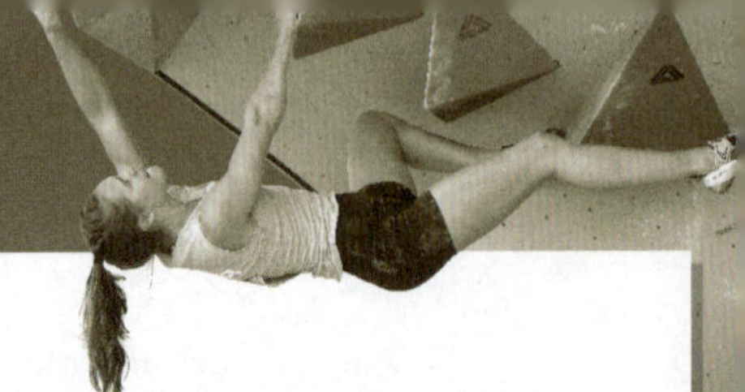

**1** ________________

In March 2019, at the age of 21, Margo Hayes became the first woman to complete three of the world's toughest climbs when she successfully reached the top of Papichulo in Spain. She had already climbed La Rambla, Spain and Biografie, France in 2017. She was only 19 when she became the first woman to climb La Ramba, which is considered one of the hardest rock faces in the world to climb. It seems this young woman from Boulder, which means 'big rock', Colorado was certain to become a record-breaking climber.

**2** ________________

She comes from a family of climbers, so that helps! Her grandfather was the expedition leader on a new route to the top of Mount Everest in 1983 and her father has climbed many of the rock walls of Yosemite Valley, California. But that's not enough. Talent and training play an essential part. Margo was a talented gymnast and at the age of six, she was aiming for an Olympic gold medal. Unfortunately, she was forced to give up gymnastics because of an injury, but by the age of ten, she had joined Team ABC, a well-known training project for young climbers in Texas.

**3** ________________

You won't be surprised to hear that Margo is extremely ambitious and very serious about her sport. She always has new goals she wants to achieve. She organises her training and climbs with the greatest precision. She believes detailed planning before a climb is essential for success. You can't risk making mistakes when you're high up on a rock face. Before she starts a climb, she chooses the route and plans every move she'll make on the rock face. She says it's an incredible feeling to finish a climb that you have been imagining in your head for so long. She enjoys her climbs and loves the feel of the rock as well as the unique views of fantastic scenery. Reaching the top is a thrilling experience.

**4** ________________

Margo's quite small – only 160 cm tall and around 45 kg in weight – but she's strong and can move her body quickly and easily into any position. She's sure that her gymnastics training has helped her climbing. She typically trains six days a week and spends 2–5 hours a day climbing both inside and outdoors. Running and working out in the gym are also included in her training programme. Her free time is spent mostly in the garden, where she keeps bees, but she also enjoys studying. She really likes Maths and Science.

What's her message for young climbers? 'Be curious and ask questions. Be kind and continually learn. Take risks and responsibility. Set goals and make a difference. Listen well and trust yourself.'

## READING

**1 Read the article. Match the headings (a–d) with the paragraphs (1–4).**

a Preparing the mind …
b How does she do it?
c … and the body
d Making history

**2 Read the article again. Correct the sentences.**

1 All Margo's record-breaking climbs were in Spain.
________________________________

2 She doesn't get ready for a climb in advance.
________________________________

3 She's the only one in her family who climbs.
________________________________

4 She has never tried any other sports.
________________________________

5 Margo spends all day, every day climbing.
________________________________

6 She discourages young people from doing her sport.
________________________________

**3** CRITICAL THINKING **Which statements would Margo probably agree with? Mark each statement yes (Y), no (N) or not sure (?). Give a reason.**

1 I often feel scared when I'm climbing. ______
Because ________________________________

2 I decide how to climb a rock when I get there. ______
Because ________________________________

3 Climbing is very hard work for the body and mind. ______
Because ________________________________

4 There's nothing better than the feeling when you reach the top. ______
Because ________________________________

5 I advise young climbers to climb with other people. ______
Because ________________________________

**PRONUNCIATION**
The /ʒ/ phoneme Go to page 119.

# DEVELOPING *Writing*

## Describing a process

1 **INPUT** **Read the text and match the steps in the process (A–F) with the photos (1–6).**

## HOW YOUR PLASTIC WATER BOTTLE IS RECYCLED

**If you can't avoid using a single-use plastic water bottle, the next best thing you can do is to recycle it. Find out about plastic recycling in your area. Do you have to put your bottle in a bin in the street or is plastic collected from outside your home? Find out which types of plastic can be recycled and follow the instructions carefully. Before sending your bottle for recycling, make sure it's clean.**

A Next, the bottles are cleaned and the paper labels, glue and other non-plastic materials are removed.

B The plastic pellets are sold to companies and will be made into things like synthetic clothes, floor mats, furniture and even recycling bins!

C When the plastic bottles have been collected, they are transported to the recycling centre.

D After drying, the bottles are melted and finally, the plastic is formed into pellets.

E The plastic is now broken down into tiny pieces and washed again because it must be perfectly clean.

F The bottles are sorted by machine into different bins depending on the type of plastic they are made from. Most bottles are made from PET. So, your water bottle goes with all the other objects made of this type of plastic. Plastics that can't be dealt with at the centre are sent to other specialised recycling centres.

2 **ANALYSE** **Match the words from the article (1–5) with the definitions (a–e).**

1 pellets ☐
2 melt ☐
3 sort ☐
4 process ☐
5 break down ☐

a heat something solid until it becomes liquid
b reduce to small pieces
c select and put with similar things
d small, hard pieces
e a series of actions

3 **PLAN** **Choose one of the processes below, or use your own idea. Do some research to find out about the process.**

- how bread is made
- how glass is recycled
- how ice cream is made

4 **Use the information you have found to make a plan.**

What you need to do first of all: ____________________

Steps in the process: ____________________

____________________

____________________

What happens to the end product: ____________________

## PRODUCE

5 **PRODUCE** **Write your description (about 200 words). Use your plan from Exercise 4. Make sure you include all the points in the checklist.**

### ✓ CHECKLIST

- Organise the process into short steps.
- Describe each step clearly.
- Explain the process in the correct order.
- Use verbs in the passive to describe the process.
- Link the steps with words like *firstly, next, after that, finally*.

## LISTENING

**1** 6.03 **Put the instructions for the card trick in order. Then listen and check.**

How to amaze your friends with a card trick:

☐ a 'I will now find your card from these ones on the table.'

☐ b 'Put your card on top of the bottom part of the pack.'

☐ c 'Choose any card from the pack. Don't tell me what it is.'

☐ d 'Is this your card?'

**2** 6.03 **Listen again. Complete the sentences with the missing sequencing words.**

1 ___________ , ask your friend to choose a card and look at it secretly.

2 ___________ , cut the pack of cards into two.

3 ___________ , ask your friend to put the card on the top of the bottom part of the pack.

4 ___________ , put the pack back together and go through the cards.

**3** 6.04 **Listen to the dialogue and put the pictures in order.**

How to pack a backpack.

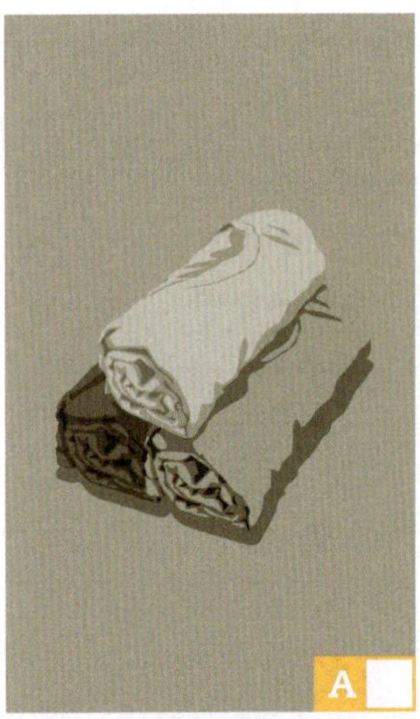

A ☐

C ☐

B ☐

D ☐

**4** 6.04 **Listen again and complete the instructions.**

1 ___________ , ___________ the trainers with small thing like socks, then place them at the bottom of the bag.

2 ___________ , ___________ the T-shirts and then roll up each one tightly.

3 ___________ ___________ , ___________ the rolls and place them on top of the trainers.

4 ___________ , ___________ them to fill in the empty spaces.

## DIALOGUE

**5** **Put the dialogue in the correct order.**

☐ **Emma** Five minutes. I'll remember that next time.

☐ **Emma** For about eight minutes.

☐ **Emma** No, I didn't. I didn't know I had to.

☐ **Emma** No, I didn't. I was far too hungry.

1 **Emma** Oh, dear. I've really made a mess of this egg. What did I do wrong?

☐ **Tim** Finally, did you wait for a minute before you started to eat it?

☐ **Tim** That's the first thing you should always do. How long did you cook it for?

☐ **Tim** That's far too long. Five minutes is all you need.

☐ **Tim** Did you wash the uncooked egg?

**6** **Complete the dialogue.**

after | finally | first | now | then

**Millie** Hi, Mum. Are you having trouble with something?

**Mum** Yes, I want to post this photo online but I don't know how to do it.

**Millie** OK, let me help you. [1]___________ click here where it says 'photo/video'.

**Mum** Ah, OK.

**Millie** [2]___________ that, click on 'upload photo'. Great! [3]___________ it's asking you which photo you want to upload.

**Mum** OK. I want this one here.

**Millie** OK, so just double-click on that. And [4]___________ write something about the photo if you want.

**Mum** All right.

**Millie** And [5]___________ click on 'post' and that's it! You've finished!

## READING AND USE OF ENGLISH

### Multiple choice

1 You are going to read an extract from *The Mind Map*. For questions 1–4, choose the answer (A, B, C or D) which you think fits best according to the text. Look back at the exam guide in Unit 5 on how to answer this question type.

## The Mind Map by David Morrison

Eva was thinking hard. She looked past Lucho. He turned and saw that she was looking at a little yellow bird which had landed on the grass behind him.

'I've seen this bird a lot recently,' he said. 'Maybe it's trying to help me.'

Eva corrected him, 'Maybe it's trying to help us, Lucho.'

Lucho smiled.

'Come on,' he said. 'Let's follow it.'

Lucho pulled Eva up by the hand and they followed the little bird over the grass, towards the door to the school building. When they reached the door, Mr Parra, the History teacher, was walking out of the building.

'How is your mind map going, you two?' Mr Parra asked.

Lucho was not sure what to say. They couldn't tell Mr Parra that the mind map seemed to be alive.

'It's going well, sir,' said Eva, 'but we've got a question to ask you. Do you know what "Ichua" means?'

Mr Parra smiled.

'Ichua is the name of the most important place in the world for the Kogi,' he explained. 'Their most important chiefs are buried there. The Kogi say it is a secret underground place full of gold, but historians don't believe that it's a real place. I see you have spent your time well in the library.'

It was Lucho's turn to ask a question. 'Mr Parra, do you know if there is a hotel in Santa Marta called the Hotel Continental?'

'Why?' Mr Parra was laughing. 'Are you planning a holiday?'

'No, sir,' answered Lucho, feeling a little stupid.

'Well, there was a hotel called the Hotel Continental in Santa Marta, near the port. But it closed a few years ago,' Mr Parra explained.

Eva watched the little yellow bird fly up to the roof of the library.

'Any more questions?' Mr Parra asked.

'Yes,' said Eva. 'Are birds important in Kogi stories?'

'Oh yes, Eva. There is a bird in every Kogi story. A bird brings a message to the jaguar or it helps the jaguar in its work. The jaguar, of course, is the most important animal for the Kogi and for many other tribes. The jaguar looks after the Kogi. Without the help of the jaguar, the Kogi believe, the sun would not rise, plants would not grow and rain would not fall.'

Mr Parra smiled.

'I must say I am very pleased that you have been working so well. Don't forget to put all the information on your mind map and bring it to class on Monday.'

Eva and Lucho watched Mr Parra as he walked away from the school building. Lucho's head was full of questions. Had he dreamed that the mind map had grown? Had he added new words in his sleep? But then, why had the message 'TAKE IT BACK' appeared on the computer screen and on Eva's mobile phone? What did the pendant want? Did he have to take it back to Ichua? But how could he? Mr Parra had said that Ichua probably wasn't a real place.

1 Eva corrects Lucho about the bird because ...

- A he doesn't know what kind of bird it is.
- B she wants him to know that she's going to help him.
- C he misunderstands how the bird is trying to help them.
- D she thinks they should follow it.

2 Which of these statements is not true about Mr Parra?

- A He is one of their teachers at the school.
- B He gave Lucho and Eva the mind map homework.
- C He is pleased the students are taking their homework seriously.
- D He was walking in the same direction as Lucho and Eva.

3 What do we learn about the Kogi from their stories?

- A They are the only tribe for whom the jaguar is important.
- B They like birds, especially yellow ones.
- C There are jaguars in all their traditional stories.
- D Nature is a very important part of their culture.

4 What does the final paragraph suggest about Lucho?

- A He thinks he might be doing things in his sleep.
- B He wanted to ask Mr Parra more questions.
- C He's sure that he's started to imagine things.
- D He's really confused about the mind map mystery.

# CONSOLIDATION

## LISTENING

1 6.05 **Listen and circle the correct option: A, B or C.**

1 How long did the story for homework have to be?
 A 50,000 words
 B 5,000 words
 C 500 words
2 What did the story have to be about?
 A ghosts
 B crime
 C romance
3 If the teacher likes his story, the boy might …
 A help the girl to write one.
 B send it to a website.
 C publish it in the school magazine.

2 6.05 **Listen again and answer the questions.**

1 Why does the boy enjoy homework that involves writing a story?
______________________
2 How does he usually get an idea for a story?
______________________
3 How long did he spend writing the story?
______________________
4 Where did he get the idea for the story from?
______________________
5 What does the girl want the boy to do?
______________________

## GRAMMAR

3 **Circle the correct options.**

1 There was an accident and a lot of people *hurt* / *were hurt*.
2 These books *are written* / *were written* a very long time ago.
3 The new school *will be opened* / *will open* by the mayor tomorrow.
4 I don't understand computers, so I always *repair my computer* / *have my computer repaired* when there's a problem.
5 In the last two years, they *have built* / *have been built* a lot of new buildings here.
6 I went to the hairdresser's and *cut my hair* / *had my hair cut*.
7 Thirty people *have taken* / *have been taken* to hospital.
8 Doctors *operate* / *are operated* on more than 30 people here every day.

4 **Complete the sentences with *who, whose, where, that* or *which*.**

1 That's the school ____________ Dad taught.
2 Mr Newson, my Maths teacher, is someone ____________ I've learned a lot from.
3 I've forgotten ____________ book this is.
4 Newquay, ____________ is a small town in the south of England, is where my sister lives.
5 Careful, it's the dog ____________ tried to bite me.
6 Look, that's the guy ____________ was on the news last night.

## VOCABULARY

5 **Complete the dialogue.**

characters | crime | ending
hero | plot | setting | villain

**Alex** I read a good book last week. It was called *Detective Grange Investigates*.
**Giorgia** What's it about?
**Alex** Well, it's a [1]____________ novel. The [2]____________ is London at the end of the 19th century. And of course the [3]____________ of the story is Detective Grange.
**Giorgia** And what's the [4]____________ ?
**Alex** Well, it's about how Grange finds out who stole some money from a rich family's house. Grange meets all kinds of different people – there are some funny [5]____________ and some horrible ones! The worst person is Dangerous Dan – he's the [6]____________ of the story. At the end …
**Giorgia** No, no! Don't tell me the [7]____________ ! I might read the book myself!

6 **Complete the words.**

1 I thought the play was a____________ fantastic.
2 Some of the things were so funny – in fact, they were h____________ .
3 One actor said something that didn't make s____________ to me, but it didn't matter.
4 One actress was very young, but she did very well – she was b____________ , in fact.
5 She took the part of the evil v____________ in the play.
6 We were all very happy that we saw the play – in fact, we were d____________ !
7 The theatre was very big – I've never seen such an e____________ theatre in my life!
8 It was a bit noisy, so sometimes I couldn't hear the d____________ between the actors very well.

## DIALOGUE

**7** 6.06 **Complete the conversation with the phrases in the list. There are two extra phrases. Then listen and check.**

it isn't strange | let me finish | the strangest thing happened | what are the chances | you'll never believe | what's strange | that was the annoying thing | I don't understand

**Jay** [1]________________ to me last weekend. I had a dream on Sunday about being lost in a completely empty city.

**Sara** [2]________________ about that? People have dreams all the time – including about being lost.

**Jay** I know. But the next day on TV there was a film where a woman was lost in an empty city, too – just like my dream. [3]________________ of that happening?

**Sara** Well, not huge, I suppose. But it's only a coincidence, isn't it?

**Jay** Well, [4]________________. There's more! You see, in the film, when the woman was lost, she started to hear a loud noise, like a wild animal or something. And [5]________________ what happened next! A tiger suddenly appeared in front of her! Now, in my dream, I started to hear a strange noise, too!

**Sara** And did a tiger appear in your dream?

**Jay** Well, [6]________________. You see, just when the noise started, I woke up! So I don't know if there was a tiger in my dream or not. But my cat was lying on my bed!

## READING

**8** **Read the book review. Choose the correct answer (A, B or C).**

1 What kind of stories was Paul Auster looking for?
   A real stories that weren't too long
   B the listeners' favourite stories
   C true stories about famous people

2 Why did he decide to put the stories in the book?
   A because he wanted to share them all with the public
   B to make some money
   C because he couldn't read them all out on the radio

3 What does the reviewer recommend?
   A to read the book from start to finish
   B to pick and choose stories from the book
   C to only read the sections you are most interested in

4 What is the reviewer's overall opinion of the book?
   A She liked it because the stories are so well written.
   B She liked it because some of the stories are very moving.
   C She liked another book of real-life stories more.

### Review: True Tales of American Life

In 1999, the writer Paul Auster was asked if he would contribute stories to America's National Public Radio. But Auster decided to ask listeners to send in their stories instead. He wanted true stories that sounded more like fiction. They could be about anything at all; they just had to be true and short. The chosen ones would be read out on the radio.

To Auster's surprise, more than 4,000 listeners sent in their stories. It would have been impossible to read them all on the radio, so Auster took almost 200 stories and put them together – and this is the book.

I liked some things about the collection, but others not so much. Because the stories were written by ordinary people, they aren't always well written (I hate to think what the ones that weren't included were like!). And I didn't think the categorisation into sections like Families, Objects, Strangers, or Animals worked. It means that if you read one story after the other, it can become a bit repetitive. What's more, some of the stories fall into more than one category.

As with any book of short stories, they don't have to be read in a particular order. You can just choose one here and there whenever you feel like it. You don't have to read the whole book straight through, and that's probably the best thing to do here, too.

What's great about these stories is their veracity – they're all true, no matter how unbelievable (and some of them really are incredible). One or two of the stories left me almost in tears, they were so moving.

So, overall, it's worth buying and reading. If you're into real-life stories like these, I'd also recommend a collection called *The Moth* – more on that next time.

## WRITING

**9** **Write a review of a story that you like (from a film, TV programme, book, or even a true story about you or a friend). Write 150–200 words.**

# PRONUNCIATION

## UNIT 1

### Linking words with *up*

**1 Match the sentence halves.**

0 I find it difficult to get [d]
1 I've got too much homework. I spend [ ]
2 Hi, Kelly! What's [ ]
3 Now that it's winter, why don't you take [ ]
4 Last night we stayed [ ]
5 We'd like you to come, but it's [ ]
6 Have you seen Jim lately? I wonder what he's [ ]
7 She's ninety now and isn't [ ]
8 I don't want to move. If it was [ ]
9 The test has started. Please pick [ ]

a up? You look really sad!
b up your pen and start writing.
c up to me, I'd stay here.
d up early in the morning.
e up to going for long walks.
f up skiing? It's so much fun!
g up to three hours a night doing it.
h up late talking about our holidays.
i up to these days.
j up to you.

**2** 🔊 1.01 **Listen, check and repeat.**

**3 Write the phrases with *up* in the column that corresponds to the correct linked sound.**

| | | |
|---|---|---|
| **t** *pronounced* | *get up* | ______ |
| **d** *pronounced* | ______ | ______ |
| **k** *pronounced* | ______ | ______ |
| **s** *pronounced* | ______ | ______ |
| **z** *pronounced* | ______ | ______ |

**4** 🔊 1.02 **Listen, check and repeat.**

## UNIT 2

### Initial consonant clusters with /s/

**1 Complete the words with the correct letters. These are all /s/ consonant clusters.**

0 I like the top that boy's wearing – the one with black and white *str*ipes .
1 A ____ong wind was blowing from the east.
2 Her favourite shapes are circles and ____ares.
3 They heard a loud ____ash as the rock fell into the river.
4 She had a headache from looking at the computer ____een all morning.
5 The fire ____ead quickly because of the heat and wind.
6 The people were ____eaming on the roller coaster ride.

**2** 🔊 2.01 **Listen, check and repeat.**

## UNIT 3

### Strong and weak forms: /ɒv/ and /əv/

**1 Match the questions and answers.**

0 What do you always buy the same brand **of**? [c]
1 What are your favourite shoes made **of**? [ ]
2 What kinds **of** clothes do you have the most **of**? [ ]
3 Do you have a lot **of** gadgets? [ ]
4 Which **of** your gadgets do you use the most? [ ]

a My mobile phone. Most **of** my friends have one so we text each other a lot.
b They're made **of** leather and they've got rubber soles.
c Chocolate! I love the taste **of** Black & Green.
d I'm quite a casual person. I've got a lot **of** jeans and T-shirts.
e Not really. Most **of** them, like the computer and games console, belong to the whole family.

**2** 🔊 3.01 **Listen and check.**

**3 Underline the weak forms (/əv/) and circle the strong forms (/ɒv/) of the word *of* in the sentences.**

**4** 🔊 3.01 **Listen, check and repeat.**

## UNIT 4
### Consonant–vowel word linking

1 Underline the words where the final consonant is linked to the vowel sound in the next word.

0 I like that film. It's about two friends who go travelling.
1 I didn't find out who wrote the message.
2 My dad doesn't walk to work anymore.
3 Her family lived in Paris before they came to London.
4 They lost everything when their flat burned down.
5 Jenny's mum gets angry when she doesn't tidy her room.
6 Can we have our break now?
7 It was so difficult to make up my mind!
8 His friends felt awful when Tom told them they'd forgotten his birthday.
9 The climb was difficult, so she gave up before she got to the top.

2 4.02 Listen, check and repeat.

3 Write the phrases with the linked sound in the correct column.

| *t* pronounced | *d* pronounced | *k* pronounced | *s* pronounced | *v* pronounced |
|---|---|---|---|---|
| ______ | ______ | ______ | *it's about* | ______ |
| ______ | ______ | ______ | ______ | ______ |

4 4.03 Listen, check and repeat.

## UNIT 5
### The schwa /ə/ in word endings

1 Complete the words with the correct spelling.

-ure (x1) | -ent (x2) | -ion (x3) | -ate (x1)
-ous (x3) | -on (x1) | -an (x1) | -al (x3)
-el (x1) | -ul (x1) | -er (x1) | -or (x1)

1 The story will capture your attent____ and imaginat____ .
2 It's a historic____ nov____ about a desper____ and danger____ man.
3 Many fam____ people live in centr____ Lond____.
4 The hospit____ provided informat____ about the accid____.
5 They used a pict____ of a beautif____ old wom____ for the advertisem____.
6 She was the obvi____ choice to direct anoth____ horr____ film.

2 Although the spelling is different, all of these words end with the same vowel sound. What is it?

3 5.02 Listen, check and repeat.

## UNIT 6
### The /ʒ/ phoneme

1 6.01 Listen and circle the one word in each group which doesn't have the /ʒ/ phoneme.

| | A | B | C | D |
|---|---|---|---|---|
| 0 | A casual | B usually | C revision | D caution (circled) |
| 1 | A sabotage | B version | C engine | D camouflage |
| 2 | A Asia | B Russia | C treasure | D collision |
| 3 | A magician | B illusionist | C occasion | D explosion |
| 4 | A pleasure | B television | C pleasant | D decision |
| 5 | A confusion | B revision | C measure | D permission |
| 6 | A unusual | B mansion | C vision | D leisure |
| 7 | A exposure | B usual | C fashion | D diversion |
| 8 | A erosion | B decoration | C illusion | D invasion |

2 6.01 Listen again, check and repeat.

3 Complete the sentences with the words in the list.

Asia | casual | collision | decision | illusionist
occasion | pleasure | ~~revision~~ | usually | version

0 I need to do a lot of *revision* because we have a test tomorrow.
1 I don't ____________ have to study more than an hour at the weekend.
2 **A** Thank you for helping me today.
**B** It's a ____________ .
3 There was a terrible ____________ on the motorway today, but no one was hurt.
4 Dynamo is an amazing ____________ .
5 I'm saving this beautiful dress to wear for a special ____________ .
6 I liked that film, but I prefer the original ____________ .
7 I've always wanted to travel around ____________ .
8 It wasn't an easy ____________ , but I finally chose a career in biology.
9 She prefers ____________ clothes and wears jeans and T-shirts most of the time.

4 6.02 Listen, check and repeat.

# GRAMMAR REFERENCE

## UNIT 1

### Present tenses (review)

**To talk about the present, we mostly use the following tenses: present simple, present continuous, present perfect simple and present perfect continuous.**

1 **We use the present simple to talk about facts and give opinions, and to talk about regular habits.**

*It **takes** around four minutes to boil an egg.* (fact)
*I **think** this is awful.* (opinion)
*I usually **go** to bed around 11 o'clock.* (habit)

2 **We use the present continuous to talk about what's happening at or around the time of speaking.**

*What **are** you **doing**?*
*A TV company **is making** a programme about life plans.*

3 **We use the present perfect simple to talk about past actions and experiences but without saying exactly when. This tense links the present and the past and we often use it when a past event has an effect on the present.**

*She**'s read** lots of articles about this and she**'s learned** a lot.*
*The storm **has caused** a lot of flooding in the town.*

4 **We use the present perfect continuous to talk about actions that started in the past and are still happening.**

*I**'ve been trying** to get fitter for several weeks now.*

### Future tenses (review)

**To talk about the future, we mostly use the following tenses: present continuous, *will* / *won't* (*do*) and *going to* (*do*).**

1 **We often use the present continuous to talk about future plans and arrangements.**

*I**'m having** a guitar lesson tomorrow morning.*

2 **We often use *will* / *won't* (*do*) to make predictions.**

*She's very clever – I'm sure she**'ll do** really well at university.*
*This is the dry time of year – it **won't rain** again until September.*

3 **We often use *going to* (*do*) to talk about intentions.**

*Next year, I**'m going to start** university.*
*Where **are** you **going to** go on holiday next year?*

## UNIT 2

### Narrative tenses (review)

**To talk about the past and to tell narratives, we mostly use the following tenses: past simple, past continuous, past perfect simple and past perfect continuous.**

1 **We use the past simple to talk about actions that happened at one moment in the past, or were true at one time in the past.**

*I **fell** over.*
*People **didn't have** easy lives two hundred years ago.*

2 **We use the past continuous to describe ongoing actions or situations around a time in the past.**

*I **was running** really fast (and I fell over).*
*Thousands of people **were living** in very enclosed spaces.*

**We also use the past continuous to talk about an ongoing action that was interrupted by another.**

*The fire started while people **were sleeping**.*

3 **We use the past perfect to describe an event that happened before another.**

*The weather **had been** very hot when the fire broke out.*
*When we arrived, the film **had** already **started**.*

4 **We use the past perfect continuous to talk about ongoing actions that began before another action in the past.**

*When I finished the race I was exhausted because I**'d been running** for more than two hours.*
*He couldn't answer the teacher's question because he **hadn't been listening**.*

### *would* and *used to*

1 **We use the expression *used to* + verb to talk about habits and customs in the past that are no longer true.**

*My mum **used to play football**.* (= *My mum played football in the past but she doesn't any more.*)
*When I was a kid, I **used to listen** to pop music.* (= *That was my habit but I don't do this any more.*)

2 **It is also possible to use *would* + verb to talk about habits and customs in the past.**

*My dad **would cook** chicken every Sunday.* (= *This was a custom of my dad's.*)
*At school, I **would** always **ask** the teacher questions.* (= *This was a habit of mine when I was a schoolchild.*)

3 The difference between *used to* and *would* is that we can only use *would* for repeated actions – we cannot use it for a permanent state or situation.

*He **used to be** a police officer.* (a permanent state)
*When I was little, I **used to play** in the garden a lot.* (a repeated action)

# UNIT 3

## *(don't) have to / ought to / should(n't) / must*

1 We use *have to* to say 'this is important or necessary'. We use *must* to say that we, or other people, have an obligation to do something.

*Our train leaves at 7 o'clock, so I **have to get up** early.*
*In our house you **must take** your shoes **off** when you come in.*
*You **must try** to work harder, Jack.*

2 We use *don't have to* to say this is NOT important or necessary.

*You **don't have to come** with us if you don't want to.*

3 We use *should* or *ought to* to tell someone that something is a good idea.

*At the beach you **should put** some sun cream on.*
*That wasn't a nice thing to say – you **ought to say** sorry.*

Remember: *ought to* isn't as frequent as *should*. It is used mostly in writing, and the negative form is rare.

4 We use *shouldn't* to tell someone that something is not a good idea.

*You **shouldn't spend** so much money on clothes.*

## *had ('d) / better (not)*

We use *had / 'd better (not)* to advise or warn people in strong terms. It is used to tell people about negative results in the future if they do / don't do something.

The form is always past (*had*) and it is often shortened to *'d*.

*You**'d better** hurry up (or you'll miss the train).*
*He**'d better not** say that again (or I will be very angry).*

## *can('t) / must(n't)*

1 When we want to talk or ask about permission, we often use the modal verb *can / can't*.

*You **can go** to the party but you **can't stay** late.*
***Can** I **borrow** your phone to make a call?*

2 To say what isn't allowed, we use *can't* or *mustn't*.

*You **can't park** here.* (This is a fact / rule.)
*You **mustn't leave** your things on the floor!* (The speaker isn't allowing something.)

# UNIT 4

## First and second conditional (review)

1 We use the first conditional to talk about real situations and their consequences. It consists of two clauses. The *if* + present simple clause introduces the possible situation or condition. The *will / won't* clause gives the result or consequence.

*If you **leave** that door open, the cat **will get** out.*
*If we **don't leave** now, we **won't get** to school on time.*

2 We use the second conditional to talk about hypothetical or very unlikely situations and their (imaginary) consequences. It consists of two clauses. The *if* + past simple clause introduces the hypothetical situation. The *would* clause gives the imagined result or consequence.

*If I **had** a cat, I**'d call** it Max. (I don't have a cat.)*
*If we **didn't have** a cat, we **wouldn't have to** spend money on cat food. (We have a cat and we need to spend money on cat food.)*

## Time conjunctions

We can join ideas about future actions or situations using words such as: *if, unless, until, when, as soon as*.

When we use these words, we use them with the present simple tense (not *will / won't*), even though the clause refers to the future.

*She won't be happy **if** you **forget** her birthday.*
*We'll be late **unless** we **leave** now.*
*I won't stop asking you **until** you **tell** me.*
*They'll be hungry **when** they **get** here.*
*I'll call you **as soon as** I **finish** this work.*

## *wish* and *if only*

1 We use *wish* or *if only* + past simple to say that we would like a present situation to be different from what it actually is.

*I **wish** I **had** more friends. (I don't have many friends.)*
*My friends **wish** they **were** rich. (They aren't rich.)*

2 We use *wish / if only* + *could* to talk about wanting to have the ability or permission to do something.

*I **wish** I **could** speak Italian.*
***If only** you **could** come with me.*

3 If there is a situation we don't like (for example, someone is doing or always does something that annoys us), we can use *wish / if only* + *would(n't)*.

*I wish you **would knock** before coming into my room.*
*If only he **wouldn't talk** about football all the time!*

## Third conditional (review)

**We use the third conditional to talk about how things might have been different in the past. The third conditional is formed with *If* + past perfect + *would (not) have* + past participle. The third conditional talks about impossible conditions (because the past cannot be changed).**

*If I'd been careful, I **wouldn't have dropped** the camera.*
(I wasn't careful, so I dropped the camera.)

*If you **hadn't woken** me up, I **would have slept** for hours.*
(You woke me up so I didn't sleep for hours.)

# UNIT 5

## Relative pronouns

**We use relative pronouns to start a relative clause.**

1 **To refer to people, we use *who* or *that*.**

*He's a writer. He wrote that fantastic story.*
➜ *He's the writer **who** / **that** wrote that fantastic story.*

2 **To refer to things, we use *which* or *that*.**

*It's a great story. It was made into a film.*
➜ *It's a great story **that** / **which** was made into a film.*

3 **To refer to possessions, we use *whose*.**

*I know a boy. His phone is broken.*
➜ *I know a boy **whose** phone is broken.*

4 **To refer to places, we use *where*.**

*This is the town. I was born here.*
➜ *This is the town **where** I was born.*

## Defining and non-defining relative clauses

**There are two kinds of relative clause: <u>defining</u> and <u>non-defining</u>.**

1 **A defining relative clause identifies an object, a person, a place or a possession. We need this information to know who or what is being talked about. When we write these sentences, we don't use any commas.**

*The woman was a genius. She wrote this book.*
➜ *The woman **who wrote this book** was a genius.*
*I saw a film last night. The film was terrible.*
➜ *The film **that I saw last night** was terrible.*

2 **We use non-defining relative clauses to add extra information which is not needed to understand the sentence. We put commas around these clauses when we write them. They are rarely used in conversational language.**

*My uncle lives in Sydney. He's a very successful writer.* ➜
*My uncle, who lives in Sydney, is a very successful writer.*

## Relative clauses with *which*

1 **When we want to refer back to a whole idea or clause, we use the relative pronoun *which*.**

*He went into the desert alone. It was a dangerous thing to do.*
➜ *He went into the desert alone, **which** was a dangerous thing to do.*

2 **We cannot use *that* or *what* in this way – only *which*.**

*Stephen King has sold millions of books, **which** (~~**that**~~ / ~~**what**~~) has made him very rich.*

# UNIT 6

## Present and past passive (review)

1 **We use the passive (present or past) to say what happens or happened to the subject of the sentence. Often the cause of the action is unknown or unimportant.**

2 **We form the passive with a form of the verb *be* and the past participle of the verb.**

*In Canada, English and French **are spoken**.*
*The roof of the house **was destroyed** in the storm.*

3 **We use the preposition *by* to say who or what does the action, but only if this is important.**

*My bike was stolen. (We don't know, or it isn't important, who stole it.)*
*The magic show was watched **by** over 500 people. (It's important to say who watched the show.)*

## *have something done*

1 **We use the structure *have something done* when we talk about someone else doing a function or service for us.**

*My granny's very old, so she has **her meals cooked** for her. (Another person cooks her meals for her.)*
*They **had their car repaired**. (They paid a mechanic to repair their car.)*

2 **It is formed with *have* + noun + past participle.**

*I **had my phone repaired** last week.*

3 **In less formal contexts, *get* often replaces *have*.**

*I'm going to **get my hair done** for the party tonight.*

## Future and present perfect passive (review)

1 **The future passive is formed with *will be / won't be* + past participle.**

*The new supermarket **will be opened** next week by a famous TV actor.*

2 **The present perfect passive is formed with *have / has (not) been* + past participle.**

*The streets of our town look awful – they **haven't been cleaned** for two weeks.*

# IRREGULAR VERBS

| Base form | Past simple | Past participle |
| --- | --- | --- |
| be | was / were | been |
| beat | beat | beaten |
| become | became | become |
| begin | began | begun |
| bite | bit | bitten |
| blow | blew | blown |
| break | broke | broken |
| breed | bred | bred |
| bring | brought | brought |
| build | built | built |
| burn | burned / burnt | burned / burnt |
| buy | bought | bought |
| can | could | – |
| catch | caught | caught |
| choose | chose | chosen |
| come | came | come |
| cost | cost | cost |
| cut | cut | cut |
| do | did | done |
| draw | drew | drawn |
| dream | dreamed / dreamt | dreamed / dreamt |
| drink | drank | drunk |
| drive | drove | driven |
| eat | ate | eaten |
| fall | fell | fallen |
| feel | felt | felt |
| fight | fought | fought |
| find | found | found |
| flee | fled | fled |
| fly | flew | flown |
| forget | forgot | forgotten |
| forgive | forgave | forgiven |
| freeze | froze | frozen |
| get | got | got |
| give | gave | given |
| go | went | gone |
| grow | grew | grown |
| hang | hung | hung |
| have | had | had |
| hear | heard | heard |
| hide | hid | hidden |
| hit | hit | hit |
| hold | held | held |
| hurt | hurt | hurt |
| keep | kept | kept |
| know | knew | known |
| lay | laid | laid |
| lead | led | led |
| learn | learned / learnt | learned / learnt |
| leave | left | left |

| Base form | Past simple | Past participle |
| --- | --- | --- |
| lend | lent | lent |
| let | let | let |
| lie | lay | lain |
| light | lit | lit |
| lose | lost | lost |
| make | made | made |
| mean | meant | meant |
| meet | met | met |
| pay | paid | paid |
| put | put | put |
| quit | quit | quit |
| read | read | read |
| ride | rode | ridden |
| ring | rang | rung |
| rise | rose | risen |
| run | ran | run |
| say | said | said |
| see | saw | seen |
| seek | sought | sought |
| sell | sold | sold |
| send | sent | sent |
| set | set | set |
| shake | shook | shaken |
| shoot | shot | shot |
| show | showed | shown |
| shut | shut | shut |
| sing | sang | sung |
| sink | sank | sunk |
| sit | sat | sat |
| sleep | slept | slept |
| speak | spoke | spoken |
| spend | spent | spent |
| spill | spilled / spilt | spilled / spilt |
| spread | spread | spread |
| stand | stood | stood |
| steal | stole | stolen |
| stick | stuck | stuck |
| strike | struck | struck |
| swim | swam | swum |
| swing | swung | swung |
| take | took | taken |
| teach | taught | taught |
| tell | told | told |
| think | thought | thought |
| throw | threw | thrown |
| understand | understood | understood |
| wake | woke | woken |
| wear | wore | worn |
| win | won | won |
| write | wrote | written |

# ACKNOWLEDGEMENTS

**Acknowledgements**

The authors and publishers acknowledge the following sources of copyright material and are grateful for the permissions granted. While every effort has been made, it has not always been possible to identify the sources of all the material used, or to trace all copyright holders. If any omissions are brought to our notice, we will be happy to include the appropriate acknowledgements on reprinting and in the next update to the digital edition, as applicable.

**Key**: U = Unit, WU = Welcome Unit.

**Text**

**U6**: Text from *The Mind Map Level 3 Lower-intermediate* by David Morrison, Cambridge English: Towards FCE. Copyright © Cambridge University Press - All rights reserved.

**Photography**

The following photographs are sourced from Getty Images.

**WU**: FatCamera/E+; kali9/iStock/Getty Images Plus; **U1**: Westend61; NoSystem images/E+; monkeybusinessimages/iStock/Getty Images Plus; **U2**: duncan1890/ DigitalVision Vectors; Mark Coggins/Moment Open; S. Greg Panosian/E+; Paola Giannoni/E+; **U3**: jojoo64/iStock/Getty Images Plus; claudiodivizia/iStock/Getty Images Plus; GoodGnom/DigitalVision Vectors; Westend61; William Perugini/ Cultura; Christoph Hetzmannseder/Moment; **U4**: Comezora/Moment; **U5**: Jeff Greenough; Steve Granitz/WireImage; Westend61; Scott E Barbour/The Image Bank; **U6**: Joseph L. Murphy/Getty Images Sport; Antonio Lopez Martinez/EyeEm; Photography by Mangiwau/Moment; JEAN-FRANCOIS MONIER/AFP; Andre Vieira/Getty Images News; aydinmutlu/iStock/Getty Images Plus.

Cover photography by Mustafagull/E+/Getty Images; George Pachantouris/ Moment/Getty Images.

The following photographs are sourced from other libraries/sources.

**U3**: konstantinks/Shutterstock; Arcady/Shutterstock; **U5**: Cover of *The Boy Who Biked the World: On the Road to Africa* (part 1), Nov 2011. Copyright © Eye Books. Reused with permission; **U6**: Realimage/Alamy Stock Photo; ton koene/Alamy Stock Photo; Charles O. Cecil/Alamy Stock Photo.

**Illustrations**

**WU**: Ben Scruton; **U1**: Daniela Geremia; **U2**: Mark Ruffle; **U3**: Martin Sanders; Ben Scruton; **U4**: Daniela Geremia; Daniela Geremia; Ben Scruton; **U6**: Ben Scruton; Daniela Geremia; Adam Linley; Martin Sanders.

Grammar Rap video stills: Silversun Media Group.

Full video acknowledgements can be found in the online Teacher's Resources.

Audio Production: Leon Chambers.